PLAYS IN REVIEW

1956–1980

British Drama and the Critics

edited by

Gareth and Barbara Lloyd Evans

Batsford Academic and Educational
London

© Barbara Lloyd Evans 1985

First published 1985

All rights reserved. No part of this publication may be reproduced, in
any form or by any means, without permission from the Publisher

Typeset by Progress Filmsetting Ltd London EC1
and printed in Great Britain by Billings, Worcester.
Published by Batsford Academic and Educational
an Imprint of B.T. Batsford Ltd
4 Fitzhardinge Street, London W1H 0AH

British Library Cataloguing in Publication Data

Plays in review 1956–1980.
   1. English drama—20th century—History and criticism
   I. Lloyd Evans, Gareth   II. Lloyd Evans, Barbara
   822'.914'09   PR737

ISBN 0-7134-4274-3
ISBN 0-7134-4275-1 Pbk

Contents

Acknowledgements

The authors and publishers wish to thank the following for permission to reproduce copyright material:
The Birmingham Post and J.C. Trewin for extracts by J.C. Trewin; *The Daily Mail* for an extract by Robert Muller; *The Daily Telegraph* for extracts by John Barber, W.A. Darlington, D.-L.S., Patrick Gibbs; *The Daily Telegraph* and Eric Shorter for extracts by Eric Shorter; *The Financial Times* for extracts by Michael Coveney, Peter Granger, T.C. Worsley, and B.A. Young; *The Guardian* for extracts by Michael Billington, Philip Hope-Wallace, Nicholas de Jongh, Benedict Nightingale, John Rosselli, and W.-M.W.; *The New Statesman* for extracts by Walter Allan, A. Alvarez, Ronald Bryden, H.A.L. Craig, Roger Gellert, D.A.N. Jones, Benedict Nightingale, Jeremy Treglown, and T.C. Worsley; *The Observer* for extracts by Ronald Bryden, Robert Cushman, Helen Dawson, Victoria Radin, and Kenneth Tynan; *Plays and Players* for extracts by Caryl Brahms, Richard Buckle, Eric Chapman, Helen Dawson, Alan Dent, Martin Esslin, Stephen Gilbert, John Holmstrom, Peter Jackson, Charles Marowitz, Peter Roberts, Jeremy Rundall, Arthur Schmidt, Lisa Gordon Smith, John Russell Taylor, and J.C. Trewin; *Punch* for an extract by Sheridan Morley; *The Spectator* for extracts by Alan Brien, Robert Cushman, Bamber Gascoigne, Kenneth Hurren, Peter Jenkins, Bryan Robertson, Hilary Spurling and Ted Whitehead; *The Star* for an extract by Robert Wraight; *The Sunday Telegraph* for extracts by Alan Brien, Anthony Curtis, Francis King, and Frank Marcus; *The Sunday Times* for extracts by James Fenton, Harold Hobson, J.C. Lambert and Bernard Levin; *The Times* for extracts by Ned Chaillet, Charles Lewson, and Irving Wardle.

Preface

The world and work of the theatre reviewer are sources of endless anguish to the theatrical profession, of bemused fascination to theatregoers, and often of unexpected value to the scholar and historian.

In a sense theatre criticism is as old as drama itself, for the creative artist, especially the playwright, in the very act of making his work public invites both favourable and unfavourable, passionate and dispassionate comment. From the time when, during the seventeenth century, the profession of theatre critic in England was given identity and formalised, there has been a ceaseless stream of comment on the latest play – good, bad, indifferent, benevolent and malevolent – comment which also contains a large body of critical reviewing distinguished by fair appraisal, unusual perception, imagination, wit, knowledge and stylistic felicity. Nowhere, however, is it possible to read, under the same covers, comprehensive sets of examples of this genre. Except in small occasional batches, there has been little collecting together of representative critical reviewing of particular periods, so that both the broad lines of approach and individual eccentricities can be seen together, compared and weighed.

The present book attempts to go some way towards remedying this, for a time period which theatre historians have perhaps over-conclusively, even a little rashly, declared as having begun at a certain specific date, May, 1956, the month and year of John Osborne's *Look Back in Anger*. The terminal date, dictated by practical circumstances of authorship, publication and length, and without intending to imply anything beyond practical considerations, has been set at 1980.

To assemble such collections is not an easy task, not least because the very subject is, by nature, inimical to what many (probably the majority) believe to be a cardinal guiding principle – the exercise of objectivity. But criticism is not an objective process, indeed it is one which achieves real distinction only by a kind of wise, inspired subjectivity, which itself demands a highly civilised and disciplined exercise of personal taste. And if criticism is itself subjective, so is the task of collecting examples – and collaborative authorship and editorship, for all its advantages, can well introduce further subjectivity.

It is not intended that the book should be a history of modern reviewing in the sense that the labyrinthine consecutives of events, fashions, fads and attitudes are followed in slavish detail. Rather the hope is that it will provide enough evidence and comment to enable the reader, first, to form an image of the characteristic modes, methods and approaches and, indeed, the obsessions and eccentricities of the major, and a few less major but remarkable, theatre critics of the period; and, second, to give the reader a general, overall sense of changing modes and attitudes in critical assessment and reviewing over a period of time. In doing this there is no intention to provide a potted history of British drama, though it is inevitable that in order to project the flux of reviewing, some reflection of the continuing flux of dramatic writing will naturally appear.

Certain procedures, some dictated by source material, but most by the authors' intention to make the book conveniently planned for the reader, have been followed:

1 All the reviews are taken from 'overnight' – i.e. daily – newspapers, weekly newspapers and/or monthly periodicals which reported on the first night performance in their first available edition. The majority are of London productions, but sometimes (e.g. Wesker's *Chicken Soup With Barley* and *Roots*) the play opened at a provincial theatre, transferred to London and received notices at either one or both venues. In a small number of cases, therefore, the first night notices are of a mixture of London and provincial productions.

2 Some reviews are given in full, some are quoted in substantial extracts and some are represented by short excerpts, even sentences or phrases. Those that are not printed in full are preceded by the word 'From:'.

3 Reviews for each play appear under the appropriate year and in month order, according to when the first night took place. It should be noted that the 'first night' and the 'press night' are not always necessarily the same thing. Increasingly, since the nineteen-seventies, theatres have separated them – the Royal Shakespeare Company's production of *Hamlet* in 1984, for example, was allocated a press night one month after the first public performance.

4 The excerpts for each year are prefaced by a short comment.

5 There has been no attempt to give equal space to each newspaper or periodical. The choice is based not on numerical allotment but, for good or ill, on intellectual and aesthetic judgement.

6 The choice of newspapers and periodicals was dictated by the intention of the authors to reveal a cross section of those sources which are most read by the perceptive theatregoer. Neither the popular nor tabloid press, nor academic nor scholarly criticism in occasional publications are included.

7 Obvious misprints in the original sources have been silently corrected. Where there is any doubt about a seeming eccentricity, the customary 'sic' is inserted in brackets.

8 As in Allardyce Nicoll's standard work, *British Drama*, the term 'British' is used so as to include playwrights of Irish origin. While this may be ethnically offensive to some, the alternative would be to omit some of the most potent dramatic work of the period.

How to use the book

The titles of the plays and their authors, the critics and their contributions, and the theatres and their productions covered in the book are listed alphabetically in the Appendixes.

Readers who wish to locate an entry, a reference or a cross-reference to a play, playwright, theatre or critic, should ascertain the date of the play or plays concerned from the relevant Appendix, then turn to the section of the main text covering that date (dates are given at the top of left hand pages, play titles at the top of right hand pages).

Introduction

In any society critics are seen as mavericks. They have no formal or institutionalised training for their job; no diploma to decorate their walls and titillate their egos. Indeed, so amorphous is the reality of being a critic that for some individual practitioner critics (as John Elsom usefully describes himself and his journalistic colleagues) the writing of criticism is a side-kick to some other more prestigious skill. One of the century's greatest – Bernard Shaw – would not have answered simply to the name 'critic': a member of the younger generation today – James Fenton – would perhaps respond to 'poet and critic'. Between these two – one from the early, one from the late twentieth century – is a substantial collection of eminent writers whose careers, on examination, include criticism that seems to be an additional function rather than a prime activity.

So, unannealed by training, the critics appear to learn their trade by stealth, instinct, experience and by an, apparently, unorganised acquisition of specialised knowledge. There are no fixed and governing principles and rules, unlike other professions where there is a large area of received wisdom, received techniques and legislated practice. The doctor, priest, lawyer, cricketer are inevitably bound to share, within their respective disciplines, many beliefs and modes of action, and they speak a language, within those disciplines, that they mutually understand. This helps, to a degree, to insulate them from the vernacular, the dialect of the tribe – they employ the language of half-secret societies.

But critics are characterised by their reluctance either to share a common attitude or to pursue similar kinds of commentary. Each critic is essentially a loner, both within his profession, and in his relationship to his readers. He seems to make his own rules, where other professions, at least in theory, follow rules laid down for them. Moreover they have, even when they demonstrably fail in assessment and judgement, a fail-safe refuge in the rules and shibboleths of their profession. Critical assessment has no back-up save the amorphous one of experience, for it is apparently based on what seems a completely subjective response.

Partly because the practitioner critic lacks the embattled, organised and protective armoury common to other professions, he is vulnerable to riposte, misunderstanding, misapprobation, even vilification. There is no council, tribunal or court of appeal which can provide an affirming wherewithal to help him to shore up his assessments, opinions and judgements. In a certain sense, the critic stands or falls, and therefore flourishes or decays, by his wits.

But his vulnerability is increased by other, more abrasive irritants. He is, for instance, assumed to share with the public at large what amounts to a kind of amateur status. He is regarded as having no special skills, only favourable opportunities to exercise what is a common function in humankind – the overwhelming urge to comment on one's fellows. Much of our everyday lives is spent in indiscriminate comment – sometimes in approval, often in disapproval – on something or someone or other, and the practitioner critic is deemed willy-nilly not only to share this common urge but to deploy essentially the same processes of assessment as everyone else.

The roots of such processes lie deep in the tangled under-growth of the human response to its environment. They have four robust strands constantly nourishing them. First – 'I know what I like'; second – 'I know what I dislike'; third – 'what I don't like is to be condemned'; fourth – 'what I like is to be praised'. In these responses lies the indiscriminate comprehensiveness of the public's critical amateurism. In them also lurks, for most people, ample justification for believing that the practitioner critic is merely an embodiment of a natural human disposition to flatter or beggar one's neighbour. Few people believe that the practitioner critic exercises anything more sophisticated than what is found in the spontaneous responses of Everyman and Everywoman, and, therefore, what they write may and must be weighed in the same balance that is used for everyday human comment, which is often 95 per cent prejudice and 5 per cent rational thought.

The never-ending suspicion with which the mass of the general public regards practitioner critics has several ingredients. First, there is the tacit, sometimes explicit, assumption that the practitioner critic is fair game for scorn, for it seems that he only differs from his fellows in that he has his opinions published and gets paid for them. There is a huge and disconcerting rancour lurking deep in the public reaction to practitioner critics and it is commonplace even for distinguished professionals whose work itself is very close to that of the critic – interpreters of great art, such as orchestral conductors – to voice sharp feelings about critics. Sir Thomas Beecham is alleged to have declared, on hearing of a proposal to set up a university chair of music criticism – 'if they must have one, I think it should be an electric chair'. And one should not ignore the part played by envy in this matter. In fact, envy that the practitioner critic benefits financially from doing what is said to come naturally is second only to the itching lust to be recognised, identified, made public. Most human beings' comments are lost in the unlistening air or on relatives, friends, acquaintances, who only half listen while assembling their own ripostes, contrary views, sensational alternatives. The urge to be noticed, known, listened to, is one of humankind's strongest emotions, as any television director or cameraman can confirm. To be asked one's opinion on camera is patently, for many people, the apogee of joy and satisfaction. A surrogate would be a 'letter to the editor', frequently written in such malevolent terms and with such dashing arrogance as few self-respecting professional practitioners would wish – or dare – to give pen to.

There is, too, another abrasive. For most people the word 'criticism' means disapproval, demolition, destruction, all of which implies a widespread belief that the critic's function is to report and comment solely on what is wrong, faulty, ill-achieved. Merciless judgement and cruel sentence rather than cool appraisal is taken to be his stock-in-trade. Small wonder that he falls under suspicion, and that the public's appetite to get back at him is sharpened.

In some measure, however, some practitioner critics invite public scorn, giving more emphasis to the *modus vivendi* of sensational journalism than to the rationale of honest criticism. Even the most intellectually and emotionally sensitive critic has, from time to time, been tempted to write for effect. This is the strongest trap laid by journalism, especially in journals and newspapers given over to titillation of public response and increase of sales. Wounding, unfair, ill-balanced comment can, alas, be found, at some time or other, in the work of most practitioner critics: it goes – as Arthur Miller's Willy Loman says – with the territory.

Yet, on overwhelming evidence, it is quite clear that on the whole pejorative (and worse) comment is the exception not the rule. In all critics' works there is a strong preponderance of commendatory, often ecstatically favourable, theatre notices. Bernard Shaw is the only possible exception. But he is a special case: he has the unique characteristic, at his best, of convincing you, even in his most rebarbative mood, that he is writing sharp, uncommon sense, and is truthful to his experience.

If the 'destructive' critic encourages public disapproval, there is another recognised type – the witty, stylish one – who is capable of mustering cadres of supporters who become gleefully excited by a firework display of words and images held under cool but imaginative control. Such critics – Agate was one, Tynan another – are tolerated, even celebrated, by aficionados for their verbal dexterity and originality. Agate gives the impression that public interest (which he revelled in) served to increase his disposition to verbal eccentricity, but Tynan, who could be as swashbuckling as Agate when he chose, rarely lost sight of his target in the interest of showing off his bowmanship. The art of theatre reviewing, certainly when it involves an obvious deployment of the tricks of wit and words, is part of the entertainment business. But the ability of some practitioners to entertain in this way highlights the dangers they face of merely showing off and so ignoring a truly critical function.

There remains, however, an area for consideration lying well outside the popular notions of the nature and status of practitioner critics. More than any other art the positive realities of criticism are hidden behind its popular image. Admittedly, there are also popular conceptions – by no means flattering – of The Poet, The Novelist, the 'Writer', but, in their case, the resulting distorted image usually remains in the background of the public's intellectual retina. Most people, if asked, are either completely dismissive or curiously apprehensive about the creative artist – who is either of no interest to them or an unfathomable mystery, whose importance they recognise but cannot understand, or shy away from understanding. But the practitioner of theatre criticism has no such luck. His place is in the pillory and no amount of invoking the plea 'this is not altogether Fool, my lord' will halt the missiles often aimed at him.

In fact the public in general seems to have little understanding of the demands made upon a critic or how those demands are satisfied. The conditions in which some critics work help to emphasise the lone wolf aura which surrounds them. They have to meet specific physical demands – newspaper presses are both hungry and impatient. A performance of a new play by, for example, an avant-garde dramatist or one who, egged on perhaps by an overenthusiastic press officer, thinks he is, is an acid test of nerve, dexterity, intellectual and emotional control and patience. Plays are often designated as 'new', not only when they have never appeared before, but because, it is claimed, either by advertising persuasion or in truth, they embody in theme or style, or both, what is boringly referred to as 'challenging' or 'radical'.

These descriptions, ironically, often turn out to mean that the play has not undergone, from its author, an essential paring, clarifying and selecting process which is genuinely innovatory. It

14

is all too easy, as any politician will confirm, to seem 'challenging' and 'radical' by the mere use of rhetoric, repetition and non-sequitur. Here the critic is faced by having to make a valid distinction between flatulent self-indulgence and robust integrity – and this in the precious interim between the end of the performance and the deadline which presses upon him. It is on such occasions of tricky decision, particularly when the digesting of a new play has become burdensome, that some critics may be observed to display an unusually intense and unwontedly warm interest in their colleagues' interval chatter. Bewildered and hungry, they seek out the crumbs dropped from their fellows' tables.

Shakespeare, too, is inclined to encourage this kind of panic herding. The majority of theatre critics in Britain, including those from London's golden circle, can be afraid, even at times somewhat contemptuous, of the works of the Bard. Their fear springs often from their embarrassed half-awareness that they are deficient in knowledge about one at least of the several contexts in which modern productions of Shakespeare, if justice is to be done, should be assessed. It is idle, for example, to assume, either that true critical balance can be maintained if the critic has only a vague notion that Shakespeare's Elizabethan context, to which the plays inevitably belong, is different from that of the twentieth century; or that critical precision can be achieved by anyone ignorant of or careless of the differences in meaning and nuance between Shakespeare's language and our own.

In any case, the time-clenched physical conditions which some critics have to contend with inevitably give rise to doubts as to whether, under such circumstances, judicious criticism is feasible. The problems raised by new productions (and by Shakespeare's plays) are therefore augmented by the plain fact that even the shrewdest critic may have little time for deliberated appraisal.

It would seem reasonable then to assume that critics writing for a weekly paper or a monthly or quarterly periodical have the advantage over their colleagues who sweat in the galleys of the dailies – an advantage, simplistically interpreted, of time in which to write 'good' and fair notices. It is, in fact, more complicated than this, and any attempt to explore the popular image of the art of criticism may rightly begin here.

Theatre criticism is not a unified entity. Indeed, the truth is that the notices appearing in the dailies, the reviews that appear in weekly papers and the (usually) lengthy critiques of periodicals, each represent a different kind of critical approach and purpose.

Tynan divides critics into two kinds, identifying two types. The first type he calls 'newsprint' critics. These include both those who write overnight or early next day notices and those who write in a more leisurely fashion for weekly publications. The second type is to be found in the pages of 'learned magazines' or are dignified by the presentation of their work 'between hard covers'. This lumping together of immediate reviewing and that written to be published several days after the first night – because they are both written for 'newsprint' – is, however, unsatisfactory and does not seem wholly to meet the facts. It ignores the differences occasioned by the varying time-gap between actual first night viewing and the written review, by what may happen during that time-gap, and also by the more relaxed, considered approach that is the prerogative of the weekly/periodical reviewer.

There are, in fact, three kinds of critical reviewing. There is the first night notice – the immediate (or almost immediate) review – written and phoned in either soon after the curtain has gone down or early next day; there is the more relaxed notice written for a weekly paper or periodical; and, lastly, there is the long-term review to be found in 'learned magazines' or between the covers of a book. As the demands on each of the writers of each of these kinds of reviews are different, the nature of the reviews itself is different and each kind must be considered separately.

The overnight/early next day notice

This is the so-called theatre notice and is the type read by most people. Its writing can be inhibited, even harassed, by time and circumstance, but it is, at its best, an invaluable and unique image of the experienced production. It is strictly a 'notice' in the sense in which a camera 'notices' by its quick, but limited attempt to capture something of the reality and the quality of what appears before its lens. The overnight critic has the (though not always recognised as such) advantage of having to 'develop' quickly what the exposed retina of his mind and feelings has captured. He has the opportunity of presenting a fresh, uncluttered image of the production. He cannot afford to squander time in attempting to hedge round his experience of the production with critical havering. Tynan saw his job as that of reporting to his readers (reporting which, without volition or control on his part, might or might not become a message to posterity) what it was like to be in a particular theatre on a particular night. The best critics rarely claim more than this. They are a sophisticated type of litmus paper, immersing themselves in the volatile depths of a production and attempting honestly to report on the changes in their intellectual and emotional colouring that occur during that immersion.

The overnight critic has to be an enormous gambler, with little opportunity to hedge his bets. His opinions and decisions have to be dangerously near to instantaneous. There can be no rough first draft of his notice to be amended later. There is no time to check the accuracy of references. There is little chance even of checking that what was seen or heard actually occurred, for the overnight critic is at the mercy of eyes and ears which can be fickle even as they watch and listen.

On the other hand the exhilarating apprehension, the sense of occasion that can accompany overnight reviewing can sharpen one's response considerably. The overnighter's relationship with his subject has more chance of being immediate and intimate, not displayed, distant and unfocused, like some remote image on radar. Indeed some of the most evocative critical notices are those which are written before the heat of experience has cooled. The passing of decades, even centuries, cannot douse the vivid fire of living performance which glows in a critical report such as Hazlitt's notice, in *The Morning Chronicle* of 15 February, 1814, of Kean's performance of Richard III. As one reads it time falls away: the twisted King played by a drink-sodden genius steps before us – 'His manner of bidding his friends good night, and his pausing with the point of his sword, drawn slowly backward and forward in the grave, before he returns to his tent, received shouts of applause . . . He fought like one drunk with wounds and the attitude in which he stands with his hands stretched out, after his sword is taken from him, had a preternatural and terrific grandeur'. Even today, nearly two centuries later, our hackles rise, and we know this is how it was.

The besetting malady of some late twentieth-century overnight critics is a loss of balance, and of nerve. There is too often a nagging inability to distinguish between irrelevant ingenuity in interpretation, production or acting, and significant originality. Too frequently reviews are either merely tantalising accounts of the plot or disconcertingly wayward parades of congratulatory or condemnatory phrases, so disposed as to draw maximum attention to themselves.

Frequently the play (as distinct from the production of it) is given second place by today's critics as they follow the erratic, often false, scent left in the wake of the latest directorial indulgence. Nowhere is this process more evident than in reviews of Shakespeare's plays. This is partly accounted for by a shift of emphasis from the traditional role of the critic as a kind of belletrist to that of a more workman-like function as a reporter of what happened in a particular theatre on a particular night. Modern critics are generally less concerned with drama and culture, less 'literary' than their forebears, whose work was as likely to contain as much literary criticism of the play as comment

17

on its realisation on stage. It may come as a shock to read the following in A.C. Ward's introduction, written as comparatively recently as 1952, to a collection of Shaw's theatre essays and reviews (World's Classics edition):

> No doubt it is inevitable that, being written by men of letters, dramatic criticism should often show a disproportionate leaning towards the play and an insufficient concern with the players . . .

The boot nowadays is on the other foot.

But the fact remains that, for all the inherent dangers of limited time and space, the overnight notice is always likely to contain the most telling, the sharpest, the freshest, the most controversial comment. The restrictions of the immediate review, much as they are likely to expose the critic's flank, can concentrate the minds of both critic and reader wonderfully. An extreme example of this, perhaps, is embodied in the words attributed to an American critic who, in his first night review of Tallulah Bankhead's Cleopatra wrote:

> Last night Miss Tallulah Bankhead barged down the Nile and sank.

The weeklies and periodicals

The first and obvious difference of weekly/periodical reviewing from the overnight notice is that the former is demonstrably not cramped by space, nor does it seem so harried by time. The reviewer, unless he is a congenital last-gasp writer, has some opportunity to speculate, to ponder, and to use the freedom to spread his thoughts and feelings more liberally.

There is too (though, for most, this is theoretical) the possibility that he may see the production more than once, so the instant response may be checked upon and if necessary corrected. Even more (and this, one suspects, on evidence, is observed more in practice than in theory) there is the undoubtedly double-edged facility of having the chance to read the reviews of his overnight colleagues before committing himself to paper.

Every reviewer is, to a degree, subject to the temptation, described by Tynan, of being a 'fairground barker disguised in the robe of prophecy', but on the whole most of the barking is done overnight and most of the prophecy achieved after days of cogitation. The weekly/periodical reviewer barks less because the interim between experience and comment causes some loss of spontaneity, some dulling of the first fine flush, the adrenalin-pumping excitement involved in transmitting the results of the immediate response. While the overnight critic often seems to shout 'Come and get it' to his reader, the weekly/periodical critic may often be tempted to write letters to posterity, as it were.

Moreover, the interim can make the critic vulnerable to a syndrome well-known to the legal profession – the inaccuracy and unreliability of evidence given when time has elapsed between observation and report. The values of reflection are, in fact, always in jeopardy because of their direct ratio to the unreliability of memory. Few theatre critics appear to use anything (though this may be, of course, mere legerdemain) more than the bare bones of notes taken during the performance; in any case, they are often loath to lose the thread of the production in attempting to record details of it.

The basic differences of approach between overnight and weekly or periodical reviewing are graphically displayed when one compares comments on the same production by the same critic for, firstly, an overnight notice and secondly, after a period of time, for a periodical.

The overnight notice:

> There is no intention to be condescending in saying that inside Terry Johnson's *Cries From The Mammal House* at the Leicester Haymarket Studio a fine play is struggling to get out. Rather it is a measure of critical indecision – I can feel the quality but the pattern is so complicated that I can't assess its worth.
>
> On the surface it really is about a zoo, its animals and its people. In a remarkably effective and economical set, with some heart-aching silhouettes of both humans and non-humans, a group of traumatic short stories is embodied. They were, I guess, meant by the author to interconnect, but they didn't for me.
>
> (Gareth Lloyd Evans, *The Guardian*, April 7, 1984)

The review for a periodical:

> Terry Johnson's *Cries From The Mammal House* at the Leicester Haymarket Theatre is a play which if it were an examination script would leave the marker in two minds – is it alpha or gamma minus? Does it flatter only to deceive or is it so much a cut above the average that you can't accept its virtues without suspicion? In fact, it's not easy to fathom. Being a man given to hazard, and, through melancholy experience, hardened to faulty divination, I brashly assert that it is alpha with a touch of minus. So much for speculation.
>
> It is about a zoo, so much is plain; about the people who run it and the animals without whom it would not exist. This is the setting, depicted with great economy and impressionism – under the circumstances naturalism might be dangerous – by the Leicester designer, Peter Hartwell and his lights colleague who silhouettes in shadow projection the more potentially violent inhabitants of the zoo – that is, the animals.
>
> In this context a number of narratives are related and embodied in dramatic form. Each one, I guess, was intended to flow from its predecessor, but this is merely part of the hazard. The play in other words lacked sharp narrative definition. But underlying messages,

sometimes (to use modern parlance) coded did eventually stack up. Each of the humans involved had a specific moral and emotional relationship to one or other animal, and, as these relationships were established and recognised, all kinds of emotions spread like a prairie fire. Human realities were gradually expressed in terms of this relationship.

(Gareth Lloyd Evans, *Drama*, Third Quarter, No 153, 1984)

What used to be called 'style' is an important signal of these differences and its effects appear early in these opening paragraphs. As the reviews continue, they grow further apart – the first is tentative, uncertain, baffled: the second, while still cautious and unwilling to be completely certain, has more balance and a calmer reflectiveness – but from the first sentence they reveal why they stand apart. It is because the first was fashioned just after the heat of performance and the second was etched in a cooler mood. In the first, one can just catch the critic's anxious attempt to hold on to the immediacy of the performance, in the second, the same critic's recollection is in relative – almost stoic – tranquillity.

The academic critic

The third type of critic/practitioner is often described as 'academic' – a word used more often with grubby overtones than approbation. Not many of the general public read them, and theatre people, barely tolerating any kind of critic, are particularly severe on them. The academics usually write in journals of limited circulation or books of dramatic history which are easily seen as elitist – read by a minority – a circumstance which only increases suspicion. Obviously this type of critic has even more time and space available than the contributor to weekly journals. But, while this may seem valuable as far as reflection and considered opinion are concerned, it can also raise problems. In the first place, with such a long passage of time between seeing the original production and writing about it, even greater errors of memory may creep in. The critic may then find himself with no alternative but to rely on cuttings – his own or those of others – of overnight notices.

Secondly, in the interim that author's whole viewpoint may well have changed, and, as a result, he will re-interpret what he remembers or what he reads in the cuttings and will select material that fits into his new viewpoint. Often such re-interpretations and selections are to one end – to support a particular thesis the critic wishes to promote. So that, in fact, the selectivity of the academic critic can raise as many difficulties as the over-enthusiasm of some first night critics.

But interesting as these contrasts are, they are secondary in importance to the newly developed and developing relationship between stage and study. The history of academic drama criticism in England is dominated by resentment, anger and dismissiveness. Indeed, one of the chief reasons for the belated appearance of drama departments in British universities (contrary to what happened in the United States) was this prevalent attitude. To a degree, academics have themselves at times been responsible for stunting the growth of formal drama education by exhibiting a superior or a dismissive or a patronising attitude towards the concrete realities of theatre production, while weaving their own webs of theory and interpretation around the texts. Even so, while academics neglected the stage, theatre people, in their turn, took up an equally pejorative, albeit defensive, attitude towards academic criticism: to them, for example, Shakespeare was strictly a man of theatre, and academic criticism was therefore deemed to be irrelevant. So, between the pontification of the scholar and the scorn of theatre men an atmosphere of suspicion and contempt was created.

Gradually, since the end of World War Two, a remarkable change has occurred in the relationship between the two. Professors can now be found (as in the case of John Russell Brown with Peter Hall) in an advisory capacity to directors. University staff gain an unexpected public exposure through being invited by prestigious radio and television programmes to express their opinions about productions. There has also been a large growth in the amount of criticism which emanates from scholarly sources and which (sometimes slavishly, not to say desperately) attempts to take account of the realities of stage-performance. This, with the rapid creation of drama departments in British universities, has led to a hitherto unheard-of collaboration between stage and study. Some degree courses in drama involve what, twenty years ago, would have seemed a startling, innovatory use of what has become known as the 'theatre-workshop situation', in which professional actors and directors from neighbouring theatres engage students in the processes by which a play reaches the stage – a practical airing of the subject which supplements (often even threatening to supplant) the academic study of it.

There are other aspects – positive, fruitful ones – to all this wooing and fro-ing. On the one hand, academics now find it difficult to escape being shown how necessary it is to experience drama on the stage as part of the process of interpretation and evaluation, and a whole new body of 'academic' criticism has developed, with scholars falling over themselves to demonstrate their commitment to theatrical realisation; on the other, British theatres now harbour many actors and directors whose careers have been touched by academic benediction. The Royal

Shakespeare Company has, one might say, a hot-line to Cambridge University operated by ex-alumni including Peter Hall, John Barton and Trevor Nunn.

There is, too, an excitement about the recent affair between theatre and study which helps to vivify and animate the silent play-text. An appreciation of the problems of actor and director can now be brought to the forefront of a student's mind as he grapples with the baffling question of Hamlet's madness or Othello's jealousy. The student nowadays is left in no doubt that a play-text is a different kind of animal from a literary text – and many find it far more exciting.

Unfortunately, however, virtue can harbour vice and the wide-eyed romance of stage and study has its darker side. Much of this is due to a fundamental difference between the skills of the academic and those of the director and actor. This difference is often obscured by the self-evident glamour, excitement, extrovert opportunities of theatre. A wise awareness of the implications of both the academic approach, and theatrical experience and sensitivity, is the most fecund way to penetrate into a dramatic text, but the glamour of theatre constantly lures the imagination away from contact with the far less spectacular but, at its best, equally valuable and stimulating process of the scholar. Perhaps this can be seen most clearly in the differing attitudes of each to the text of the play.

The great majority of theatre directors and actors, however much they may declare that they wish to preserve the integrity of what the author has written, have no compunction in altering the text. It cannot be too frequently stressed that a text, to most actors or directors, is an expendable commodity, and certainly not a sacred cow! At best it is given a respectful hearing, but, more often, it is regarded merely as the starting block for the director's racing, colourful and inventive imagination, and, in a director-dominated theatre, such as we have today in the United Kingdom, it tends to be seen merely as a kind of aide-memoire – a sort of map. Tyrone Guthrie is not the only spectacular example of this but also reveals how a director's preoccupation with his own creativity can addle historical fact.

> Performance in the theatre seems to me the right way to make such comment upon works which were written in dramatic form, which exist as the raw material for performance. Shakespeare, for instance, wrote his plays, often in a hurry, for a specific group of players. So little was he interested in the plays as literature that there is no record of their being printed, or published, during his lifetime. And when, shortly after his death, his two friends Heminge and Condell endeavoured to get together the texts of his plays for publication, they could only find prompt scripts full of errors, omissions and, we may

be sure, 'improvements', added in rehearsal or performance.

(Tyrone Guthrie, *A Life in the Theatre*, 1960)

This is not a simple matter of accepting that any individual director will naturally have his own unique vision of any text, but a far more complex one of realising that sometimes this vision is not even a version of the author's original. Rather it becomes an imposed image, which the text, by commission but usually by omission, is then employed to justify.

This process is particularly easy to trace in productions of our English classics. Indeed, so clear is it that productions of Shakespeare, for example, are often designated and recalled by the director's name – Brook's *A Midsummer Night's Dream*; Nunn's *A Comedy of Errors*; Barton and Hall's English histories. Today the chief players' names are often not easy to recall, and the author's taken for granted, but the director is dignified (some might say deified) by having the whole affair – play, text, production and all – attributed to him. A notable example of this is Peter Hall's superb productions of Pinter's plays – his name, in the reviews, often being given equal weight with that of the author.

The true actor's instinct is almost always to simplify – to achieve the maximum explosive force with the minimum of material and energy. He will often achieve this paring down of his source by cutting (usually with the connivance of the director) or by a substitution of what he believes to be complex language and thought patterns in the text by others more generally and quickly understood by himself and, he hopes and believes, by his audience. The art of acting is essentially the art of selection, simplification and concentration. That this can be in direct contrast (even opposition) to the academic's procedure and ethos, which is, essentially, amplification, explanation and logical persuasion, can be seen in the following comments on the 'English' scene in *Macbeth* [IV.3].

First, the actor:

He is a virgin, therefore all the things he says he would do with women are a sort of masturbatory fancy; similarly all the things he says about power and wealth must be a knowledge of the megalomania that is in him. But, in rehearsal I discovered that both must be shown – this knowledge AND the fact that he is putting it on to test Macduff. It must be two-dimensional acting.

Curiously, at the end of the England scene, when Macduff has had his harrowing news, Malcolm's immediate reaction is 'What man! . . . etc'. In other words the megalomania in the man cannot help him using this awful thing to spur not only Macduff but also himself. This is why he says 'This tune goes manly'. Undeniably there is in the man a ruthless ability to take a situation and turn it to his own use.

In the England scene when I hear the news about Macduff's

23

children, in order to get myself into the right emotional state I have
quickly to flash a kaleidoscope set of pictures through my mind of my
own children and what my emotions would be if something ghastly
happened to them. It happens always at the same place, when
Macduff says 'I cannot remember such things'. In rehearsal you
almost have to shut out the other actor and make just a selfish
recollection for yourself.

(Ian Richardson in Shakespeare and the Actors by
Gareth Lloyd Evans, Shakespeare Survey No.21, 1968)

Then the academic:

The (English) scene can also be defended as a 'mirror for magistrates'
– a discussion on the contrast between true royalty and tyranny that is
very germane to the matter. It can demonstrate effectively how
Macbeth's misrule has made even the good suspect the good of
treachery. Perhaps, too, as Professor Knights has suggested, the scene
acts as a choric commentary: 'We see the relevance of Malcolm's
self-accusation. He has ceased to be a person. His lines repeat and
magnify the evils that have already been attributed to Macbeth, acting
as a mirror wherein the ills of Scotland are reflected. And the
statement of evil is strengthened by contrast with the opposite virtues.'

(Kenneth Muir, Macbeth, The Arden Shakespeare, p. LXX)

Finally, the director/critic:

Malcolm is meant to be a young man who is deliberately virtuous,
level-headed moreover, and astute. And however unheroic such a
figure may seem to the romantically-minded playgoer, Shakespeare
will have it that this is the man to save Scotland. Given an actor of the
right authority for Malcolm, the scene can be made interesting
enough. A thing in it to make clear and stress carefully is the
opposition between the natures of the two men and their ways of
approach to each other: Macduff outspoken; Malcolm reserved,
over-cautious at first, though never cold. From its beginning, indeed,
the scene is, beneath the surface, well charged with emotion.

(Harley Granville-Barker, Prefaces to Shakespeare,
(Vol. VI, p. 83)

An awareness of and participation in all processes, used
judiciously and sensitively, can illuminate drama; but it is idle to
pretend that it is an easy task to yoke them – the Shire horses of
the academic stable were not intended to run the same course as
the quivering thoroughbreds of the theatre.

The new academic criticism, born of the animosities of the past
and still suffering from the uncertainties of its present status, is
still a babbling babe, inexperienced, relatively unknowing, wayward and given to wild bouts sometimes of enthusiasm and
sometimes of disapproval. But time may well amend all this and
help to nurture a truer, more shrewd, balanced and therefore profitable relationship between academic and theatrical.

The professional's qualifications

Most of the public, however, make no distinction between the differing kinds of critical activity. The empty but stubborn authoritarianism of 'I know what I like' is what rules their responses and is as paramount and immutable a reaction to academic criticism as it is to first night or weekly reviewing. The task therefore of attempting to prove that the professional practitioner is likely to be more sensitive and accurate in his critical appraisals than the average theatregoer is daunting, not to say thankless. It is nevertheless as necessary to make such an attempt as it is to recognise the compatibilities and incompatibilities of the world of the theatre and the world of the critic.

Any professional 'qualifications' of the practitioner critic are seldom thought or written about – to most people the practitioner seems to act subjectively on instinct, without control or discipline. But this does not mean that qualifications do not exist and that they cannot be discerned in the work of the best critics. Indeed, a critic without them is as handicapped as a mathematician who can't add up.

Enthusiasm

All the great practitioners have possessed one quality which theatregoers, when acquainted with it, find very surprising. The surprise is encapsulated in the belief that, given what they believe to be the critic's melancholy task of eternal fault-finding, he must find theatregoing at best a bore, at worst a physical and spiritual pain. But the very fact that the critic is prepared, night after night, to subject himself to theatre is a firm denial of this supposition (the financial inducements to endure nights of boredom are not over-persuasive in Britain). The best practitioners have a zest, even an obsession for theatregoing, in which even incipient boredom can be subsumed in expectant passion. Disapproval of any single production by a critic has no correlation with the immense pleasure and satisfaction that the overall experience of theatre gives him. It is, indeed, like a successful marriage in which the consummate assurances of true, lasting love override the rough irritations that intermittently inflame daily co-habitation.

> Eric Keown testifies to '. . . the feeling of innocent excitement . . . as the curtain rises, on whatever play. Unless he can preserve this undimmed, the critic would do better to shell peas or go into Parliament'.
>
> (Quoted in J.C. Trewin (ed.), *Theatre Programme*, 1954, p. 291)

Pleasure and satisfaction in theatre, then, is implicit in the zest which is the primary characteristic of the best critics. Shaw, Tynan, Agate, Hobson all possessed it. It animates their style, it sharpens their wits, it cossets their sensitivity and it enables them even in the bleakest of theatre experiences to preserve their balance and to remember their passion.

The false practitioners – and many exist – have no continuing zest. For some this is through no fault of their own, forced as they are to split their activities into inimical sections and functions. The worst defaulters are to be found among those journalistic unfortunates who range across the gossip columns, the sports page, the political spot and the arts page. Their hearts are not in theatre. Their editor has, willy-nilly, shunted their pens into that particular siding, until another line is open again.

Experience

Enthusiasm in itself, however, is not enough. It needs to be maintained by continuing and uninterrupted experience of theatre. The critic must persistently exercise his professional skill in a disciplined way so that his critical judgement has behind it a form of guarantee that, at least, he is in close and easy acquaintance with his subject – a relationship often, perforce, denied to even the most avid 'I know what I like' theatregoer. The most telling evidence of the necessity of uninterrupted practical commitment is to be found in the work of a number of late twentieth-century critics (for example Bernard Levin) who have, at some point, abandoned criticism temporarily for some other activity. In some cases they have eventually returned to the fold, and this return is almost always, at first, accompanied by a sense of tentative appraisal, of enervating remoteness from the subject. Whatever else may be claimed for or hurled at the critic, he is only successful and to be trusted so long as there remains in his work a kind of single-mindedness. The critic who takes his eye for a time off the ball runs the danger of confusing his critical eye with peripheral images and ideas, and, returning to his craft and art after a sojourn in some other literary bourne, almost invariably brings with him an ambience irrelevant to critical appraisal. He has to regain his single-mindedness. It is not easy.

Neville Cardus, as distinguished a critic of music as of cricket, recognised and magnificently evoked the close relationship between the exercise of the cricketer's bat and of the conductor's baton. The arts and crafts of batsmanship and of conducting are both close and, perhaps surprisingly, involve a great deal of critical sensitivity. The nature of the batsman's stroke is, in its result, a critical comment on the ball that's bowled as is the conductor's baton on the orchestration of the composer. Both may remain great even when prevented from exercising their craft and art, but rarely, when they first return to their profession, is their form and manner certain, until practice and renewed experience restore balance, perception and sensitivity. The theatre critic is in an analogous condition – absence does not diminish genius but it makes return a difficult task.

Knowledge

But neither is the mere act of consistent attendance at first nights, and commenting upon them, enough. There are other areas of experience that mark off the professional critic from the amateur. Although they can be simply summed up as 'knowledge' their varied aspects and implications are complex. Their possession amplifies criticism, giving authenticity to opinion, credibility to judgement. One of them, essential as a sound basis for any theatre reviewer, is some knowledge of the mechanics of theatre. An understanding of, and an ability to distinguish different acting techniques, an informed eye for the compatability of set design and production style (a much neglected skill), an informed acquaintance with lighting techniques – all of these, and other matters, constitute a 'knowledge' that the critic should be able to deploy with natural ease and authority. In fact, a characteristic of much contemporary criticism is, on the evidence of reviews, its comparative unease with, and/or avoidance of, such matters. Many critics are too often occupied with directorial interpretation and sociological significance to the detriment of any other considerations. They seem not to appreciate the fact that their critical appraisals and conclusions can be hopelessly distorted unless the theatre's environment and the art and craft of acting are taken into consideration.

But this know-how is not the only one, nor perhaps the paramount one for the professional critic. His 'knowledge' should also embrace both the cultural and the sociological context of his society. It is fairly easy today to be passionately au fait with the sociological context – in fact it is difficult to avoid it. Probably in view of the preponderence of sociological drama today, this is inevitable. But it is quite another thing to be on good terms with society's, and particularly drama's, cultural heritages and lineage. This is all the more necessary because contemporary theatre is a flux, restless, adept at presenting one face to the world today and quite another tomorrow. The contours of contemporary drama, like those of contemporary society, have changed radically from thirty years ago and seem likely to change even more in the next thirty years, and it is the critic's job to be sensitive to and understanding of that change; but to be so, he must have some knowledge of what preceded the contemporary scene.

If we look at tragedy, for example, a critic who wishes to assess what has happened to tragedy in modern drama, but whose knowledge does not extend to past conceptions and examples of tragedy, lacks a vital dimension of critical perception. Seen in the perspective of both its Greek classical and English renaissance forms and content, traditional tragedy has little relevance for the modern author and the traditional tragic hero little place in modern plays. He has disappeared, with the lessening of belief in the influence of supernatural destiny and in individual responsibility. He has been replaced, both in society and the drama that reflects that society, by a virtually anonymous protagonist, the responsibility for whose plight is mostly placed, not on his own weakness of character, but on the shoulders of a society which is almost always depicted as inimical, unfair and dispossessing.

Macbeth's cry, 'I have no spur to prick the sides of my intent, but only vaulting ambition', sounds strange, certainly to modern ears – an outmoded confession of personal responsibility for his actions: the 'juggling fiends' he visits can no longer be accepted by most as agents of a destiny which haunts the imagination. They have become mere half-comic remnants of a primitive folk-lore. The power of the supernatural cannot flourish in a godless society, and the unpalatable notion of personal responsibility belongs to another world, where, if an individual commits a crime, the cause is equally disposed between his stars and his own soul. Joe Orton's contemptuous and ironic words give the modern counterpart:

> Mike (laying the gun aside): He's dead.
> Joyce: But he can't be. You haven't killed him?
> Mike: Bring a sheet. Cover his body.
> Joyce: I've a bit of sacking somewhere.
> Mike: I said a sheet! Give him the best.
> (He goes into the bedroom and drags a sheet from the bed which he puts over Wilson's body.)
> Joyce: What excuse was there to shoot him?
> Mike: He was misbehaving himself with my wife.
> Joyce: But I'm not your wife. And he wasn't.
> Mike: He called you Maddy.
> Joyce: Somebody must've told him about my past. You know what people are. (Pause.) Did you have anything to do with his brother's death?
> Mike: Yes.
> Joyce: This is what comes of having no regular job. (Pause.) Is the phone working by the Nag's Head?
> Mike: Yes.
> Joyce: Go to the telephone box. Dial 999. I'll tell them I was assaulted.
>
> (Joe Orton, *The Ruffian on the Stair*,
> *Collected Plays*, p. 61)

An awareness and knowledge of this huge shift in the nature of tragedy will lead the critic today to take cognisance of other signals of change, both in society and its drama – the blurring of public and private morality for example, the reliance on expediency as a justification for action, and, sadly, the emaciation of language.

Moreover, the modern critic has also had to come to terms with another shift in the motivation for writing plays today. More and more they spring from the playwright's head fully armed with contemporary issues and -isms. They mirror the immediate social and political preoccupations of their creator and, all too often, are slavishly concerned with the immediate, present-tense, status of humankind and its environment. In these plays there is almost always a diminution of what J.B. Priestley calls the 'magic' of theatre, whose aim was essentially to entertain and beguile, and, even if it wishes to educate or persuade, to do so only by stealth. In short, the functional rather than the aesthetic rules modern drama. Priestley's words doubtless sound old-fashioned and outmoded to modern aficionados to whom the art of dramatic writing is valued and justified only to the extent to which it openly serves what they deem to be the needs of society. His plays, Priestley wrote,

> . . . moved audiences to laughter and tears, which is what should happen in the theatre. Though my plays have ideas in them, I have never regarded the theatre as a medium for ideas – the plays and the actors are there to move people.

Trevor Griffiths unconsciously provides an ironic context for Priestley's words in his assertion that, if he believed he could do more towards changing Britain by 'working on the streets, or in the political parties', he would give up writing plays (quoted in Hayman, *British Theatre Since 1955*, 1979, p. 82).

Because of the close involvement of contemporary drama with socio-political matters the practitioner critic has had to make an assessment of a kind never before so keenly and comprehensively demanded of the profession. He requires not only knowledge of, and sensitivity to, the shifting sands of society, but also self-knowledge. He is under pressure to question his own political and social status. And this invariably causes his slip to show. It is much easier today to discover a critic's 'colouring' than it was three or four decades ago. It needs no groping now – it shows.

A feeling for the past
Western societies in the last four decades of the twentieth century give every evidence of being addicted to allowing the present to monopolise their cultural thinking and feeling. This tendency is

29

accompanied by a deliberate rejection of yesterday and an equally deliberate refusal to think of tomorrow. For many people, but particularly the teenage and late teenage generations, the future is a dangerous blank, the past an unknown darkness: only the NOW has any meaning – although perhaps 'meaning' is too rich a word to describe the persistent stark craving for instant stimulus, instant response, of the growing majority.

The lure of the present is accompanied by either ignorance, avoidance of, or a calculated, sometimes superficial, distortion of the past. For many people it is a tight-shut unreadable book: for them what they call 'the olden days' actually happened only a few years ago: even last week's events are a dim memory. As for what lies centuries behind – it is mysterious, unapproachable, meaningless and irrelevant – it is as apocalyptically baffling as a black hole in the heavens.

Even in education a sense of history is conspicuously less evident in both teacher and taught than it was four or five decades ago. This reveals itself in several ways, but notably in a failure to respond to verbal associations which require even the most modest awareness of the past. It has also become, except in exceptional cases, impossible to emphasise an idea, characterise a modern situation, illuminate a contemporary individual of importance, by a comparative reference to the past, even the near-past. In England hazy areas of history have become particularly opaque since the post-war progressive denigration of the so-called 'imperial past'. Many English people today try to push history out of their minds, both because they are sensitive to being on a losing streak in the world today and because of the rise to prominence of ideologies, with which they sympathise, that preach the annihilation of class, hierarchy, elitism while proselytising for egalitarianism. The adherents of an egalitarian corporate state regret, even hate, a past which seems to them directly, vividly and cruelly to confirm their angry beliefs.

A disturbing corollary to this is an assumption that any perception of the past must presuppose a rejection of the present. To be dubbed a 'traditionalist' is a mark of disapproval, not least in the world of dramatic criticism. Even so, it is impossible to deny that we are, biologically and culturally, a product of our past and that the richer seams of our so-called 'culture', far from being an invention of the more relatively sophisticated media of today, are the accumulated deposits of our yesterdays.

This syndrome has had its influence on critical writers. To be blinkered into tunnel vision by the sociological trappings of modern drama; to attribute innovations to modern dramatists without any of the validation that only a knowledge of dramatic history can supply; to claim originality for stage business, set-design, acting technique, costumes, directional interpretations, without any confirming evidence from theatrical history – are common characteristics of modern criticism. Many would declare that they are unnecessary to honest response; only a few seem to realise that, without them, critical assessment is built on quicksand.

Examples abound in twentieth-century criticism of the imprecision and warping of judgement that a failure to enlist the past can result in. There are two notable ones. The first implies a blindness to the fact that history – and certainly theatrical history – does not advance in neat and measurable jumps, but is a chaotic mixture of skidding, overlapping, and even sometimes crab-like movement: the second is concerned with the critics' frequently unquestioning acceptance of the treatment of historical matter in plays, where either the author's knowledge of that matter is in itself unreliable or where, while claiming to be presenting the truth in his play, the author openly acknowledges that he is distorting historical fact to make his point.

The first can be seen in the critics' reaction to John Osborne's *Look Back In Anger*, the second in their assessment of Bond's *Bingo*.

Osborne's *Look Back In Anger* was first produced in 1956. It begat very mixed reviews yet there was a strong consensus of opinion that, for good or ill, the play signalled – even, perhaps, started – a revolution in English theatre. Nothing would ever be the same again. History was changed overnight. The present had taken over and the future had better look out.

> The whole picture of writing in this country has undergone a transformation in the last few years or so, and the event which marks 'then' off decisively from 'now' is the first performance of *Look Back In Anger* on 8 May 1956.
>
> (John Russell Taylor, *Anger and After*, p. 9)

The interest and passion aroused both by the play and by certain slightly frantic media accounts, together with its undoubted influence on the work of other young 'angry' writers, cannot be ignored, but their significance and relevance have, arguably, been over-rated and misinterpreted. There is, for example, little correlation between the stir it aroused and its innate artistic quality. It is now widely admitted to be clumsily written – neither has it worn well, as recent productions have unwittingly but cruelly revealed. The original vast claims made for its innovative brilliance were, to be fair to him, not only repudiated by Osborne himself (though he modified this opinion later) – it is 'a formal, rather old-fashioned play' – but have not stood up to historical testimony. Osborne's chief character – Jimmy Porter – was hailed as the first anti-hero, but this conveniently ignored the claims of Stanley Kowalski in *A Streetcar Named Desire* (first produced New York 1949) with whom Porter shares, if only superficially, a number of common characteristics.

Look Back In Anger was described by enthusiastic devotees like the theatre critic John Russell Taylor, as providing a mouthpiece for a whole disillusioned post-war generation but in truth it neither was, nor is, possible to be sure what generation or class that was supposed to be. Some of Osborne's admirers were of his age-group yet, curiously, when they write of the play's speaking on behalf of a vast concourse of disaffection, they always seem to distance themselves from it – it is always 'them' not 'us' whom it represented.

A case could be made out that Jimmy Porter is not so much speaking for a generation as, simply, for himself – himself being Osborne. Indeed many, even today, find it difficult not to confuse the author's name with that of his creation, Jimmy Porter, and his anger is now seen to be motivated more by self-indulgence than by anything else.

> Jimmy: . . . Every time I sat on the edge of his bed, to listen to him talking or reading to me, I had to fight back my tears. At the end of twelve months, I was a veteran.
> (He leans forward on the back of the armchair.)
> All that that feverish failure of a man had to listen to him was a small frightened boy. I spent hour upon hour in that tiny bedroom. He would talk to me for hours, pouring out all that was left of his life to one, lonely, bewildered little boy, who could barely understand half of what he said. All he could feel was the despair and the bitterness, the sweet, sickly smell of a dying man.
> (He moves around the chair.)
> You see, I learnt at an early age what it was to be angry – angry and helpless. And I can never forget it. (Sits) I knew more about love . . . betrayal . . . and death, when I was ten years old than you will probably ever know all your life.
> (John Osborne, *Look Back In Anger*, Act 2, Sc. 1)

Again, large claims were made for its innovative, straight-from-the-shoulder, solar-plexus language. It was described as a 'breakthrough' in dramatic speech: never before, some said, had such raw naturalistic language, fierce and fearless, been heard on the English stage. But time, yet again, has shown how manufactured, in a self-conscious undergraduate way, the language is. It always seems on the point of breaking into rhetorical literary eloquence, and, curiously, tends to give Jimmy Porter the aura of the class he seems to love least – the middle class.

The intervening years between 1956 and today have taken their toll of the play, in the sense that they have shown how the claims made on behalf of its influence were out of all proportion to its alleged qualities. It may be objected that it is easy to be right by hindsight – but hindsight is, after all, only another word for a sense of historical perspective. If, for example, in 1956, some of the more prestigious, eloquent and admiring critics of *Look Back In Anger* had coolly attempted at least to put the play in an historical context, they would have noticed a play of the thirties called *Love on the Dole*, first produced in Manchester (1934) and then in London (1935). It is a skilfully assembled play; its 'hero' is easily linked to a disaffected social class; his anger is more easily identified than Jimmy Porter's; what is claimed for the character of Jimmy – representativeness – is more strictly true of Larry Meath in the earlier play; and the raw naturalism which Osborne is said to have introduced is to be found, with varying degrees of 'rawness', both in it and in some late nineteenth-century plays. The redoubtable Miss Horniman (1860–1937) who, among other notable contributions to English theatre, encouraged a school of young provincial playwrights – the Lancashire group – in the early part of the century, wrote at the time:

> If Lancashire playwrights will send their plays to me I shall pledge myself to read them through. Let them write not as one dramatist does, about countesses and duchesses and society existing in imagination, but about their friends and enemies – about real life.
>
> (quoted in Rex Pogson, *Miss Horniman and the Gaiety Theatre*, Manchester, 1953)

One of the results of her declaration was the production of a play which, in its time, occasioned as much startled comment as did *Look Back In Anger* – and for similar reasons. It was Stanley Houghton's *Hindle Wakes* (1912).

Today's sociologically involved plays owe a great deal to the lead given by Osborne in creating a protagonist (hardly a hero) who shouted at his society, his relatives, his wife and his wife's mother, loudly announcing what he thought of them. If we can believe Jimmy Porter (though some have always found his anger mere rhetoric) most things in his society except himself were rotten. There was a fortuitous element in the fact that Jimmy Porter was created at a time when the growing effects of the Welfare State gave many people, of all generations, a kind of guarantee that society owed them a living, and when the advance into political power of socialism, with its emphasis on egalitarianism, made the 'elitism' of being a tragic hero (in the traditional sense) almost a criminal act. Besides, permissiveness was in the air, censorship was in a state of siege, doing one's own thing was a popular cry, and blunt speaking, which usually meant either the lowest common denominator of language or a kind of cheeky, witty brassiness (like Jimmy's) came to be regarded by a vociferous minority as the only authentic speech of today and probably tomorrow. Jimmy Porter did not create the conditions about which he vents his anger in *Look Back In Anger* any more than the heroes of *Love on the Dole* or *Hindle Wakes* did, but all three found some positive response from society. The advantage that *Look Back In Anger* had was that the response was the stronger because the political clout of those who either thought they were, or actually were, disaffected, had become and was becoming greater.

However, *Look Back In Anger* as an emblem of what later resulted in a bloodless social revolution, and Jimmy Porter as a catalytic representative of an angry generation, has stuck fast in the minds and pens of many critics and theatre historians ever since. The accepted opinion of the play (rather than the play itself), distorted as it may well be, must in its turn be held responsible for pushing many young dramatists along certain narrow socio-political roads. Today's young writers have, however, advanced much deeper into the thickets of social commitment than did Osborne, his colleagues and immediate successors. Whereas they were content to arouse gut-reactions which encouraged some audience-sympathy, playwrights now want us to take decisive action: their plays are an incitement to audiences to go out and change society. Edward Bond, Howard Brenton, Caryl Churchill, David Edgar, John McGrath, Trevor Griffiths are among the most vociferous of a host of activist dramatists, and the most naggingly explicit of them is Bond: 'Theatre is a way of judging society and helping to change it . . .'

Any consideration of Bond's plays drops us bang in the middle of the whirlpools aroused by the dramatic use of history, the uncertain eddies it creates between fact and fiction and the critical assessment of them. Bond is a notable example of the buccaneer's way with history. He doesn't ignore it, but makes it walk the plank of concepts, values, shibboleths, opinions – of which those contemporary with the events knew nothing, or knew them in forms very different from the modern shape he gives them. His attitude towards history seems subtle, but this is deceptive. There is, rather, a raw permissiveness in his treatment of the past in order to make it bow to his own expression of the present. A number of his plays have a 'historical' setting, though often of a kind that is unrecognisable as in-focus images of past events and people. 'The past', he declares with deceptive generosity, 'is also an institution owned by society' and a good deal of his dramatic energy and skill is squandered in forcing that 'institution' to display its subservient 'owned' status, so ratifying his verdict.

He uses a variety of techniques to achieve this victory over the past. In *Early Morning*, for example, he caricatures with unmerciful exaggeration accepted notions of nineteenth-century people, notably Queen Victoria and Disraeli, Gladstone and Prince Albert. This is intended to de-mythologise established images, but Bond seems unaware of the fact that he is only replacing them with myths of his own making. The result of this process of giving history a comprehensive transplant is intellectually specious, often baffling, but always theatrically sensational, theatrically compulsive. For example, the portrait of Shakespeare in *Bingo* verges on dramatic caricature. In this play Bond gives Shakespeare a share of personal responsibility for certain social and public events considered, by Bond himself, to be both inhuman and immoral – a responsibility which is inevitably derived from Shakespeare's 'bourgeois' involvement in land-enclosure on the Welcombe Estates in Stratford-upon-Avon; he makes Shakespeare realise his bourgeois guilt in having inhumanly, even mindlessly, exploited the undefended, dispossessed and persecuted and finally arranges for him to commit suicide. In short, Bond has transformed him into a conscience-stricken middle class exploiter.

Such audacious manipulation of history, however, leads to a loss of credibility on several counts, all of them a by-product of Bond's stated desire to face opposite ways simultaneously. On the one hand he claims, fairly enough, the artist's right to use history 'for my own dramatic convenience' and he certainly does this: on the other, however, he claims to have based the play on 'material facts so far as they're known'. This is demonstrably untrue: Bond embodies the personality of Susanna (Shakespeare's daughter) in the guise of an elderly servant, William Combe (a powerful landowner and acquaintance of Shakespeare) becomes several men, and the Globe Theatre is burnt down by Bond three years before it actually happened. Such misuses of historical facts, and there are many others, distort the 'material facts' on which he claims the play is based, and, as a result, impose a strain on the audience's credence of the theme the play is promoting. It is quite naive of Bond to admit these misuses in order to pre-empt 'petty criticism' of the play.

> Judith is the only daughter in the play. I gave the more comforting and strengthening role that I think Susanna played in his life to an old woman servant. I did this for my own dramatic convenience. The old woman's son is a victim of Shakespeare's business world. By making her close to Shakespeare I had a bridge between the two elements of the play, but I kept what I think is the true psychological situation: one woman (Susanna, or in the play the old woman) was close to him, and another (Judith, and probably also his wife) was estranged.
>
> I've done something similar with my account of the enclosure which involved Shakespeare. Combe represents several men, and the undertaking signed in the second scene by Combe and Shakespeare

was in fact between Shakespeare and a representative of the enclosers called Replingham (though Combe confirmed it later). Shakespeare's last binge was with Jonson and Drayton. Only Jonson is shown in the play. I've also altered some dates. For example, Shakespeare's theatre was burned down in 1613 not 1616. I made all these changes for dramatic convenience. To recreate in an audience the impact scattered events had on someone's life you often have to concentrate them. I mention all this because I want to protect the play from petty criticism. It is based on the material historical facts so far as they're known, and on psychological truth so far as I know it. The consequences that follow in the play follow from the facts, they're not polemical inventions. Of course, I can't insist that my description of Shakespeare's death is true ... I can only put the various things together and say what probably happened .... My account rather flatters Shakespeare. If he didn't end in the way shown in the play, then he was a reactionary blimp or some other fool. The only more charitable account is that he was unaware or senile. But I admit that I'm not really interested in Shakespeare's true biography in the way a historian might be. Part of the play is about the relationship between any writer and his society.

(Edward Bond, Preface to *Bingo*)

This question of what is 'petty criticism' becomes more pointed when Bond further claims in his preface that the play is based on 'psychological truth so far as I know it'. What kind of 'psychological truth' can possibly emerge from Susanna's translation into an old servant, from Bond's declaration that his version of Shakespeare's death (suicide) is 'what probably happened' and that 'if he didn't end in the way shown in the play, then he was a reactionary blimp or some other fool'?

Bond's right to use quasi-factual, even completely fictional material, is not in question. A beguiling waywardness with historical record has always been, to a degree, acceptable for entertainment or for urging some ideology, point of view or persuasion. Drinkwater's *Abraham Lincoln*, Besier's *The Barretts of Wimpole Street*, Eliot's *Murder in the Cathedral*, Brecht's *Galileo*, each in its different way testifies to the malleability of historical events and personalities. But Bond wants both to have his cake and eat it, to use history as the handmaid of modern ideology, while at the same time claiming a sort of objective historical truth for his visions.

Theatrical energy, verbal gallimaufry and intellectual agility, however, have helped Bond not only to establish his own controversial, ideologically-centred drama, but have also aided the growth of an enveloping and gripping cultural atmosphere to which a conspicuous number of critics have succumbed. He has affected the stance of dramatic criticism by a kind of goading insistence that art is really a part of the social services. He himself has abandoned the aesthetic for the social function of art, and the persuasive theatrical sensationalism of his plays has enabled him, like some latter day Pied Piper, to make his critics dance to his tune – or even to lead them by the nose!

Many critics, then, have struggled, sometimes frantically, to keep in step with their dramatist contemporaries in accepting changes that have taken root and sprouted since the 1960s. As a result one of the most enriching qualifications of a critic, manifest or implied, since the very inception of newspapers and periodicals – an easy commerce between history and value-judgement – is now fast disappearing. What Samuel Johnson regarded as the *sine qua non* would find no place in most modern criticism:

> If we were to act only in consequence of some immediate impulse and received no direction from internal motives of choice we should be pushed forward by an invincible fatality, without power or reason for the most part to prefer one thing to another, because we could make no comparison but of objects which both might happen to be present ... the present is in perpetual motion, leaves us as soon as it arrives, ceases to be present before its presence is well-perceived, and is only known to have existed by the effects which it leaves behind.

Such an apotheosis of common sense would irritate those whose modus vivendi is encapsulated in the words of David Edgar:

> ... the new theatre must be everything the old theatre is not. It must be serious in content, but accessible in form. It must be popular without being populist. It must be orientated towards a working-class audience. It must be temporary, immediate, specific, functional. It must get out of theatre buildings. It must be ideological and proud of it ... It must not be escapist; it must take our times by the throat ... the central artistic problem is portraying people's behaviour as a function of their social nexus rather than individual psychology.
>
> (James Kinson, ed., *Contemporary Dramatists*, 1977)

It is partly because the modern age has either never considered the concept given words by Johnson, or has totally rejected it, that the late twentieth century seems to have marooned itself, vulnerable and militant, on a diminishing atoll of time and value, having forgotten where it came from and fearful that the next wave will bring oblivion. Increasing numbers of our dramatists and theatre critics subsist precariously on day-to-day pickings, imagining, often fervently, that they sit at a banquet.

A further example of the theatre critic's susceptibility to the dramatist's demands is in the matter of artistic values – or lack of them – particularly as far as notions of dramatic form are concerned. This is revealed, ironically enough, even in the works of our most competent and reliable theatre critics. One wonders how Michael Billington's illustrious predecessors on *The Guardian* would react to his summing up of the state of the theatre for the year 1983.

> Looking back over my theatre-going years, I detect a couple of cheering trends. One is an increasing preoccupation with form on the part of several dramatists. Another is the ability of at least three of our mid-thirties playwrights (Hare, Hampton, and Edgar) to write works that can fill large stages and large auditoria.
>
> (Michael Billington, *The Guardian*, 30 December, 1983)

Billington seems to have a decided enthusiasm for contemporary 'functional' drama and reviews it with insight. Indeed, his writing takes on an added glow in 'the heat generated by dramatists who want to analyse, castigate and change society. But he also often responds sensitively to any non-'functional' plays that slip through the net. All the more surprising, therefore, to find him, in his round-up of theatre in 1983, lauding what he calls 'an increasing preoccupation with form on the part of several dramatists'. This sounds like an expression of approval at the unexpected reappearance of a neglected minor ingredient in the dramatist's range of choices, in their quest to communicate. This impression is reinforced by Billington's assertion that 'attention to form is not compromise: it is simply a means of communication'.

But what is any alleged piece of art without form? Where, in fact, does chaos end and the achieved order of art begin, if not at the frontier where form exists? Is not a formless play no play at all? And to describe form as simply one 'means of communication', as if there were an alternative, is tendentious – a grunt 'communicates' something, but what? Billington's celebration of a return to form could be heartily welcomed, but for him to cheer it, as if its absence had been a mere lapse of interest rather than a gap in nature, is tantamount to lauding a train driver for discovering railway lines.

Michael Billington, B.A. Young, Benedict Nightingale and Irving Wardle are the chroniclers of the drama of the seventies and eighties least suffering from tunnel vision, yet one sometimes wonders whether even they have considered that there may be a direct corollary between absent or dramatic form and the most prevalent thematic content of so many contemporary plays. Form, to a growing number of people, apparently implies cramping discipline, restriction, authoritarianism, and elitism. Such qualities are frequently explored, exploited and jeered at in contemporary drama and the rejection of form is as much a socio-political act as it is an artistic dereliction. And whether or not that alliance is deemed holy or unholy depends very much on one's stance in the face of history. Nothing, in fact, in the past thirty years, in the relationship of theatre criticism to its society and to its drama, has been more profound than this demonstrable shift to avoid, minimise, ignore if possible, the almost palpable ghost of the past.

Language

Perhaps the greatest danger any writer faces is to be misunderstood, and no writers are more vulnerable to this than critics. The most obvious precaution is to exercise great care in the use of language, to put clarity before effect, and to be brief.

But the use of language has implications beyond even these important considerations. The critic has to persuade, and he is just as likely to attempt this by force of expression as by force of argument. It is not enough even to be clear and brief – the reader has to be waylaid, engaged and held: the prospect displayed to him or her must be interesting, attractive, beguiling.

Although the main purpose of a theatre notice is to report an individual experience of a performance on a particular occasion, there is another deeper, less obvious purpose. It is to evoke, as far as is possible, something of the flavour, the distinctive tang of the performed play. All the great critics, and in particular those of the so-called Romantic period of the late eighteenth and early nineteenth centuries, have had a breath-catching ability to graft, so to speak, the performance's character and spirit on to the imagination of the reader: the 'reported' notice thus becomes a vivid evocation of the performance itself much as, in Enobarbus's description, Cleopatra's progress down the Nile in her royal barge undergoes an implied change, as he speaks, from objective past tense to subjective present tense. Similarly, nowhere is the critic's language at a higher degree of controlled creativity than when it is, like Enobarbus, annihilating the gap between past and present, between observation and re-creation. Ronald Bryden shows that this art is not dead:

> With a click of lights, a room jumps into being. An echoing grey chamber, reminiscent of that lichened brain-dungeon where, last year at the Aldwych, Beckett's Hamm and Clov railed against the dying of the light in *Endgame*. Only these walls are as bare as chalk, these furnishings a blackened, broken-backed three-piece and dresser, remnants of some Seven Sisters Road auction. They lessen the scene's bareness no more than the chewed stools and duckboards in one of the larger animal-houses at the zoo. An old man in a flat cap and dirty tennis shoes is quarrelling with a younger over the newspaper; he wants to snip out an advertisement; for cut-price Navy surplus flannel vests. His son, a sullen little Carnaby Street dandy, hogging the racing page, snarls back. The battle for the mastery of the cage is on; will continue, you know, until some intruder has either conquered or slunk away, defeated. A pungent smell of cats, decay and hostility, of

cheap toiletries and enigma, assails your ring-side nostrils. It is the smell of Pinter.

(Ronald Bryden, *The Unifnished Hero and other essays*, p. 91)

A critic who is capable of effecting this transformation is taking a big step towards capturing and holding his reader. But there is a potential liability, an ironic one, in that the notice will be in danger of diverting attention from critical appraisal and comment to its own skilful accomplishment, to its own performance.

The critic can go some way towards avoiding this by attempting to create a balance of content and communication, and the nearer he is able to achieve this the closer will his notice be (however abbreviated by time and space) to the old-fashioned, now out of fashion, essays. Two of the great practitioners of the essay, sadly it seems among the last, were J.B. Priestley and Virginia Woolf, who are read as much for their manner as for their matter and in whom shrewd comment and fecund imagination are in fine harmony. Indeed, in the earlier decades of the twentieth century, critics were almost always also regarded as belletrists – 'a category, like the maiden aunt's, that is now almost extinct' (Evelyn Waugh on his father) – and were immediately distinguishable from the majority of academic critics by their constant care for presentation, for the nuances of language. The academic sometimes does not seem to worry whether his work is 'properly dressed' or dowdy or untidy, but the sensitively literate journalist/critic who has a care for his job is always aware of the need to don exactly the right wardrobe for the task in hand. The academic expects to persuade by intellectual force, the shrewd journalist never ignores evocative presentations.

Theatre critics in the past always occupied a very high position on the graph of stylistic distinction and verbal sensitivity. Indeed, the critic's intimacy with the world of show business may well have disposed him, and sometimes still does, to a kind of self-conscious showmanship which he must be at pains to tether and control. But there is also a defensiveness in the way critics sometimes use words, as if a magic circle of wit, metaphor, pun, felicitous phrase, can give protection from any opprobrium his notice is likely to attract. Even Shaw sometimes gives the impression that he sandbags himself behind his language to escape the fury of counter attack.

What I cannot understand is why Miss Granville was cast for the queen. It is like setting a fashionable modern mandolinist to play Haydn's sonatas. She does her best under the circumstances; but she would have been more fortunate had she been in a position to refuse the part.

(G.B. Shaw, *Hamlet* at the Lyceum
2 October, 1897)

40

But conversely a skilful use of words has enabled many a critic to penetrate more deeply, often by implication, than is at first apparent to the reader. Sharp judgement (which is not by any means always the same as justice) has often hid its blade in an elegant sheath. Irony (a dying art), satire (often, these days, confused with invective), and parody (a rare gift), have all been deployed, and still sometimes are, with aplomb, efficiency and relish by the best critics to sweeten condemnation. James Fenton, one of the newer generation of critics, in this sentence pushes responsibility for the dismissive implication of his remark away from himself and on to the very actor he is reviewing!

> Dinsdale Landen's performance and make-up is probably some kind of personal attack on Denis Healey.

The most frequent display of agility in the use of the English language is to be found in theatre reviews. And, indeed, from time to time, the language's subtle, even profound, versatility is harboured in them. Hazlitt on Kean, Shaw on Terry, Tynan on Olivier, display a range of tension and tones of expression which illustrates the huge area of verbal dexterity available to the critic. Indeed, though all the other necessary qualifications be present, if the critic cannot write in a way which, in Sir Philip Sidney's phrase, 'keeps children from play and old men from the chimney corner', then that critic is, in modern parlance, a dead duck.

In the closing decades of the twentieth century, art has become progressively valued only in terms of its relationship to society, as a branch of the social services. Agate, who could say this of Priestley's *They Came To A City*, might well have been rendered speechless at almost any play by a contemporary dramatist.

> I realise that while *They Came To A City* would have had mighty little chance played to an audience of Walkleys and Beerbohms, it goes down immensely with young people devoid of dramatic perception but interested in the housing problem and wondering whether they should put their prefabricated homes together in Neasden or Gerard's Cross.
>
> (James Agate, *Ego 8*, 1946)

The advance into social relevance by artists and critics has been accompanied by a diminution in the felicity and flexibility of their language. Critical reviewing has lost a good deal of its flight-power since the 1950s and is now habitually and earnestly earth-bound. No contemporary critic of worth since Tynan can be confidently identified by a highly individual use of language, nor can, therefore, be unquestionably deemed a stylist. It is not their way in these latter days to re-work, to conjure, the spirit of a play. They anatomise it, being perhaps more surgeons than artists.

The kind of critic, therefore, of half a century ago, who was both essayist and, to a degree, creative artist, is a comparative rarity today. This change is important. It manifests itself in different critics in different ways. Tynan almost self-consciously tried to remove his belletrist garb to take on the uniform of social activist. Fortunately for his critical reputation and for the perceptive reader, he failed, and his later criticism still glows and glints with that verbal and intuitive largesse which first alerted Agate to his potential. J.W. Lambert, conditioned by his own acute musical sensitivity, and therefore disposed to 'aesthetic' appraisal, is, one senses, uneasy when faced with any play fiercely dedicated (as is the manner) to being a mirror to or scourge of society. He displays a valiant and rational attempt to treat them fairly, but his style gives away the secret of where his heart is: a winged phrase, a flight of metaphor, will suddenly swoop across his review. It is as if his intuition and imagination say – enough is enough, man does not live by bread, welfare, manifestos and social conscience alone.

Most of the younger generation shows no such reluctance or reservation. Of them, James Fenton is the most obvious and potent example of the extent of the change. Hilary Spurling writes, of a collection of Fenton's reviews, that he only rarely notices an actor and that even when he does 'his terms are more often abstract than concrete and frequently political' (The Observer, July 31, 1983).

Younger critics (like Fenton) seem just as anxious to be seen as committed to functional drama as do the majority of new playwrights. The critics' subjectivity now differs in nature from that of their near forebears. Ivor Brown, Agate, C.E. Montague, A.B. Walkley exhibited not so much an anxiety to be understood and agreed with, as a kind of relaxed gentility: their subjectivity was a meticulously displayed and carefully groomed expression of their own likes and dislikes. This was 'taste', fostered and developed by assiduously acquired knowledge, elegantly supported by experience.

> Miss Bannerman has acquired a wonderful carriage of the head – half the drawings by Charles Dana Gibson, so popular a few years ago, and half Herkomer's idea of the *maintien* of great ladies. She exhibits a very perfect sense of well-bred comedy, and makes not the smallest concession to any kind of bourgeois decency. There is so much sparkle about her performance that whenever she appears it is as though the lights in the theatre have suddenly gone up. Constance Collier, as her *vis-à-vis*, was richly comic. She trailed behind her clouds of the pork-packing business, yet wore her clothes and her manners with an air. She was, you felt, vulgar only of the soul. Her archness, her fatuousness, the ridiculousness of the Duchess's passionate forties was a joy.
>
> (James Agate, *Ego 9*, p. 226)

Today when subjectivity is a function of social conscience, there is less concern as to whether individual 'taste' is displayed or not and as 'style' today tends towards the functional, it is, as a result, amorphous: and it is the force and direction of corporate opinion which establishes a common kind of subjectivity. A substantial minority of the earlier generation of critics – particularly the successful ones – were living up to an image of the groomed man of letters. At home in those areas of society where style, in every manifestation, was appreciated and civilised judgement approved, they were regarded, and behaved as, connoisseurs. Few of today's critics have perpetuated that image. They are more like journeymen and are, moreover, one feels, proud to be so.

The X Factor

No critic can cross the line which separates pedestrian opinion from inspired appraisal without possessing a sensitive intuition. It is not enough to try gradually and painstakingly to come to a conclusion about an actor, actress, director, designer, or playwright: their qualities have, to some extent, to be nosed out. The critic must learn to interpret the message that sniffing the air of the theatre brings to him. Instinct is a precious and essential element in the critical process, and it is as valid for the critic to employ it as it is for the actor and playwright. Such instinct can be kept in trim by experience, but it cannot be so acquired. It is, like theatre, a kind of magic, as potent in its way as that which surrounds a star, or makes a play a winner or a production a hit. The mid-century critics had frequent recourse to it and their notices show its effect: one senses in their words and phrases a unique excitement such as the gambler experiences when his bet gives every indication of paying off and out.

But intuition's role is not simply to pick likely winners or give the thumbs down to probable losers. It can encourage perception and nourish an aperçu. Agate's censure of Alec Clunes for leaving out the jingle about 'imperious Caesar' in his Hamlet is a lesson in understanding and critical sensibility:

> That Shakespeare could, wittingly or unwittingly, at this juncture, contrive something that is less than great poetry and more than doggerel, something with the hint of the nursery rhyme that *in its place* is better than grandiosity's tumbling seas – this is sheer miracle.
>
> (James Agate, *Ego 8*, 1946)

That 'more than doggerel' which 'in its place' is able to chime with deep emotional exactness is

> Imperious Caesar, dead and turn'd to clay,
> Might stop a hole to keep the wind away.
> O, that the earth which kept the world in awe

43

Should patch a wall t'expel the winter's flaw.

(Shakespeare, *Hamlet*, Act 5, Sc. 1)

Only a writer who was prepared to rely on some smack of divination in pursuit of a critical truth could have written this. And only a writer whose intuition is able to perceive the soul as well as the visual effect of a performance could have written this: she was 'half dabchick and half dragonfly' (Agate on Vivien Leigh in Wilder's *The Skin of Our Teeth*).

Critical principles

The question which hangs most nearly over the head of the theatre critic is, 'What are your critical principles?' Lurking inside it is the implication that no satisfactory answer can be expected; the question often masks the implicit demand, 'What gives *you* the right to pass judgement?' A more reflective curiosity will also want to know whether the critic's 'principles' enable him to have a sense of responsibility towards his readers, or the theatre, or the acting profession, or society at large – singly or together.

The question may be easily posed but easy answers are impossible. The fly in the ointment is 'responsibility'. What kind? Is the critic to be responsible for 'educating' the public's taste, for encouraging, even advising, the theatrical profession, for proselytising the 'serious' place of drama and theatre in society, for reminding dramatists and theatre people of their 'duty' to society?

Strikingly, one has only to change one word in this assembly of presumed options – that is, 'critic' for 'director' – and wider areas of speculation are revealed, the rarely acknowledged common territory between two apparent irreconcilables. Directorial interpretation of a play is, in a deep sense, a form of critical comment; the chief difference is ironic in that the director's critical comments are embodied in and disguised by and, to a degree, made beguiling by performance. The director is thus cossetted behind, and is protected by, a screen of actors who often take the full weight of any public disapproval or discontent. The critic has no such crash barriers and, while he waits for the inevitable fierce questioning of his 'principles', few seem disposed to turn to the director and ask, 'What are your directorial principles?'

Suspicion and envy of the critic's apparent power create a burning curiosity to know what qualifications are required to enable him to wield his awful and unmerciful sword. In most other professions, degrees and diplomas – those portentous symbols – often quell all response save a kind of fearful respect. D.Litt, Ph.D., M.A., and so on, can be comfortably, if awesomely, reassuring to a curious questioner, but in a few public activities, including, in bizarre fellowship, local government and theatre criticism, a degree can be as a stone hung round the neck. The writer of an article – 'The Socialist Republic of Islington' (Andrew Stephen, *Sunday Times*, May 13, 1984) – on those seeking election to local government, comments, with what might be either irony or implacable conviction:

> To many of them, academic qualifications were also something apparently better hidden. Degrees, after all, instantly catapult the holder into the middle class in social qualifications.

This makes the process sound like a kind of social treachery and (in the mores of today) intellectually disqualifying. Similarly any critic who hoists the flag of a degree to his mast is inviting broadsides. Indeed the theatre critic is double-damned – first for being a critic at all, and, second, for violating the curious shibboleth much revered by theatre people (even that few but growing number who have accepted honorary degrees from those academic institutions hot to keep up with fashionable contemporaneity), that academic status is incompatable with 'real' critical activity. Clearly the possession of formal qualifications does not of itself imbue the critic, so far as the majority of people are concerned, with any ability to have or to hold acceptable principles.

But at a deeper level, the query about principles proceeds from a curiosity to know what makes the critic tick. Is the critic 'honest'? Is the critic 'sincere'? Do his 'opinions' and 'theories' chime with the questioner's? What is the critic's approach? Is he atheist, Mohammedan, vegetarian, Catholic, racist, Left, Right, old, young, crippled, Jewish, Irish, Welsh – and so on? The 'principles' sought multiply in clichéd words – barnacles of prejudice, pre-judgement, and pre-supposition. The search for 'principles' is, in effect, a search for the inchoate, complicated, elusive reality which is the critic's personality.

But a less militant and inchoate questioning of a critic's principles has been usually directed at his religious, moral or political stance. Here there is division by generation gap. The older generation is more concerned with the first two, the younger with the third. 'What are your critical principles?' is the way an older generation disguises its root query, 'Do you believe in God, in public and private morality?' Whereas today the younger generation is really asking, 'Where do you stand – left-wing, right-wing, or middle of the road?'

This divided approach has, at its base, one of the major problems of this century. In a society now short of public orthodox religious observances the vague but nagging sanction of 'authority' has wilted and decayed. Putting it baldly, the ten commandments, a public code of morality, a belief in heaven and

45

hell, in damnation and salvation, are now all lost leaders. Each once had its place in a system of cultural checks and balances, but they are rapidly being replaced by secular, personal, permissive expediencies, which incontinently shove behaviour along and force a new 'morality' into action. The motto of this new 'morality' is 'Everyman for himself' or 'Devil take the hindmost' or, at its most brash – 'Sod you – I'm alright'.

The battle between the old and the new 'moralities' exposed itself in a debate which billowed and bellowed about the abolition of stage censorship in the 1960s. Traditional, deeper, some may claim, moral, considerations were skated over and the storm blew itself out in a puffing and blowing about obscene words, profane words, libellous statements, taboo subjects, leaving the bulkier problems undisturbed. The opposers of censorship cried that there was a desperate need for society to be 'free' to experience anything the dramatist chose to offer it. The conscientious response from the other side – the case for a public code based on conventional/traditional/received moral principles, was never fully made, and so was doomed. The young lions, in the end, had it their own way.

In some respects the lifting of censorship has had beneficial results, as many of the thin-lipped and ludicrous restraints exercised by the Lord Chamberlain's office were wiped out. But there have been, almost equally, some baleful effects, on language and theme particularly – an uncheckable permissiveness for example, of far greater menace, being more lip-smacking than lip-pursing. It is to the credit of the majority of critics in the period under review that their notices have shown a distinctly cautious and responsible attitude towards such effects. Edward Bond's *Saved* and Edgar's *The Romans in Britain* were subjected to very sharp and relevant questioning about those incidents which made both plays a *succès de scandale*, and the latter the subject of a court action.

An ideal cadre of critics, then, would be neutral, loftily objective, disdainful of over-enthusiasm and disposed to back away from delivering verbal upper cuts. Such an ideal is a practical impossibility; even more, it would be undesirable since it would (as was said at the death of one of our greatest actors, Garrick, by one of our greatest critics, Dr Johnson) 'diminish the gaiety of nations'. Such objectivity would need only one kind of critic – and how flat, stale and unprofitable, let alone dull, that would be.

To try to establish a highway code – a set of rules to which all critics should subscribe – will only lead one up a cul-de-sac. The critic, like Everyman, is at the mercy of all the many tensions, prejudices, predilections that flesh is heir to and, again like

Everyman today, he has no firm, public structure – religious, moral, or otherwise – to bolster him up.

It seems then, that critical principles can gain little from the amorphous cultural reality of modern society. They can shape themselves only in the shifting quicksands of individual personality and the reader is therefore at the mercy of each individual critic's system of values, which is likely to be as complicated, ambiguous, contradictory as the next person's. The only possible and credible moral control available therefore to a critic is honesty – but honesty, not to some theory, foible, conviction or -ism but to his own perception of what he experiences on a particular stage, on a particular night, in a particular theatre, and to his ability to convey that to the reader.

This honesty must embrace two kinds of integrity. The first, expressed by Shaw, is incorruptibility: 'The cardinal guarantee for a critic's integrity is simply the force of the critical instinct itself. If my own father was an actor–manager and his life depended on his getting favourable notices of his performance, I should orphan myself, without an instant's hesitation, if he acted badly.'

The second, announced far less melodramatically by Agate, is to exercise the fairest appraisal the critic can muster: 'Decide what the playwright was trying to do and pronounce how well or ill he has done it . . . Determine whether the well-done thing was worth doing at all.'

These two convictions add up to the most credible and viable 'principles' available in an imperfect world. Even so, they are still often undermined by the critic's human frailties. They confirm that critical expertise is essentially based on an aspiring and subjective art and craft, whose credibility is achieved not by formalised laws but, as Shaw says, 'by the force of the critical interest itself'. That force is generated, sustained and applied not only by a highly sensitive but also by a firmly disciplined exercise of will, knowledge, experience, imagination and felicitous communication. If the word 'principles' has to be used at all there are no more viable, no more stringent ingredients than these.

It is in fact in a rigorous attempt to muster these qualities in pursuit of truth that the justification lies for the existence of critics. Not only that, those critics who come closest to exercising them best can give a depth of meaning, understanding and authority which is quite beyond the reach and vociferous claims of the 'I know what I like' hosts – which include most of us.

PLAYS IN REVIEW
1956–1980

1956

In the whole of recent British theatrical and dramatic history no date has been loaded with such significance as 1956. Equally, no play has been encumbered with such responsibility for initiating, and eventually representing, a break with past dramatic modes and a model for the future as Look Back In Anger. *Journalistic historical judgement has steadfastly upheld these views, but a sober, less flushed approach, taking more notice of the play's innate qualities than of the excited propaganda which surrounded it, shows that, as usual, iron-clad attributions to moments in history have feet of clay. Neither the play, nor its successors, nor what was claimed for it, have withstood time without considerable reservations. And, indeed, in hindsight, it can be seen that its reception by the critics after the first night in May 1956 displayed far more contention than agreement. Nevertheless, no other play of that year possessed what was regarded then as a dry raw naturalism of language and a hard-hitting theme. There is a certain blandness about even such titles as* The Chalk Garden, Nude With Violin *or* Romanoff and Juliet. *And the combination of the play's brazen directness and its speedy if reckless acceptance as a social document gave it a lofty and not entirely undeserved pre-eminence over other plays of the year.*

Look Back in Anger
John Osborne
May 1956   The Royal Court

... this is a play of extraordinary importance. Certainly it seems to have given to the English Stage Company its first really excited sense of occasion. And its influence should go far, far beyond such an eccentric and isolated one-man turn as the controversial *Waiting for Godot*.

The reasons for this are not far to seek. However one may object to the illogicality of much of Mr Osborne's detail in the matters of background painting it is true that for the first time he has raised the curtains to show us those contemporary attitudes that so many of the post-war generation have adopted and in particular that "raspberry blowing" belligerency – it is the young's particularly prickly form of honesty – which is, the result of a calm but absolute disillusionment. It is life, in fact, as many representatively dour and graceless young people now live it.

(From: Derek Granger, *Financial Times*, 10 May, 1956)

This first play has passages of good violent writing, but its total gesture is altogether inadequate . . . The piece consists largely of angry tirades.

(From: unsigned, *The Times*, 9 May, 1956)

If I were Mr George Devine I should regard *Look Back in Anger* as something of a test case. This is just the sort of play which the English Stage Company was created to produce; and it was created in the belief that a great capital like ours could produce an audience loyal and interested enough to invest a few shillings a week in supporting experiments like this one. If there is such an audience, let them show their interest by filling out the performances of this play. If there is not, let us all stop pretending there is, and complaining that no one comes along to do just what Mr Devine is now doing.

Of course, *Look Back in Anger* is not a perfect play. But it is a most exciting one, abounding with life and vitality, and the life it deals with is life as it is lived at this very moment – not a common enough subject in the English theatre. The three young people who are crowded together in a top flat in some Midlands town, are being slowly destroyed. Jimmy Porter, the protagonist, is a brilliant young intellectual adrift, and since he can find no other way of using it, he is employing his intelligence to punish himself and everyone round him. It is a dazzling performance, and he knows it (he is not an attractive hero). It is also a monstrous one, and he knows that, too. But he can't stop it; the self-destroyers never can. He has seen through all the tricks of self-deception by which we people persuade ourselves that life is worth living, and debunks them in a brilliantly funny series of tirades. His is the genuinely modern accent – one can hear it no doubt in every other Espresso bar, witty, relentless, pitiless and utterly without belief. Since he cannot find himself a place, he must compensate by making fun of all those who can; and his wit bites home.

It is painful as well as funny, and someone must suffer for it, the one who is nearest, in this case his wife. She has had the misfortune to be better born socially than he and he uses this incessantly and brutally – but any other excuse would do. All she can do is suffer the assault, helped out by the inarticulate Cliff

Lewis, the dumb and loyal friend who is always the necessary third in this kind of marriage. Mr Osborne understands some aspects of life deeply, and renders them truly, and one of his particular merits is to dare to go further in showing us the things that people do to one another than is usually revealed on the stage.

Not a pleasant play, then. The battle goes on repetitively in its squalid setting. The wife is temporarily driven out; her best friend replaces her, and she too gives up. There is not enough action and it is not all convincing. But what remains completely convincing is the mood and the contemporary language in which it is expressed. Mr Osborne's mistakes of construction are so howling that I am inclined to believe that we have all missed his intentions here. He is an actor himself, and must know that you can't keep building up expectancy for characters who never appear (unless their non-appearance is their point). Then he fails to base his hero's predicament on any dramatised motives. Motives are written into the text, true; but they are not working in it, fomenting it and aërating it. In the naturalistic form he has chosen (perhaps mistakenly), we inevitably ask questions which aren't answered. A sweet-stall, for instance, is such an odd choice of occupation for an intellectual *manqué* that we need an explanation. We need lots of other explanations, too, and feel cheated not to be given them. The biggest cheat of all is Mr Osborne's end. He has too successfully persuaded us of his hero's state of mind, to palm us off with a phoney reconciliation.

All the same, don't miss this play. If you are young, it will speak for you. If you are middle-aged, it will tell you what the young are feeling. It is particularly well acted by Mr Devine's resident company. Mr Kenneth Haigh's young intellectual completely convinced me; he missed none of the savage humour and was endlessly resourceful in getting variety. Above all he avoided, as the part demanded, drawing sympathy to himself. The sympathy goes to his wife, and Miss Mary Ure, dumbly taking it, gave one of her best performances; while Mr Alan Bates was admirably self-effacing as the third member of the ménage. Miss Helena Hughes and Mr John Welsh completed the strong cast. The true and vivid interpretation of the actors was the best of tributes to Mr Tony Richardson's intelligent direction.

(T.C. Worsley, *New Statesman*, 19 May, 1956)

The author and the actors too did not persuade us wholly that they really 'spoke for' a lost, maddened generation. There is the intention to be fair – even to the hated bourgeois parents of the cool and apparently unfeeling wife who is at length brought to heel by a miscarriage. The trouble seems to be in the overstatement of the hero's sense of grievance: like one of Strindberg's woman-haters, he ends in a kind of frenzied preaching in an empty conventicle. Neither we in the audience nor even the other Bohemians on the stage with him are really reacting to his anger. Numbness sets in.

Kenneth Haigh battled bravely with this awkward 'first-play' hero without being able to suggest much more than a spoilt and neurotic bore who badly needed the attention of an analyst. No sooner was sympathy quickened than it ebbed again. Mary Ure as the animal, patient wife, Helena Hughes as a friend who comes to stay and reign in the sordid attic and Alan Bates as a cosy young puppy, that third party who sometimes holds a cracking marriage together, were more easily brought to life. Tony Richardson's production and a good set by Alan Tagg help out this strongly felt but rather muddled first drama. But I believe they have got a potential playwright at last, all the same.
(From: Philip Hope-Wallace, *Manchester Guardian*, 10 May, 1956)

The fact that he writes with charity has led many critics into the trap of supposing that Mr Osborne's sympathies are wholly with Jimmy. Nothing could be more false. Jimmy is simply and abundantly alive; that rarest of dramatic phenomena, the act of original creation, has taken place; and those who carp were better silent. Is Jimmy's anger justified? Why doesn't he *do* something? These questions might be relevant if the character had failed to come to life; in the presence of such evident and blazing vitality, I marvel at the pedantry that could ask them. Why don't Chekhov's people *do* something? Is the sun justified in scorching us? There will be time enough to debate Mr Osborne's moral position when he has written a few more plays. In the present one he certainly goes off the deep end, but I cannot regard this as a vice in a theatre that seldom ventures more than a toe into the water.

Look Back in Anger presents post-war youth as it really is, with special emphasis on the non-U intelligentsia who live in bed-sitters and divide the Sunday papers into two groups, 'posh' and 'wet'. To have done this at all would be a signal achievement; to have done it in a first play is a minor miracle. All the qualities are there, qualities one had despaired of ever seeing on the stage – the drift towards anarchy, the instinctive leftishness, the automatic rejection of 'official' attitudes, the surrealist sense of humour (Jimmy describes a pansy friend as 'a female Emily Brontë'), the casual promiscuity, the sense of lacking a crusade worth fighting for, and, underlying all these, the determination that no one who dies shall go unmourned.

One cannot imagine Jimmy Porter listening with a straight face to speeches about our inalienable right to flog Cypriot schoolboys.

You could never mobilise him and his kind into a lynching mob, since the art he lives for, jazz, was invented by Negroes; and if you gave him a razor, he would do nothing with it but shave. The Porters of our time deplore the tyranny of 'good taste' and refuse to accept 'emotional' as a term of abuse; they are classless, and they are also leaderless. Mr Osborne is their first spokesman in the London theatre. He has been lucky in his sponsors (the English Stage Company), his director (Tony Richardson), and his interpreters: Mary Ure, Helena Hughes, and Alan Bates give fresh and unforced performances, and in the taxing central role Kenneth Haigh never puts a foot wrong.

That the play needs changes I do not deny: it is twenty minutes too long, and not even Mr Haigh's bravura could blind me to the painful whimsey of the final reconciliation scene. I agree that *Look Back in Anger* is likely to remain a minority taste. What matters, however, is the size of the minority. I estimate it at roughly 6,733,000 which is the number of people in this country between the ages of twenty and thirty. And this figure will doubtless be swelled by refugees from other age-groups who are curious to know precisely what the contemporary young pup is thinking and feeling. I doubt if I could love anyone who did not wish to see *Look Back in Anger*. It is the best young play of its decade.

(From: Kenneth Tynan, *The Observer*, 13 May, 1956)

1957

Osborne's second great success – The Entertainer – was a dominant theatre experience in 1957. But although some critics saw in it the same acidic motivations which had made Look Back in Anger a kind of cause célèbre, there can be little doubt that it was the character of Archie Rice and Olivier's consummate realisation of it which largely accounted for its success. It helped to establish the actor as the possessor of the greatest effective range of versatility since Garrick, and his acting conveniently dazzled the eyes and enthralled the ears so that the very obvious structural weaknesses of the play were discerned only by a few. Some of these attributed the flaws to Osborne's half-hearted digestion of Brecht's influence – which, as time went on, came more and more to occupy what some thought an unjustifiable prominence in the theory and practice of British Theatre.

Another theme whose buzzing for attention became more insistent in 1957 was 'Absurdism'. Its insistence was increased by a play which, almost alone, challenged The Entertainer's hold on the theatre-going public – N.F. Simpson's A Resounding Tinkle. Claims were made for it as the first English 'Absurdist' play, but Tynan best caught its quality by declaring that it derived from 'the best Benchley [i.e. Robert Benchley, the American humourist], the wildest Thurber cartoons and the cream of the Goon shows'.

The co-habitation of 'Brechtian', 'Absurdist' and 'Kitchen-sink' drama in discussion, theorising and practice makes it clear, despite the monopolistic position accorded to Look Back in Anger as the harbinger of the new overwhelming 'kitchen-sink' naturalism, that other formidable issues were in the air. As a slightly ironic tailpiece it should be noted that it was the English Stage Company at the Royal Court – hailed as the home-fastness of kitchen-sinkery – which also domiciled Simpson's A Resounding Tinkle and another 'Absurdist' offering, Nigel Dennis's stage-version of his novel, Cards of Identity. This was a nine days' wonder in which Osborne shone as an actor!

1957

The Entertainer
John Osborne
April 1957   The Royal Court

It is no great play but no bad evening either.
(From: Philip Hope-Wallace, *Manchester Guardian*, 11 April, 1957)

I suppose Archie stands for the little man of today who cannot
cope . . . He [Olivier] ran the whole gamut and struck every note
except the one *right* one, which I think he is congenitally incapable
of striking; he cannot be *vulgar*. [Olivier's Rice is] a remarkable
failure . . . I could not believe in his genteel accent. It was all like
charades at the castle.
(From: Richard Buckle, *Plays and Players*, May 1957)

Mr John Osborne's new play at the Royal Court Theatre will have
the happy result of confirming all sorts of opposite-minded
people in their opinions. It will confirm those who saw in his first
play a genuinely new and exciting talent; it will confirm equally
those who questioned his ability to construct a play. It will confirm
the pessimists in their belief that the commercial managements
don't know their business because they have neglected an author
who can, as it turns out, fill a theatre for five weeks before the
play opens. And it will confirm the optimist too, because one of
our two leading actors whom any commercial manager would
give his eye-teeth to persuade into a play, prefers to support Mr
Osborne and the English Stage Company.
  The first thing to be said about *The Entertainer* is that it is
stamped throughout with the unmistakable and authentic personal accent of its author's individual style. It is the same voice
speaking as we heard in *Look Back in Anger*, making the same kind
of protest. In the theatre where we hear so many banalities, so
much utility dialogue and stock line of language, it is a delight in
itself to hear a genuine personal style. This play differs from the
last by being an attempt to move out from the realistic four-wall
convention. And it is, I suggest, in this attempt that the play has
got itself bogged down. For in fact it falls pretty squarely between
the two stools. For seven-tenths of its length it is in fact a family
drama (not very ably conducted), and of the remaining fraction,
one part is highly successful, two parts not.
  The dazzling successful part, as everyone now knows, is the
superb impersonation by Sir Laurence Olivier of a seedy
music-hall comedian treading the boards of some low suburban
hall. This is a virtuoso turn so staggeringly perfect and exact, and
so funny, that it is even in danger of throwing the play by its sheer
excellence . . .

Mr Osborne's vision of England is expressed through three generations. There is Grandad, continually reminding us in the words of his old songs that life is not what it used to be, that our glory lies in the past; there are the middle-aged Father and Mother living mechanically on tired routines, on tattered and tatty patterns of gentility and patriotism – and on gin; and there are the young people who are simply – there is no need to avoid the phrase – angry. Of these groups only the middle one begins to be successfully handled. Grandad, in spite of all the resources of the resourceful Mr George Relph, is, frankly, a purely conventional character, who easily, and indeed very early, becomes a bore. The long opening scene between him and the daughter is so much waste. The necessary information in it could be conveyed by any competent working dramatist in a page of dialogue. Nor in later scenes does Grandad enrich the texture with anything except clichés.

Of the two young people the girl does from time to time express a current mood. Her first outburst is in admiration of her brother Frank, who spent six months in jail as a conscientious objector, as against her other brother Mick who is on the pages of the evening papers as a hero for some exploit in Egypt, and is thereby raising the easy, flag-waving sentimentality of her parents. And later she has one or two other characteristic outbursts. But Mr Osborne is singularly careless (perhaps deliberately so in pursuit of some Brechtian purpose?) about placing and defining his characters. This girl Jean is engaged to a 'posh' type, but the engagement is in danger or is broken. She has been teaching painting to a class of juvenile delinquents whom she despises. She has been attending demonstrations in Trafalgar Square, but in a very half-hearted, unengaged sort of way. It is all extraordinarily negative and driveless – without this nihilism being built up as the point of her. Too much of the time she is used as a mere feed to her father. Miss Tutin makes what she can of the outbursts, but for the most part she has a thankless task. . . .

This inability to place his characters, to give them the emotional weight where it is needed if they are to affect us, is visible even in the best creation in the play, the Entertainer himself. Archie Rice, the sad and seedy performer in public, is evidently in private life something very different from the conventional idea of that kind of man. He is capable of turning on his wife with a line of invective as pungent, educated and contemporary as Jimmy Porter's. He is given lines such as 'Observation is the basis of all art' or 'Engaged? Rather suburban for intellectual types like you?' Now, a man capable at the same time of comments such as those, and of the public performances we have seen him give, needs a bit of explaining. Certainly very much more than Mr Osborne bothers to give, and decidedly at an earlier stage than he gives it.

The fact is that Mr Osborne has not yet taught himself the most elementary of the playwright's techniques. In addition to this question of the weighting and placing of explanation – all the sleight of hand of 'preparation' – his narrative technique barely exists. It would be a great pity if, encouraged by his too enthusiastic admirers, he should simply come to despise these technical devices. It is fashionable to regard them as only a set of tricks. But they are in fact the grammar of his craft. If he will learn them, it will strengthen not weaken his plays.

(From: T.C. Worsley, *New Statesman*, 20 April, 1957)

Mr Osborne's favourite dramatic *milieu* is the slums of culture. In *Look Back in Anger* his vituperative and poverty-stricken hero reads the best book reviews, though I remember with a touch of disappointment that he took no interest in dramatic criticism. In Mr Osborne's new play the theatre is prominent enough, but dramatic criticism is still absent. For the entertainer, Archie Rice, belongs to that section of the drama, the decaying music halls, the twice-nightly nude revues, into which the dramatic critic is rarely invited to enter.

In these seedy surroundings, Archie Rice, with his dreadful jokes, his puffed, glazed face, his second-rate tap dancing, his doubtful songs, and desperate sauciness ('I have a go, don't I, ladies? I have a go'), his awful leers, and the terrible heartiness with which he tries to cover up a turn that falls flat, attempts night after night to amuse small, apathetic audiences who are only there to see the nudes come on again.

There can hardly be a greater torture than to fulfil a destiny like that, to seek with a sickening confidence twelve times a week, for the laughter that never comes, and then to pretend, to yourself, and your audiences, and your family, that you don't care anyway, because anything that was ever real in you, and capable of response to true emotion, as distinct from what can be got out of the gin-bottle, died long ago. To carry on like this, year after year, is also a form of heroism; and when Archie at the end, the police waiting to take him for unpaid income tax (surely he couldn't have been liable for much?) utters for the last time his 'I have a go, don't I, ladies? I have a go', the words rise over the sordid battlefield like at tattered banner.

* * *

I do not believe that a man like Archie, with no strength of character, and no positive conviction of any kind could have borne his disasters with such bruised panache. That is why I call Mr Osborne's play sentimental. But its theatrical effect is enormous. Splendid as Sir Laurence is when showing us Archie on the stage, he is even finer when he gets home to his squalid drunken family. There are ten mintues, from the moment when he begins telling his daughter, with a defiant, ashamed admiration, of a negress singing a spiritual in some low night club, to his breakdown on hearing of his son's death, when he touches the extreme limits of pathos. You will not see more magnificent acting than this anywhere in the world.

In showing the terrible quarrelling of an unhappy home, Mr Osborne for long stretches throws his sentimentality aside. He writes with a true and frightening fidelity. His players give performances of the highest class. Dorothy Tutin is poignant in one of those frequently unworded parts which Mr Osborne composes so skilfully for young actresses. Brenda de Banzie brings out the pitiful inadequacy of the drab wife, George Relph as Archie's father perfectly establishes the old man's irritated longing for the past, and Richard Pasco gives to the grandson an impressively kindly bitterness.

(From: Harold Hobson, *Sunday Times*, 14 April, 1957)

Archie is a droll, lecherous fellow, comically corrupted. With his blue patter and jingo songs he is a licensed pedlar of emotional dope to every audience in Britain. The tragedy is that, being intelligent, he knows it. His talent for destructive self-analysis is as great as Jimmy Porter's. At times, indeed, when he rails in fuddled derision at 'our nasty sordid unlikely little problems', he comes too close to Jimmy Porter for comfort or verisimilitude. He also shares the Porter Pathological Pull towards bisexuality, which chimes with nothing else in his character, though it may be intended to imply that he has made a sexual as well as a moral compromise. . . .

In short: Mr Osborne has planned a gigantic social mural and carried it out in a colour range too narrow for the job. Within that range he has written one of the great acting parts of our age. Archie is a truly desperate man, and to present desperation is a hard dramatic achievement. To explain and account for it, however, is harder still, and that is the task to which I would now direct this dazzling, self-bound writer.

(From: Kenneth Tynan, *The Observer*, 14 April, 1957)

A Resounding Tinkle
December 1, 1957   The Royal Court

An anti-play, I should explain, is one which holds its audience through ignoring rather than conforming to theatrical conventions. It is valuable chiefly as a corrective to fixed values and received ideas.

(From: Patrick Gibbs, *The Daily Telegraph*, 3 December, 1957)

The method is that of the seemingly inconsequential. The connexion between one speech and another in a scene as it unfolds is not apparent till the end of it, is sometimes not apparent till the end of the evening. The play has been thought of not in terms of scenes or acts, but singly, continuously, as it were monolithically. Like a sculptor before his block, the playwright stands there, chiselling; with each line as he writes it a splinter is set flying. The splinters fly, pile up, and their only importance is that they have been got rid of.

(From: unsigned review, *The Times*, 2 December, 1957)

About the highest tribute I can pay N.F. Simpson's *A Resounding Tinkle*, which was tried out at the Royal Court last Sunday, is to say that it does not belong in the English theatrical tradition at all. It derives from the best Benchley lectures, the wildest Thurber cartoons, and the cream of the Goon Shows. It has some affinities with the early revues of Robert Dhery and many more with the plays of M. Ionesco. In English drama it is, as far as I know, unique. It is also astonishingly funny, and a superb vindication of the judicial acumen that placed it third in *The Observer* play competition.

To sustain anarchic humour for a full evening is among the hardest things a playwright can attempt. Once having espoused the illogical, the irrelevant, the surreal, he is committed: a single lapse into logic, relevance, or reality, and he is undone. A playwright of Mr Simpson's kind comes defenceless to the theatre. He has voluntarily discarded most of the dramatist's conventional weapons. He can have no plot, since plots demand logical development. Lacking a plot, he can make no use of suspense, that miraculous device which, by focusing our attention on what is going to happen next, prevents us from being intelligently critical of what is happening now. Mr Simpson can never free-wheel like that. At every turn he must take us by surprise. His method must be a perpetual ambush. All playwrights must invent, but he must invent incessantly and unpredictably. It is the only weapon left him – he is otherwise naked. As naked, perhaps, as a British Foreign Secretary without an H-bomb; yet unilateral disarmament, even in the theatre, is an extremely disarming thing. At least, the audience seemed to find it so.

What they saw, hilarious though it was, notably differed from the play to which we of *The Observer* awarded the prize. Mr Simpson had revised and reshuffled it, and there were moments when I felt like the American director who, revisiting one of his old productions, found it necessary to call an immediate rehearsal 'to take out the improvements'. The original text began in the suburban home of Bro and Middie Paradock, a young married couple disturbed by the presence, in their front garden, of an elephant they had not ordered. The question soon arose of how to name it. Middie conservatively favoured 'Mr Trench', their usual name for unexpectedly delivered animals, a suggestion which the radical Bro countered with bravura alternatives such as ''Tis-Pity-She's-A-Whore Hignett'. The debate was interrupted by the arrival of two Comedians, who were lodgers in the kitchen, from which they emerged from time to time to discuss, with examples, the nature of comedy. This arrangement set up what I may call, with a deep breath, a sort of counterpoint. Mr Simpson has since decided to lump all the Comedian scenes together into his first act, while reserving the Paradock scenes for the second. I take this to be a back-breaking error, and when the English Stage Company decides (as it surely must) to put on the play for a run, I hope it will amalgamate the two texts and insist on a new ending.

Even as it stands, this is a revolutionarily funny piece of work. In a programme note Mr Simpson declares his indebtedness to the simple fact that the earth, given luck, can support life for another twelve hundred thousand years. How, for so long, are we to keep ourselves amused? This is the problem that faced the tramps in *Waiting for Godot*. An astonished patience is Mr Simpson's answer, as he implies when one of the Comedians doubts the audience's ability to sit through a play full of pauses and the other replies by asking him whether he has ever complained of buying a sponge full of holes.

I prefer Mr Simpson's assumption, which is that we are all on the brink of boredom, to that of most comic writers, which is that we are all on the brink of hilarity. Bro Paradock (Nigel Davenport) is a splendidly sour creation, drab, leather-elbowed, and disgruntled, comic because he reacts with no surprise to circumstances of absolute fantasy. Neither he nor his wife, Middie (Wendy Craig, a pretty study of controlled disgust), is perturbed when their Uncle Ted turns out to be a woman; and he has nothing but quiet scorn for the man who calls and asks him, at six o'clock in the evening, to form a government. (As he says, that's the Prime Minister's job.) About a fifth of Mr Simpson's family portrait is *voulu*, polysyllabic and of a determined quaintness. The rest is pure plutonium, by which I mean something rarer than gold.

(Kenneth Tynan, *The Observer*, 8 December, 1957)

1958

The theatrical record of this year starkly shows the error of assuming that dramatic history since the Second World War is a progress from the complete dominance of one genre to another – from, as it were, West-endery to kitchen-sinkery, to Absurdism, to Brechtianism, to Theatre-of-Cruelty, et al. In fact certain dramatic genres seem to have domination over certain areas of time, but it is, in reality, more often the brilliance of a single play rather than the general quality of a group which creates a sense of oneness and this false impression. In 1958 several genres are identifiable and subject to contention. The Birthday Party and Five Finger Exercise *were, by some critics, cheerfully accommodated by 'Absurdism', stretching its territories to encompass both the impenetrable and the zany. In passing it should be noted that Pinter's first full-length play was regarded as a disaster by the critics.* Chicken Soup with Barley and A Taste of Honey *were made to live together under the shelter of 'working-class realism' though, in truth, in the Delaney play, there was as much fantasy as realism. It was undoubtedly the crucial creative interference with the author's text by the director Joan Littlewood, famed for her vibrant obsession with 'popular' theatre, which incited some critics to make a connection between Wesker's golden-hearted socialism and Delaney's young, poignant mixture of sentimental comedy and pathos. To this day few know how much of Delaney's text was left untouched and unaltered by Littlewood: indeed what is called Delaney's 'realism' may well have been Littlewood's 'Magnified realism' (John Russell Taylor's description) and the original of a somewhat different order of the imagination.*

Also, in this year, were Beckett's Krapp's Last Tape *and Behan's* The Hostage – *the one a writer who cannot safely be accommodated by any genre, the other deriving largely, despite inflated claims made for him, from a very Irish tradition of semi-poetic realism laced with political wryness.*

And finally a survivor, almost a critically discarded relic of the thirties and forties – T.S. Eliot and The Elder Statesman. *Less prescient critics almost automatically assigned it to that* genus rara, *'poetic drama', failing to realise, as many of their predecessors had done, that this pigeon-hole could not really contain the verbal restlessness and sensitivity, restraint, ambiguity and sometimes haunting music of the greatest experimenter, overall, with dramatic language since Shakespeare.*

Indeed, in one sense – where good quality and variety are concerned – 1958 was the annus mirabilis, *not 1956. The theatre-goers had an* embarras de richesse *– perhaps it took two years for the catalytic effects of* Look Back in Anger *to work: or perhaps, considering how much appeared that did not derive from* Look Back in Anger, *a mini-renaissance would have happened anyway.*

The Birthday Party
Harold Pinter
May 1958   The Lyric, Hammersmith

. . . it turned out to be one of those plays in which an author wallows in symbols and revels in obscurity. Give me Russian every time.

(From: W. Darlington, *The Daily Telegraph*, 20 May, 1958)

What all this means only Mr Pinter knows, for his characters speak in non-sequiturs, half-gibberish and lunatic ravings.

(From: M.W.W., *The Guardian*, 21 May, 1958)

One of the actors in Harold Pinter's *The Birthday Party* at the Lyric, Hammersmith, announces in the programme that he read History at Oxford, and took his degree with Fourth Class Honours.

Now I am well aware that Mr Pinter's play received extremely bad notices last Tuesday morning. At the moment I write these lines it is uncertain even whether the play will still be in the bill by the time they appear, though it is probable it will soon be seen elsewhere. Deliberately, I am willing to risk whatever reputation I have as a judge of plays by saying that *The Birthday party* is not a Fourth, not even a Second, but a First; and that Mr Pinter, on the evidence of this work, possesses the most original, disturbing, and arresting talent in theatrical London.

I am anxious, for the simple reason that the discovery and encouragement of new dramatists of quality is the present most important task of the British theatre, to put this matter clearly and emphatically. The influence of unfavourable notices on the box office is enormous; but in lasting effect it is nothing. *Look Back in Anger* and the work of Beckett both received poor notices the morning after production. But that has not prevented those two very different writers, Mr Beckett and Mr Osborne, from being regarded throughout the world as the most important dramatists who now use the English tongue. The early Shaw got bad notices; Ibsen got scandalously bad notices. Mr Pinter is not merely in good company, he is in the very best company.

*　　　*　　　*

There is only one quality that is essential to a play. It is the quality that can be found both in *Hamlet* and in *Simple Spymen*. A play must entertain; it must hold the attention; it must give pleasure. Unless it does that, it is useless for stage purposes. No amount of intellect, of high moral intent, or of beautiful writing is of the slightest avail if a play is not in itself theatrically interesting.

Theatrically speaking, *The Birthday Party* is absorbing. It is witty. Its characters – the big, oafish lodger in the slatternly seaside boarding house whose lethargy is subject to such strange bursts of alarm, the plain, middle-aged woman who becomes girlishly gay, the two visitors, one so spruce and voluble, the other so mysteriously frightened – are fascinating. The plot, which consists, with all kinds of verbal arabesques and echoing explorations of memory and fancy, of the springing of a trap, is first-rate. The whole play has the same atmosphere of delicious, impalpable, and hair-raising terror which makes *The Turn of the Screw* one of the best stories in the world.

*　　　*　　　*

Mr Pinter has got hold of a primary fact of existence. We live on the verge of disaster. One sunny afternoon, whilst Peter May is making a century at Lord's against Middlesex, and the shadows are creeping along the grass, and the old men are dozing in the Long Room, a hydrogen bomb may explode. That is one sort of threat. But Mr Pinter's is of a subtler sort. It breathes in the air. It cannot be seen, but it enters the room every time the door is opened. There is something in your past – it does not matter what – which will catch up with you. Though you go to the uttermost parts of the earth, and hide yourself in the most obscure lodgings in the least popular of towns, one day there is a possibility that two men will appear. They will be looking for you, and you cannot get away. And someone will be looking for *them*, too. There is terror everywhere. Meanwhile, it is best to make jokes (Mr Pinter's jokes are very good), and to play blind man's buff, and to bang on a toy drum, anything to forget the slow approach of doom. *The Birthday Party* is a Grand Guignol of the susceptibilities.

(From: Harold Hobson, *The Sunday Times*, 25 May, 1958)

Harold Pinter's first play comes in the school of random dottiness deriving from Beckett and Ionesco and before the flourishing continuance of which one quails in slack-jawed dismay. The interest of such pieces as an accepted genre is hardly more than that of some ill-repressed young dauber who feels he can outdo the *école de Paris* by throwing his paint on with a trowel and a bathmat; and indeed – to come back to the terms of playmaking – as good if not a better result might have been achieved by summoning a get-together of the critics circle or the vegetarians unions, offering each member a notebook and pencil and launching thereafter on an orgiastic bout of 'Consequences', with the winning line to be performed by a star-cast midnight matinee at Drury Lane.

But I have now said enough about the word-playing qualities of this arbitrary, barren and mercilessly inward-growing style; to make any further inquiry into its methods and meanings would be a bigger bore for me as it would certainly be for you. The fact that Mr Pinter has stolen a march on his predecessors by lacing his own mad, wearying and inconsequential gabble with an odd strain of Jewish banter must merely be put down to a question of time-lag. As far as the rest, the only surprising thing about it is that no one has yet offered it a prize.

What the evening is about is a more fiendish matter altogether, and except to say that it takes place in a Bratby–Eskue interior prodigally furnished with packets of cornflakes and detergent, the message, the moral, and any possible moments of enjoyment, eluded me utterly.

Apart from a seaside deckchair ticket-collector (Mr Willoughby Gray) and a spritely bare-legged floozy (Miss Wendy Hutchinson) all the characters seemed to me to be in an advanced state of pottiness or vitamin-deficiency, and quite possibly both at once.

The fact that their united barminess could be separated into that of a crazed landlady without lodgers (played with wild, grotesquestry [sic] by Miss Beatrix Lehmann); by Mr Richard Pearson as a shambling victim of neurotic inertia, and by Mr John Slater and Mr John Stratton, hailing respectively from Jewry and Ireland, seemed to be of slowly diminishing interest as the evening wore on.

The gifted Mr Peter Wood produced, but how the piece claimed the services of anyone is beyond me.

(Derek Granger, *Financial Times*, 20 May, 1958)

The Birthday Party is like a vintage Hitchcock thriller which has been, in the immortal tear-stained words of Orson Welles, 'edited by a cross-eyed studio janitor with a lawn-mower'.

(From: Alan Brien, *The Spectator*, 30 May, 1958)

1958

A Taste of Honey
Shelagh Delaney
May 1958   Theatre Royal, Stratford East

A Taste of Honey is a boozed, exaggerated, late-night anecdote of a
play which slithers unsteadily between truth and fantasy, between
farce and tragedy, between aphrodisiac and emetic. Helen is a
grammar-school girl with a music-hall tart of a mother, and a
nightmare Negro lover, and a strip-cartoon dude of a stepfather,
and a police-court pansy of a best friend. Each character swells
into focus through a different distorting lens. The play is written
as if it were a film script with an adolescent contempt for logic or
form or practicability upon a stage, and Miss Joan Littlewood has
produced it with the knockabout inconsequence of an old-
fashioned Living Newspaper tract. Twenty, ten, or even five years
ago, before a senile society began to fawn upon the youth which is
about to devour it, such a play would have remained written in
green longhand in a school exercise book on the top of the
bedroom wardrobe.

(From: Alan Brien, *The Spectator*, 6 June, 1958)

If I tell you that the heroine was born of a haystack encounter
between her mother and a mental defective; that a Negro sailor
gets her pregnant and deserts her; and that she sets up house,
when her mother marries a drunk, with a homosexual art student
– when I tell you this, you may legitimately suspect that a tearful
inferno of a play awaits you. Not a bit of it.

The first half is broad comedy (comedy, perhaps, is merely
tragedy in which people don't give in); almost too breezily so; and
Joan Littlewood's direction tilts it over into farce by making Avis
Bunnage, as the girl's brassy mother, address herself directly to
the audience, music-hall fashion. The second half is both comic
and heroic. Rather than be lonely, the gutsy young mother-to-be
shares her room (though not her bed) with a skinny painter who
enjoys mothering her and about whose sexual whims ('What
d'you do? Go on – what d'you do?') she is uproariously curious.
Together they have what amounts to an idyll, which is interrupted by mother's return with her puffy bridegroom, who likes
older women and wears an eyepatch – this brings him, as he
points out, at least halfway to Oedipus. By the end of the evening
he has left, and so, without rancour, has the queer. A child is
coming: as in many plays of this kind, life goes on. But not
despondently: here it goes on bravely and self-reliantly, with a
boisterous appetite for tomorrow. . . .

There are plenty of crudities in Miss Delaney's play: there is
also, more importantly, the smell of living. When the theatre

66

presents poor people as good, we call it 'sentimental'. When it presents them as wicked, we sniff and cry 'squalid'. Happily, Miss Delaney does not yet know about us and our squeamishness, which we think moral but which is really social. She is too busy recording the wonder of life as she lives it. There is plenty of time for her to worry over words like 'form', which mean something, and concepts like 'vulgarity', which don't. She is nineteen years old: and a portent.

(From: Kenneth Tynan, *The Observer*, 1 June, 1958)

Chicken Soup with Barley
Arnold Wesker
July 1958   The Royal Court

... his potential as a dramatist is undoubtedly great.
(From: Peter Jackson, *Plays and Players*, September, 1958)

It is a play that finds some difficulty in concentrating its meaning, but the author has something to say.
(From: unsigned review, *The Times*, 15 July, 1958)

Best moments, which were very good indeed, were not those of serious political inspiration or discussion, but the humorous genre scenes of Jewish family life and young Communist cameraderie.
(From: Patrick Gibbs, *The Daily Telegraph*, 15 July, 1958)

Mr Wesker's socialism is more emotional than intellectual; he is concerned less with economic analysis than with moral imperatives. His rhetoric sometimes rings hollow, and what distinguishes his style is not so much its subtlety as its sturdiness. All the same, nobody else has ever attempted to put a real, live, English Communist family on to the stage; and the important thing about Mr Wesker's attempt is that they *are* real, and they *do* live.
(From: Kenneth Tynan, 12 June, 1960, on the production of the Trilogy at the Royal Court; reprinted in *Left and Right*, 1960)

1958

Five Finger Exercise
Peter Shaffer
July 1958   Comedy Theatre

By the end one knows that Mr Shaffer may easily become a
master of the theatre.

(From: Harold Hobson, *The Sunday Times*, 25 July, 1958)

At its best this play provides a devastatingly true picture of the
way human beings suffer and yet remain isolated and totally
unable to understand one another.

(From: Peter Roberts, *Plays and Players*, September 1958)

I belong to the generation which thoroughly enjoys a good play. I
make this damaging admission in the full awareness that it puts
me out of court with all of those who take their theatre with a
proper seriousness. And to make my position unequivocally clear
let me add that I am using the phrase 'a good play' in the
vulgarest sense, as Aunt Edna would use it. I do not go to the
theatre to be educated or to be alienated. I am all for what Mr
Lindsay Anderson calls 'sloppy identification', I am. Naturally
there are distinctions to be made. There are bad 'good plays' as
well as good ones and to indicate what I mean I should call
Priestley's *Dangerous Corner* and the late Ronald McKenzie's
Musical Chairs good ones.

Now, there has just opened at the Comedy a very good 'good'
play, *Five Finger Exercise*. It is an unpublicised first play by an
unpublicised writer, Mr Peter Shaffer, and I confidently and
warmly recommend it to everyone who shares my taste. It has
distinct affinities with both of the plays I have mentioned, in
theme to the Priestley, in atmosphere to the McKenzie. Neither
the subject nor the milieu nor the characters are particularly
original. It is (I almost blush to record it in these days) a family
play, and that family is (now indeed I do blush) both English and
middle-class. What distinguishes it is the treatment. Mr Shaffer
can write, and can write well enough to bring new life to familiar
situations. The English middle-class family is certainly a long
fought over emotional battle-field. But the skirmishes are new to
each set of participants, and what we require of a playwright is
that he makes his new for us. Mr Shaffer does. The conflict in his
conventional family may be conventional. But then such conflicts
are. The point is that he has the ability to give them depth. Not
depth of complexity but depth in time. From the very first we feel
that this group of people has been really living together, scraping
against each other, year after year. We come in at a chosen point
in a continuous history. The past vibrates in the present, and it is

this which makes for the kind of reality that really matters in a play about a family. . . .

Adrianne [sic] Allen's role as the mother does not allow her to expose her face so nakedly. At first sight she seems to be walking through her part. She doesn't seem to be speaking her own words. She doesn't seem to be picking her own route through the smart, contemporary furniture. She seems to see the other characters as cues rather than people. But soon it becomes apparent that she is operating the most subtle double-bluff. She is the woman inside the woman she plays. And when she strips off, the revelation is doubly terrible. . . .

Mr Shaffer's dialogue has pace and bite though no great wit. His faults are glibness and whimsy. But he has kept his suburban cabbage patch to almost window-box size – and every leaf and caterpillar is minutely observed.

(From: T.C. Worsley, *New Statesman*, 26 July, 1958)

The Harringtons are a cannibal family in Suffolk. Snap-crackle-pop like the talking cereal, they spoon each other down reluctantly with cream and sugar at breakfast. At lunch, rather more enthusiastically, each carves from the one on his left a generous bloody helping. Through the long, indigestible after-noon, they drink each other with a splash of soda. They love being eaten almost as much as they love eating. When one opens his mouth the others rush to put their feet in it. And at night they toss and turn, dreaming painfully of somebody they ate. In other words, they are a normal happy family – at least as incarnated on the stage by our modern young playwrights today.

If Peter Shaffer had been content to write another propaganda tract in the Age War, then *Five Finger Exercise* could have been dismissed with a mild pat on the head. But his great achievement has been to convince us that the family really is normal. Like all cannibals, the Harringtons are decent, ordinary, respectable people who are only unconventional in their menus. Mr Shaffer takes no sides, follows no party line. He has no hero and no villains. He does not blame Society, or the System, or Religion, or Sex. Life is the disease and more life is the cure.

Each member of the family can see the fatal spot between the eyebrows of the rest. But his own weakness seems to him his strength. The father is a self-made man – and like all self-made men he adores the cracks and bulges in his own jerry-built façade. His boast is that he doesn't understand anything except money. 'You're proud of it,' the son bursts out. 'As if it defined you. I'm the Man Who Doesn't Understand.' And yet the father's know-ledge of money is still knowledge of something real – he knows the cost, if not the value, of his family's flaws. He knows that his wife's veneer of culture is painted on like lipstick. He knows that his son's sensitivity is just another form of cowardice. And you can feel whole rows of the orchestra stalls identifying with him.

Roland Culver's performance in the role is the finest piece of Method acting in Britain today. Critics who ought to know better have been blinded by his long columns in *Who's Who in the Theatre*. He has been described as 'cruelly miscast'. If that is miscasting, then it is about time every actor in Shaftesbury Avenue swopped parts with his neighbour. With his mournful, eroded Macmillan face, the face of a fossilised arrowhead, he suffers the tortures of an inarticulate St Anthony. In baffled anger, in stony contempt, in pitiable palliness, in defeated apathy, Mr Culver is a real man trapped in an invisible net of cause and effect. I can hardly believe that he will re-create these unbearable blind strugglings night after night and live.

(Alan Brien, *The Spectator*, 25 July, 1958)

The playwright examines a frustrated household of ostensibly well-to-do and happy people. True, Mr Harrington, who has made the money, is touchy about being thought common. Mrs Harrington is compensating for a not very happy marriage by becoming an intellectual snob. The son, just up at Cambridge, is dangerously like 'a mother's boy', to put it no more plainly.

The pony-loving adolescent daughter is probably the least tangled. And the catalyst? A smooth, mature young German tutor, who gives himself out as an orphan. He worships this family of his adoption; and they batten on him – rather as some tongue-tied families will use a dog to test otherwise inadmissible feelings and attitudes of affection. Slowly, much too slowly, the ugliness of the pattern of jealousies and loneliness is opened up – to be brought to a violent and by no means ineffective breaking point.

What then is missing? The ability to create sympathy. Mr Shaffer can analyse his rather pathetically shallow characters persuasively enough. But between 'pathetic' and 'sympathetic' there is that all important inch – which is never crossed here, unless it is so momentarily by the son of the house (Brian Bedford) and the enigmatic German romantic (in a striking performance by Michael Bryant which held the house). These are first rate; Juliet Mills as the girl has a charming success of another kind; and Adrienne Allen as the mother, and Ronald Culver as the father both tied up in incommunicable agonies of jealously do not fail – though one hardly calls them ideally cast. The study earns respect. For myself, I must say that it did not catch me up into emotional surrender or belief.

(From: Philip Hope-Wallace, *The Guardian*, 17 July, 1958)

The Elder Statesman
T.S. Eliot
August 1958   Lyceum, Edinburgh
September 1958   Cambridge Theatre

It has happened exactly as we expected it would happen. T.S. Eliot's *The Elder Statesman* – at the Lyceum – is the finest modern English play seen at any Edinburgh Festival since *The Confidential Clerk*. It is strong and sure in conception and evocative in writing, at once a touching drama and a stimulating piece of literary criticism. In the Festival production there are two good performances, a third which is superb, and none which is positively bad. The director, E. Martin Browne, has kept an exquisite balance between Mr Eliot's poetry, pathos, and philosophy, and even his pedagogy is charmingly and modestly recalled by Hutchinson Scott's setting for the second act, which shows a summer-house in the grounds of a sanatorium.

This summer-house is thrown into the form of a Greek temple, and the fascinating thing about it is that its latticed roof is broken and decayed. It is well known that in *The Elder Statesman* Mr Eliot has in contemporary terms retold the story of *Oedipus at Colonus*, and, with an Ibsenite skill of construction, implied that of *Oedipus Rex*. Only a dramatist of Mr Eliot's stature could afford so delicately to suggest that although he tells both stories well, Sophocles told them better. . . .

Oedipus brought upon Thebes a plague; and Claverton has put a blight on everyone he has touched, on the old Oxford friend he unconsciously turned into a swindler, on the foolish girl whom he deceived, and on the son whom he has not been able to deceive. It is one of the qualities of this play, as of all outstanding plays, that it leaves a large margin for speculation. Whether Claverton's dead wife also had been one of his victims is as unsettled a question as how many children had Lady Macbeth. And why do the people that Claverton ruins do so well in the world? Has Mr Eliot a contempt for riches? It would be in the conventional character of a poet if he had: but one remembers that for a poet he has all his life shown an uncommon tenacity in sticking to a well-paid job. And why is it so subtly and so insistently made clear that Claverton, not really knowing any more than Oedipus what evil he has done, has never been a quite first-rate man?

Is there here, or is there not, an implication about Oedipus himself? These questions admit of a wide solution: and the prompting of them adds a peripheral pleasure to the satisfaction of a play both peaceful and profound.

*   *   *

The opening duet between Claverton's daughter Monica and her fiancé deals in those tinkling repetitive trivialities by means of which Mr Eliot loves to approach the theme of his plays. Here again is an echo, and not too happy a one, of *The Cocktail Party*. But with the entrance of Claverton himself, not old, but very, very ill, the poetry strengthens as it darkens. There is a passage about the desolation of railway waiting-rooms after the last train has gone which shows how well Mr Eliot remembers the geography of 'The Waste Land' even though *The Elder Statesman* is about how to escape from it.

(From: Harold Hobson, *The Sunday Times*, 31 August, 1958 – Lyceum, Edinburgh)

... the third act flowers into the best scene the dramatist has written in his later style.

(From: J.C. Trewin, *Plays and Players*, October, 1958 – Lyceum, Edinburgh)

The Elder Statesman comes to London with the reputation of having been the most pre-booked play of the Edinburgh Festival. It presents the passionate playgoer with an inescapable question. Is there a place, outside the English Stage Company, for the Theatre of the Poet – that there is great need for the poet in the theatre is not in question – and it is just my luck to find myself cast as The Oracle without The Answer Pat. The problem does not lie with the dramatist with the eye to see, the ear to hear, and the heart to feel, whose insight can turn people into poems – muddled, maybe, but poignant and glorious poems – so that their predicaments rise with them into the realms of high tragedy or highly comical tragedy according to the genre in which they are conceived. For to these writers a dramatic situation generates an incandescence which sets the stage alight with the tensions of people in opposition to one another or to fate, and what they do and say and feel in their moment of truth will be common to all mankind. The Theatre then is perhaps above all places the province of the poet whose vision passes into the characters he creates and is so deeply integrated that he speaks to us only with their voices and through them.

But the Theatre of the Poet is something very different. For here it is the Poet himself who speaks to us, not, as it were in the words of his characters, but in despite of characterisation.

Here it is the word and its arrangement in the phrase that is important and the people in the play are nothing but the author's loudspeakers; necessary nuisances to be bundled on and off as summarily as Nannie's anger, falling upon a nursery offender.

And in passing we must not forget that the poet, treading the tightrope of his sentences with his obsession for finding the perfect word and setting it in the perfect place, is a greater show-off than any over-excited child high on his own spirits, in every sense, 'above himself'. . . .

Why, then, did I, who so greatly love my Fry and my O'Casey, and somewhere in between, my Ionesco and my Godot; why did I hate *The Elder Statesman*?

Not for its matter. For if it said anything at all it was 'love one another'. The advice is admirable if not new and heaven knows the world could ponder worse. . . .

No, it was the stilted manner of the delivery of the message that maddened me; the way that it was always the writer, never the people in the play – or almost never – who appeared to be addressing us or one another; the cursory working-out of a plot, the obscurity of purpose and the lack of any communicated conviction.

Yet Mr Eliot is a fine, illuminating and convincing poet on the page – here is no writing-down, no literary slumming. And if I cannot understand a thought in one of Mr Eliot's poems it is not because it has been stated without care and passion, but simply that my mind is not in a sufficient state of grace to receive it.

(From: Caryl Brahms, *Plays and Players*, November, 1958 –
Cambridge Theatre)

Last week, for the third time in twelve years, the Edinburgh Festival presented the world *première* of a play by T.S. Eliot. It has not always been the same play, though sometimes it has seemed so: in this author's imagination the same themes compulsively (and not always compellingly) recur, among them a guilt-bearing death in a man's past, the human need for contrition and absolution, and the paradox whereby true selfhood can be attained only through self-abnegation.

The Elder Statesman contains all these, together with a rich haul of familiar stylistic devices. Images calculated to evoke well-bred dread cluster together ('The laughter in the doorway, the snicker in the corridor, the sudden silence in the smoking-room'); percipient aphorisms alternate with verbal horseplay, as when an old lag remarks:

Forgery, I can tell you, is a mug's game.
I say that with conviction. Ha ha! Yes, with conviction.

And Mr Eliot's trick of iteration frequently verges on outright parody:

I see more and more clearly
The many many mistakes I have made
My whole life through, mistake upon mistake,

73

    The mistaken attempts to correct mistakes
    By methods which proved to be equally mistaken.

At moments like this *The Elder Statesman* comes dangerously near to the competition pages of the *New Statesman*.

But if the old Eliot is well in evidence, the voice of a new Eliot is also heard, unexpectedly endorsing the merits of human love. It is a safe bet that the word 'love' occurs more often in the present play than in all the author's previous work put together: the new Eliot has majored in the Humanities as well as the Eumenides. Often in the past, as the latest Eliot unfolded chill and chaste before us, we have inwardly murmured: 'Poor Tom's a-cold'. Now, by comparison, he is positively aflame.

Encouraging though we may find this step in his spiritual development, it is not by itself enough to make good theatre. In some ways, indeed, it has the opposite effect: Mr Eliot's Indian-summer love-lyrics have little distinction, either literary or dramatic. A new simplicity has certainly entered his style, but so has simplicity's half-wit brother, banality; and at times one longs for the old equivocations, for just one kind of characteristic ambiguity.

This banality extends to the plot. Lord Claverton, politician and tycoon, has retired to a convalescent home, accompanied by his beloved and adoring daughter. Two figures from his past return to plague him, each a reminder of an occasion when he behaved dishonourably. One of them, a prosperous crook from Latin America, was with him when, as an undergraduate motorist, he ran over a man and failed to stop; true, the victim was dead already, but technical innocence, as Claverton knows, is poles apart from moral innocence. His second tormentor is a rich, ageing *chanteuse* whom long ago he seduced and paid off in order to avoid a breach-of-promise action. Other, affiliated sins come home to him. The crook might not have turned to crime, might even have got a First, had not Claverton introduced him to the pleasures of the *luxe* life. Moreover – last item in the catalogue – the old man has sought to dominate his son, who has become in consequence a mutinous wastrel.

By way of expiation Claverton makes a full confession of his misdeeds to his daughter and her fiancé. Duly absolved, having found his true self by sloughing off the sham, he goes off to die mysteriously beneath a great beech tree in the grounds of the sanatorium. He has learned patience and strength; the two lovers, left alone, celebrate their union in language more suggestive of Patience Strong.

It does not help to point out that Mr Eliot has based his play on *Oedipus at Colonus*, in which the guilty, discredited king journeys with his faithful daughters to the sacred grove. Translated into a world of board-rooms and pin-striped trousers, Sophocles becomes Pinero on stilts – the old story of the great man whose past catches up with him, the hero who has Lived a Lie. The more we remember the Sophoclean background, the more we are conscious of the disparity between Claverton, with his puny sins and facile absolution, and the tremendous obsessing agonies of Oedipus. One's conclusion must be that out of the wisdom of his years and the intensity of his cerebration Mr Eliot has come up with a gigantic platitude. Towards the end, to be sure, he casts over the play a sedative, autumnal glow of considerable beauty, and here and there a scattered phrase reminds us, by its spare precision, that we are listening to a poet. On the whole, however, the evening offers little more than the mild pleasure of hearing ancient verities tepidly restated.

The production, by E. Martin Browne, is careful and suave, with settings by Hutchinson Scott that loyally hint at Attic temples and holy grottoes. Paul Rogers lends Claverton a fine shaggy sonority and the right look of stoic dismay, as of a man staring past the fire into his thoughts. Anna Massey, of the beseeching face and shining eyes, is a first-rate stand-in for Antigone, and Alec McCowen is bonily brilliant as the rebel son.

(Kenneth Tynan, *The Observer*, 31 August, 1958 – Lyceum, Edinburgh)

Somehow Mr T.S. Eliot melts the marrow in the bones of critics. When Don Quixote de la Faber comes blindly clanking across the waste land, the fog streaming from his outsize armour, the gallant yeamen [sic] of England break their pencils across their knees and throw themselves beneath his proud hooves. They are so afraid that they will miss the point that they desperately make all the points he muffed. They rewrite his plays for him. They magnify his puppets into people. They create an imaginary genius called 'T.S. Eliot – playwright' and clamber over each other to call us all to worship at the shrine of the Invisible Dramatist.

Eliot's latest play, *The Elder Statesman*, has been so far for the critics the *pièce de non-résistance* of the Edinburgh Festival. It would be unfair to assert that Mr Eliot already writes English as though it were a dead language – but his prosy dramatic verse is at best dangerously wounded. And there is little pleasure to be gained from watching him reverse over the dying victim.

An old political peer crawls off to an unholstered bolthole in the country – a sort of baron's Butlin's camp – where rigor mortis will quietly creep from his stiff upper-class lip to the last empty suburb of his freezing corpse. Among the sacred groves two profane old loves sprout like ghosts. There is the grammar school swot he debauched at Oxford – an unsuccessful forger who became a South American millionaire. There is the tarty blonde he seduced at the stage door – a chorus girl who became a professional merry widow. Together they twist the screw of emotional blackmail and in the gleaming mirrors of their eyes he sees himself as he really is. Leaning over his coffin are his two children – a daughter who loves but does not understand and a son who hates but does not understand. Before he dies outside the summer house temple, he makes confession and feels for the first time the warmth of comprehension. This is the plot. But already the précis is better than the practice.

E. Martin Brown [sic] has directed all but two of the cast to speak at dictation speed like an exercise in teaching English by radio. The opening scene between Anna Massey as the daughter and Richard Gale as her fiancé might be by Charles Morgan out of Agatha Christie. The slow-motion trivialities float down like confetti while the Young England couple join hands over the anvil. 'It . . . is . . . simply . . . a . . . question . . . of . . . you . . . staying . . . to . . . tea' they dictate to each other, while the hushed house holds up each word to the light seeking for a revelation. Mr Gale is as stiff, glazed and cold as a monument: Miss Massey, with her puffed cheeks and popping eyes, is torn between ham and hamster – for the more technique she pours into this tiny role the more it overflows into melodrama.

The two ghosts are allowed to rattle their glacial verse a little more naturalistically so that the quickness of the foot sometimes deceives the ear. But William Squire prances and cavorts like a refugee from a horror film in which Peter Lorre was filling in for Boris Karloff. And Dorothea Phillips is believable only within the conventions of a matinee comedy with intellectual pretensions – I expected her to enter swinging a Palgrave's *Golden Treasury* chirruping 'Anyone for Tennyson?'.

The Elder Statesman is a zombie play designed for the living dead. Occasionally across the pallid mortuary scene flits an ironic joke or a haunting phrase but the smell of formaldehyde hangs heavy in the air. It is a play in which Mr Eliot mistakes snobbery for ethics, melodrama for tragedy, vulgarity for wit, obscurity for poetry and sermonising for philosophy. Only Paul Rogers as the deliquescing peer sits it all out with a certain neuralgic grandeur and poker-faced stoicism. In his muted trumpet voluntaries even lines like 'This is the peace which ensues upon contention when contention ensues upon the truth' ring out with a brassy music of their own.

(Alan Brien, *The Spectator*, 5 September, 1958 – Lyceum, Edinburgh)

The Hostage
Brendan Behan
November 1958   Theatre Royal, Stratford East

. . . one does not quite know whether one is supposed to regard the work as a serious play with music or a musical comedy with a serious theme.

(From: Lisa Gordon Smith, *Plays and Players*, December 1958)

. . . a curious entertainment which has a vitality that excuses a multitude of shamelessly loose touches.

(From: unsigned review, *The Times*, 15 October, 1958)

Brendan Behan admits he always writes his curtain speech before he writes the play. It would have been helpful if he had followed this through by also writing the reviews. For what is *The Hostage*? Is it a Sing-song Synge-song in a Dublin brothel, a Beggars' Uproar in an Irish stew? Is it the Marx Brothers in the IRA or Max Miller meets Arthur Miller at the GPO? Or the coming-out party of a whistling jail-bird who has been too often hungover and hanged-over? Or the phantasmagoria of a broth of a buoy, bobbing queasily on the waves of sex and politics, and clowning to keep his courage up and his breakfast down? Certainly, it is the most preposterous, comic and unnerving evening in London.

The Hostage is set in a bomb-shattered bedroom of a bawding house. The kilted and cloaked owner speaks Gaelic with an Oxford accent and bagpipes round the corridors marshalling the whores and pimps and drunks and queers into an imaginary Republican army. Then one day the IRA actually appear. They quarter on him a skinny, baffled young Cockney national service man who is to be executed as a reprisal for the hanging of an IRA gunman in Northern Ireland. Around this boy the whole household revolves in an eightsome reel of songs and dances and jokes and anecdotes and arguments. The whole thing has the air of having been written that afternoon. There are jokes about the league of Empire Loyalists, and Mr Dermot Morrah's series in the *Daily Express*, and the American rocket to the moon. It also has the air of having been written while the Lord Chamberlain was out of town. And every point is turned towards the audience, then hurled straight across the footlights.

Miss Joan Littlewood has given *The Hostage* a braw Brechtian production. The cast do not pretend to be people. Instead they are actors putting on the surface quirks and eccentricities of people the way a music-hall comic puts on a funny hat. The audience is as much part of the performance as the audience in a game of charades. And Pat, the old swollen nose of a caretaker, acts as a sort of master of ceremonies from inside the play by deflating each pomposity with a crafty corner-of-the-mouth comment. When the mad laird says he would hang crucified in the town square for the Cause, Pat is politely concerned – 'Let's hope it's a fine day,' he says. There is no suspension of disbelief because there is no pretence that this is anything but a theatrical performance. But there is also no suspension of belief because it is impossible to begin to enjoy the hodge-podge and hullabaloo unless you appreciate Behan's philosophy of life. Underneath the compulsive jocular grin of the born farceur, Behan is forcing us to re-examine our prejudices and assumptions. The joke, like the dream, is a way of turning grit into pearls; a way of disguising our faces so that we can bear to look at them in the mirror. But at least we have got rid of the grit, and we do look in the mirror.

To some extent Behan is repeating the theme of O'Neill – to live we need illusions as we need clothes. We choose a sympathetic role, then play it like Method actors, so that we come to believe we *are* the role. But Behan widens his angle of vision to reveal the make-believe of societies as well as individuals. His whores and pimps and civil servants and IRA staff officers are dressing up as romantic revolutionaries partly because they cannot stand themselves as they really are. But also partly because a provincial, tumble-down society cannot find any more useful and valuable a costume for them. They are being manipulated by outside powers as well as by inside fears. And in the specific context of *The Hostage*, Behan is arguing that both the oppressor and the oppressed are slaves to their own illusions and the illusions their ruling classes force upon them. The references to Cyprus and Suez are deliberately provocative and political. And the young English hostage, who is as apathetic in his beliefs as his Irish captors are pathetic in theirs, brings down the second-act curtain with a consciously unsympathetic sneer at 'the niggers of Notting Hill'. Brendan Behan has said that he is waiting for the critics to tell him what his play meant. There you are, Mr Behan, that's what you meant. And I don't care if you didn't know it.

The Hostage is the sort of political pantomine which would have been impossible on the stage ten years ago. But *The Threepenny Opera* kicked a hole in the balderdash about the theatre being a magic world which transported us out of ourselves. And the Royal Court has presented a series of plays which more and more emphasised that the actors are there to communicate to us, not to each other. Brendan Behan has not completely mastered his job. In *The Hostage* he too often caps and recaps his jokes, hammers his characters in and out of shape, twists and tangles his plot, from the sheer joy of having a platform to entertain upon. And Joan Littlewood has shaken the bottle rather too vigorously so that at times there is more head than body in the glass. But despite a tendency towards Old Mother Riley among some of the cast, the Theatre Workshop have given this a memorable production especially in the performances of Murray Melvin, as the NAAFI Romeo trapped among the Capulets, Avis Bunnage, as the old bag of tricks, and Howard Goorney, as the ponce who acts as chorus.

(Alan Brien, *The Spectator*, 17 October, 1958)

From a critic's point of view, the history of twentieth-century drama is the history of a collapsing vocabulary. Categories that were formerly thought sacred and separate began to melt and flow together, like images in a dream. Reaching, to steady himself, for words and concepts that had withstood the erosion of centuries, the critic found himself, more often than not, clutching a handful of dust. Already, long before 1900, tragedy and comedy had abandoned the pretence of competition and become a double act, exchanging their masks so rapidly that the effort of distinguishing one from the other was at best a pedantic exercise. Farce and satire, meanwhile, were miscegenating as busily as ever, and both were conducting affairs on the side with revue and musical comedy. Opera, with Brecht and Weill, got into everybody's act; and vaudeville, to cap everything, started to flirt with tragi-comedy in *Waiting for Godot* and *The Entertainer*.

The critic, to whom the correct assignment of compartments is as vital as it is to the employees of Wagons-Lits, reeled in poleaxed confusion. What had happened was that multi-party drama was moving towards coalition government. Polonius did not know the half of it: a modern play can, if it wishes, be tragical-comical-historical-pastoral/farcical-satirical-operatical-musical-music-hall, in any combination or all at the same time. And it is only because we have short memories that we forget that a phrase already exists to cover all these seemingly disparate breeds. It is Commedia dell'Arte. *The Hostage* is a Commedia dell'Arte production. . . .

Some of the speech is brilliant mock-heroic; some of it is merely crude. Some of the songs are warmly ironic; others are more savagely funny. Some of the acting is sheer vaudeville; some of it (Murray Melvin as the captive, and Celia Salkeld as the country girl whom, briefly and abruptly, he loves) is tenderly realistic. The work ends in a mixed, happy jabber of styles, with a piano playing silent-screen music while the Cockney is rescued and accidentally shot by one of the lodgers, who defiantly cries, in the last line to be audibly uttered: 'I'm a secret policeman, and I don't care who knows it!'

Inchoate as it often is, this is a prophetic and joyously exciting evening. It seems to be Ireland's function, every twenty years or so, to provide a playwright who will kick English drama from the past into the present. Mr Behan may well fill the place vacated by Sean O'Casey. Perhaps more important, Miss Littlewood's production is a boisterous premonition of something we all want – a biting popular drama that does not depend on hit songs, star names, spa sophisticated, or the more melodramatic aspects of homosexuality. Sean Kenny's setting, a skeleton stockade of a bedroom surrounded by a towering blind alley of slum windows, is, as often at this theatre, by far the best in London.

(From: Kenneth Tynan, *The Observer*, 19 October 1958)

Krapp's Last Tape (with Endgame)
Samuel Beckett
November 1958   Royal Court

Samuel Beckett's two threnodies made me feel like death – literally like Death. As I climbed the stairs from the Royal Court I could taste the decay in my mouth, I could hear the wax in my ears, I could smell the bacteria in my lungs, and I could sense the humming energy of the pioneer corps of disease as it divided my body into captive provinces. It seemed criminal negligence on the part of the management not to provide me with a leper's bell to ring before me as I humped this condemned body through the crowd. Mr Beckett's message is not simply that it is later than you think but that it always has been later than you thought. Birth is simply a temporary reprieve. Godot died before you were born. And the longer you wait the nearer you get to the day of execution.

Krapp's Last Tape and *End-Game* are exercises in peevish despair. The first has a deliberately ape-like ancient who scuttles around a darkened stage slobbering over obscene bananas and cackling at recordings from his youthful diary. Age is pushing him back down the greasy pole of evolution and he listens to his early thoughts with the sort of puzzled hysteria that a Neanderthal man might display as he ran through a copy of *Citizen Kane*. It is a striking and memorable image, but a static and petrified one. It is one frame caught from a reel. It is a page torn from James Joyce and given a temporary illusion of originality by a few wry exclamation marks from Beckett in the margin. *Krapp's Last Tape* is just a kind of Molloy [sic] Bloom ingeniously transferred to the stage by Cocteauesque tricks with a tape recorder. Patrick Magee, arthritic knuckles scraping the boards and strangled vocal cords

scraping the ear-drum, is a refugee from a nightmare – vivid but
unreal, haunting but insubstantial, ape without essence. . . .

Both plays left me saddened – partly because, as Beckett
intended, I became once again conscious of my own mortality.
But mainly because I became even more conscious of Beckett's
refusal of immortality as a dramatist. *End-Game* and *Krapp's Last
Tape* are both highly subjective correlatives for the author's fears
that his own talent may be as diseased as the world it refuses to
mirror. As the flood-waters rise he burns his bridges, scuttles his
boats, punctures his water-wings and tries to forget how to swim.
Art is the last illusion and Beckett seeks to destroy even that by
creating deliberately inartistic works of art. He is a literary suicide
desperate to die alone. We have waited for Beckett too long – he is
on his way back before he has begun.

(From: Alan Brien, The Spectator, 7 November, 1958)

Slamm's Last Knock, a play inspired, if that is the word, by Samuel
Beckett's double bill at the Royal Court:

*The den of Slamm, the critic. Very late yesterday. Large desk with throne
behind it. Two waste-paper baskets, one black, one white, filled with
crumpled pieces of paper, at either side of the stage. Shambling between
them – i.e., from one to the other and back again – an old man: Slamm.
Bent gait. Thin, barking voice. Motionless, watching Slamm, is Seck.
Bright grey face, holding pad and pencil. One crutch. Slamm goes to black
basket, takes out piece of white paper, uncrumples it, reads. Short laugh.*

SLAMM (*reading*): '. . . the validity of an authentic tragic vision, at
once personal and by implication cosmic . . .'

*Short laugh. He recrumples the paper, replaces it in basket, and crosses
to other – i.e., white – basket. He takes out piece of black paper,
uncrumples it, reads. Short laugh.*

SLAMM (*reading*): '. . . Just another dose of nightmare gibberish
from the so-called author of *Waiting for Godot* . . .'

*Short laugh. He recrumples the paper, replaces it in basket, and sits on
throne. Pause. Anguished, he extends fingers of right hand and stares at
them. Extends fingers of left hand. Same business. Then brings fingers of
right hand towards fingers of left hand, and vice versa, so that fingertips
of right hand touch fingertips of left hand. Same business. Breaks wind
pensively. Seck writes feverishly on pad.*

SLAMM: We're getting on. (*He sighs.*) Read that back.

SECK (*produces pince-nez with thick black lenses, places them on bridge
of nose, reads*): 'A tragic dose of authentic gibberish from the
so-called implication of *Waiting for Godot.*' Shall I go on?

SLAMM (*nodding head*): No. (*Pause.*) A bit of both, then.

SECK (*shaking head*): Or a little of neither.

SLAMM: There's the hell of it. (*Pause. Urgently.*) Is it time for my
Roget?

SECK: There are no more Rogets. Use your loaf.

SLAMM: Then wind me up, stink-louse! Stir your stump!

Seck hobbles to Slamm, holding rusty key depending from piece of string round his (Seck's) neck, and inserts it into back of Slamm's head. Loud noise of winding.

SLAMM: Easy now. Can't you see it's hell in there?

SECK: I haven't looked. (*Pause.*) It's hell out here, too. The ceiling is zero and there's grit in my crotch. Roget and over.

He stops winding and watches. Pause.

SLAMM (*glazed stare*): Nothing is always starting to happen.

SECK: It's better than something. You're well out of that.

SLAMM: I'm badly into this. (*He tries to yawn but fails.*) It would be better if I could yawn. Or if you could yawn.

SECK: I don't feel excited enough. (*Pause.*) Anything coming?

SLAMM: Nothing, in spades. (*Pause.*) Perhaps I haven't been kissed enough. Or perhaps they put the wrong ash in my gruel. One or the other.

SECK: Nothing will come of nothing. Come again.

SLAMM (*with violence*): Purulent drudge! *You* try, if you've got so much grit in your crotch! Just one pitiless, pathetic, creatively critical phrase!

SECK: I heard you the first time.

SLAMM: You can't have been listening.

SECK: Your word's good enough for me.

SLAMM: I haven't got a word. There's just the light, going. (*Pause.*) Are you trying?

SECK: Less and less.

SLAMM: Try blowing down it.

SECK: It's coming! (*Screws up his face. Tonelessly.*) Sometimes I wonder why I spend the lonely night.

SLAMM: Too many f's. We're bitched. (*Half a pause.*)

SECK: Hold your pauses. It's coming again. (*In a raconteur's voice dictates to himself.*) Tuesday night, seven-thirty by the paranoid barometer, curtain up at the Court, Sam Beckett unrivalled master of the unravelled revels. Item: *Krapp's Last Tape*, Krapp being a myopic not to say deaf not to say eremitical eater of one and one-half bananas listening and cackling as he listens to a tape-recording of twenty years' antiquity made on a day, the one far gone day, when he laid his hand on a girl in a boat and it worked, as it worked for Molly Bloom in Gibraltar in the long ago. Actor: Patrick Magee, bereaved and aghast-looking grunting into his Grundig, probably perfect performance, fine throughout and highly affecting at third curtain-call though not formerly. Unique, oblique, bleak experience, in other words, and would have had same effect if half the words *were* other words. Or any words. (*Pause.*) . . .

SLAMM: But a genius. Could you do as much?
SECK: Not as much. But as little.
Tableau. Pause. Curtain.

(From: Kenneth Tynan, *The Observer*, 2 November, 1958)

1959

This was the year of Wesker's Roots, the second instalment of his famed Trilogy. As with Look Back in Anger, in a different but equally peremptory way qualities were attributed to the play that it did not possess. Critical opinion ranged from the obviously under-informed notion that it was the first time the 'working-class' had been given a voice on the stage to very inflated claims for its socio-political dynamism.

Time shows it to have been neither. Rather, it now stands as an unsteadily written and largely emotional evocation of Wesker's own impeccably sincere convictions about social deprivation and his slightly embarrassing simplifications of political history – a flaw that haunts all three parts of the Trilogy. Galsworthy in Strife served the working class better, not because he was more caring, but because he had a greater discipline over his imagination and technique. However, this hugely underrated dramatist was forgotten, as, indeed, were Stanley Houghton (Hindle Wakes) and Walter Greenwood (Love on the Dole), by those anxious to find a uniqueness in Wesker that didn't really exist. The play was pushed into approbation by two factors – first, a speech, an aria of rhetorical emotiveness, and second, its performance by Joan Plowright. Indeed a marked characteristic of the plays of the sixties and seventies is the number which contain such arias, whose effect on audiences is to distract their attention from what, on examination, is a surrounding area of unexceptionally average accomplishment.

Roots did not have it all its own way. John Arden appeared on the scene to confuse the world of criticism – a process to be continued throughout his career. Simply, it could not weigh him up, and Serjeant Musgrave's Dance weighed heavily on any attempts at judgement. The Times's unsigned review could not recall a week of worse plays at the time it appeared and considered it confused and confusing. Some of its import escaped, on his own admission, Philip Hope-Wallace, who found it 'something short of a great play'. The severe Mr Alvarez of the New Statesman complained that 'the puzzle is to know how and where it went wrong' and Harold Hobson found it 'Another frightful ordeal'. In short the play's reception is a splendid example of how volatile the critical world is. Still, there was always One Way Pendulum which nearly all critics found funny – but couldn't agree why!

Roots
Arnold Wesker
May 1959   Belgrade, Coventry
June 1959   Royal Court

There can be no doubt about the enthusiastic reception which greeted *Roots*, a new play by Arnold Wesker at the Belgrade Theatre, Coventry, last night. This is distinctly a 'message' play and the audience loved its downright mixture of earthy humour, stylised characterisation and preaching. The pulpit is occupied with verve and sincerity by Joan Plowright as the daughter of a farming family who – by what sounds like a pretty intensive kulchur course from one who sounds and probably is meant to sound like an insufferable intellectual London Teddy boy – finds herself alienated from her grass roots. Why can we not speak ourselves into living? Words to speak our meanings are our salvation, she preaches, and echoes her absent mentor. To her the roots of her family clutch at nothing for they are not watered by the sweet flow of man speaking to man. The play's dialogue which runs between a faulty naturalism and an uneasy theatricality is echoed by a set which very effectively uses realism and back projection. Perhaps because of the nature of the theme in which one virile protagonist is set against a group which has to be in a state of bovine undevelopment the action is spare and the movement, except for the final act, is slow. But the slowness is redeemed by some excellent acting by Patsy Byrne, Gwen Nelson and Jack Rodney. It may seem churlish to carp about a play written with an urgent sincerity about a basic dilemma, but it fails to convince largely because it veers a little crudely between polemics and nose-to-the-ground farmyard 'life'.

The producer is John Dexter.

(Gareth Lloyd Evans, *The Guardian*, 26 May, 1959)

In its genre of the kitchen-sink-propaganda play, *Roots* is a major achievement. Perhaps it could never have been written without the precedence of *Look Back In Anger*, but Mr Wesker is a better writer than John Osborne.

When Jimmy Porter rants and raves in *Look Back In Anger*, we know he is pleading a special case – Mr Osborne's case. But Mr Wesker's simple country girl is angry for all of us and at all of us who will die rather than think for ourselves.

(From: Robert Wraight, *Star*, 1 July, 1959)

[*Roots*] is exactly the kind of thing Shaftesbury Avenue never finds room for. It is original, entertaining, with a hard core of social criticism, well produced and acted admirably by the

85

Coventry Company. It might easily have been Cold Comfort: it is in fact rural kitchen sink.

The action takes place in the cottages of Norfolk farm labourers. They have electric light, some of them; and some of them have the telly. They suffer from a mysterious complaint called gut-ache and seem not to have heard of the National Health Service. What Mr Wesker is doing is quite simple: he is exposing the impoverishment of English working-class life, no longer necessarily economic impoverishment but, in the deepest sense, cultural, his title is an exercise in irony; beyond all this he is attacking his characters' own dumb acceptance of this condition, their very ignorance that they are impoverished.

The nature of the material sets Mr Wesker obvious problems which he very rarely surmounts. The characters, all but one, are dumb oxen in Wyndham Lewis's sense of the word; moreover their vocabulary is so sparse as to make them almost inarticulate; and, it must be admitted, the Norfolk dialect is the slowest means of expression outside Texas. Nevertheless, Mr Wesker triumphs, because of his own unsentimental sympathy, partly because of the character of the agent of light in the play.

This is Beatie Bryant, the one member of the family who has broken away. She has gone to London, become a waitress and has fallen in love with a young socialist intellectual, Ron, who has shown her a whole new world of experience. The action of the play consists in Beatie's and the Bryants' waiting for her Ron to arrive. He doesn't; as the family sits round the table set for high tea, his letter arrives instead: he is breaking off the engagement. It is a nice touch of Mr Wesker's that we are made to realise that Ron himself is a phoney; but still, Beatie has to accept the fact of her own inadequacy, an inadequacy arising from the thinness of the soil in which her roots are set; and it gives her – and Mr Wesker – the chance to launch out into an impassioned onslaught on the shallowness of her environment.

Beatie is beautifully played by Miss Joan Plowright. She attacks her part with a gusto that is always under control, and she quite splendidly renders Beatie's bewildered uncomprehending love for her Expresso-bar [sic] Romeo and her numbed realisation, in the end, both that she has failed him and that he has betrayed her. But she is admirably supported by the other players, and especially by Miss Gwen Nelson as her mother. This is by far the best and most faithful play about British working-class life that has appeared for a long time.

(From: Walter Allen, *New Statesman*, 11 July, 1959)

The setting is a farm labourer's kitchen – scruffily cosy, meagrely cluttered, with hand-me-down furniture, zigzag linoleum, gaudy wallpaper, a clock and a radio both designed like jerry-built Greek temples, and (of course) the over-stuffed sink. Mother, with cottage-loaf figure and Yorkshire-pudding face, is taking a purely token sit-down on the edge of her chair. Daughter, in a housecoat and bathing hat, is trying to explain the appeal of good music. As the gramophone spins out the two interlocking themes of the farandole from *L'Arlesienne*, the daughter begins to prance around in her bare feet, eyes closed, fingertips widespread, in a parody of the ballet. Mother jogs her old bones and mutters indulgently, 'She's like a young lamb'. Curtain to the second act of *Roots*.

I should have thought that such a scene would have spread prickles of embarrassment through the audience such as the Royal Court has not felt since that bear-and-squirrel romp in *Look Back In Anger*. Can this really be the high peak of the best play so far from one of our most talented young playwrights? Can this really be the finest minute so far of one of our most talented young actresses? I don't know what reply you were expecting but it is a resounding 'Yes'. . . .

Roots is the second play of Arnold Wesker's trilogy which began with *Chicken Soup and Barley*. None of the same characters appears on stage – though Beatie's Pygmalion lover, whose failure to turn up leaves her defenceless against her family, is presumably the same self-pitying, self-lacerating, young intellectual who ended by hacking out his own roots in the first play. Here Mr Wesker does not have the advantage of characters who talk with the racy, vivid articulateness of the Jewish East End. Yet the dialogue has enormously improved in its dramatic impact. I cannot understand those critics who complain that it is boring and trivial. Mr Wesker has realised the central truth about working-class talk which has been missed by most other Royal Court dramatists. Such talk is not meant to be under the control of intellect pushing the frontiers of experience forwards with each safari into the unknown. Even in the Welfare State, a large section of the population still lives on a hostile and unmapped planet where the invisible dragons of disease and loneliness and poverty wait outside the light of the camp fire. Conversation is the interchange of ritual, repetitive magic formulas which dull the edge of their fears. *Roots* not only captures the occasional surface eruptions of humour and anger but also exposes the banked fires beneath the surface.

It is basically a left-wing play. But it carries a conviction which few such overtly political plays achieve because it does not start off with the assumption that the working class are noble victims of a selfish conspiracy. In a long, eloquent speech, Beatie forces her sullen relatives to acknowledge that today of their own free will they are deliberately choosing to be an audience for third-rate, mass-produced culture and to make millionaires out of the pedlars who dope them. Mr Wesker's point is well-made and well-taken – the job of the left wing today is not demagoguery but pedagogy. The people of England must be taught the words to understand their own thoughts.

(From: Alan Brien, *The Spectator*, 10 July, 1959)

Serjeant Musgrave's Dance
John Arden
October 1959   Royal Court

. . . one cannot recall a week of worse plays . . . good realistic dialogue . . . an atmosphere which is mysteriously pregnant with suspense [but] these dramatic virtues unfortunately get smothered in a mass of character defects.

(From: unsigned review, *The Times*, 23 October, 1959)

Serjeant Musgrave's Dance by John Arden, who wrote *Live Like Pigs*, is a long and challenging play. Even now, at curtain-fall, some of its import escapes me, but for the best part of three hours it has worked on my curiosity and often put that ill-definable theatrical spell on my imagination. I think it is something short of a great play. But wild horses wouldn't have dragged me from my seat before the end.

The first two-thirds is like an eerie Victorian melodrama (the sounds which supervene on the slow, silent, strike-bound colliery town in the 1880s made me think of 'The Bells'). A party of Redcoats, three odd sorts and a fiercely religious serjeant, come to the town on what at first seems like a recruiting drive, though the surly strikers and their pastors and masters assume for different reasons that the soldiers are there to be 'used'. They are billeted in the ale house and it gradually becomes clear that they are deserters, led by a maniac, driven out of his mind – or the prison of his sense of duty – by appalling memories of a massacre in some Colony.

Serjeant Musgrave's mission is a reversal of all soldierly values; violent, coercive pacifism, which is to be preached like the word of Jehovah at the point of a gun. He duly has his great inside-out recruiting jamboree, but already his great, revealed, heaven-sent plan has gone aglay. The brand of Cain is on the lot of them. Fighting breaks out among the missionary party. Musgrave ends behind bars.

The play is written with an acute sense of language, which somehow fits the period without conscious archaism. There are occasional deviations into the jingles of folk ballad, but in the main the writing is remarkably strong, yet unpretentious. It gives the actors every chance, and Ian Bannen, in particular, as the fanatical Serjeant, gives a magnificent performance. Werner Krauss, whose death was reported this week, would have given just such a fine fierce heavy mould to the role.

Donal Donelly, Frank Finlay, and notably Alan Dobie bring great conviction to the three other ranks, and Freda Jackson as the ale-wife and Patsy Byrne as the barmaid could hardly be better.

Lindsay Anderson produces with strength and economy in the earlier scenes, which are beautifully set and lighted (decor by Jocelyn Herbert).

(Philip Hope-Wallace, *The Guardian*, 23 October, 1959)

No one would quarrel with Mr Arden's intentions; the horror and contamination of violence is a subject which, as the Aldermaston march showed, a good many people take very seriously indeed. But there is a significant gap between good intentions and effective drama.

The author apparently has come under the influence of Büchner; he, too, tries to kaleidoscope scenes into each other, sliding from action to introspection and back. But in Mr Arden's hands, the method is used merely for its obvious symbolism, not at all for its psychological insights. Büchner's symbols arise out of the intensity of his characters' perceptions, Arden's out of the intensity of his own good will. He insists so much on his own meaning that his characters never get a chance to develop. They have simple purposes but no complexity of life, like so many puppets. Even the serjeant's nightmare vision of the end of the world is simply plain oratory, compelling enough as prose sense, but with none of the nakedness, fear and compulsion of a dream. For symbolism to become drama the characters must take charge of the meaning, not *vice versa*. . . .

Part of the blame for the evening's failure lies with the director, Lindsay Anderson. Visually, his production was sharp and exciting enough. With Jocelyn Herbert's beautifully spare sets it could hardly have been otherwise. Unfortunately, he did not use his best actors, Ian Bannen and Freda Jackson, with the same verve. For the timing was far from faultless. Instead of marshalling both scenes and actors so that they moved with the dramatic concentration that Arden's writing – like Büchner's – demands, Mr Anderson deliberately slowed everything down. Even the most trivial bits of dialogue were punctuated by those tiny pauses in which the actors turn, or move up stage, or gesture, as though about to embark on some long set speech. The talk bogged down in endless hesitation. The action, too, dragged repetitively. . . . Finally, having used Dudley Moore's music so effectively to create a background of emotion, it is a pity he did not bring it in where most needed: to set off the bits of doggerel with which Mr Arden studs his text. But still, with a little more critical awareness from the author and a more positive production, *Serjeant Musgrave's Dance* might have been a very good play.

(From: A. Alvarez, New Statesman, 31 October, 1959)

Another frightful ordeal. It is time someone reminded our advanced dramatists that the principal function of the theatre is to give pleasure. It is not the principal function of the theatre to strengthen peace, to improve morality, or to establish a good social system. Churches, international associations, and political parties already exist for those purposes. It is the duty of the theatre, not to make men better, but to render them harmlessly happy. It will then help to achieve those higher purposes which, properly speaking, are no part of its concern. For when men are harmlessly happy, there is some sort of chance that they will be charitable to each other. Then possibly these other things may be added unto us.

It is therefore simply no good at all for John Arden to come along to the Court Theatre, and employ actors, and a director, as skilled as Lindsay Anderson to tell us that war is wrong. We know that already. If we are to be told it again, we must be told entertainingly. For two long acts this play, with its deserting redcoats, its northern town in the grip of strikes and winter, its gloom and its darkness, may be said to be sinister, strange, even ominous: but entertaining it is not. The third act is a different matter, for then we discover that the great advocate of peace in the play is very near religious madness. That at least is unexpected. But it does not make an evening.

(Harold Hobson, The Sunday Times, 25 October, 1959)

One Way Pendulum
N.F. Simpson
December 1959   Royal Court

A play wholly composed of *non-sequiturs* is as hard to digest as a play wholly composed of puns.

(From: unsigned review, The Times, 23 December, 1959)

N.F. Simpson's *One Way Pendulum* is a very funny play. For this reason, since humour is a mysterious and rather alarming phenomenon, it deserves serious and even solemn consideration. Moreover, it is at the Royal Court, a theatre renowned for putting on plays with a meaning. When this theatre, therefore, presents a play which is ostentatiously meaningless, flamboyantly nonsensical, even the most guileless heart becomes suspicious. All through Christmas I have felt as if I were walking among minefields.

A French critic whom most English people do not read remarked of a French dramatist whom most English people underrate that his great merit was that he did not put all his goods in the shop window. The plate glass display was dazzling, but greater riches lay in the interior. Behind the brilliant detail, there was something else: a personality, an attitude towards life, a deeper and all-embracing feeling.

Could one say the same of Mr Simpson? He juggles dexterously with the incongruous. Into an ordinary suburban household he introduces the bizarre and the baroque: a woman in a wheel chair planning journeys to St Pancras and Sirius: a young man training a series of weighing machines to sing the Hallelujah chorus: a man who is building the Old Bailey in the sitting room: a housewife who pays a daily woman to help her with, not the cooking, but the eating: and a girl who wants to have arms as long as a gorilla's. The humour of all this – and it is very humorous – arises from the fact that it is accepted as perfectly ordinary and normal. If an elephant walked through his front door, Mr Simpson might ask it to stay to tea, but he would not be in the least surprised.

*   *   *

One laughs as one laughs at a succession of first rate funny stories. If they have no theme and illustrate no point do they not, after a time, become wearisome? It is literally true that laughter can make the jaws ache as well as neuralgia. It would be sad if, after having an uproarious time at Mr Simpson's play, one had to go, not home, but to the dentist's. . . .

We are accustomed to the laughter that covers a broken heart. It gives a pleasant sentimental feeling. But Mr Simpson's laughter, *if* it has significance, is laughter that covers a cracked brain.

The cracked brain of humanity, the obsessional delusions of ordinary men and women: Old Baileys, gorillas, weighing machines, holocausts of Jews, massacres – they are all forms of madness, of the same madness. We are all mad. But if we are all mad, then Mr Simpson is mad, too. And if Mr Simpson is mad, then his allegation that we are mad – if that is what he does allege – means nothing. But if we are not mad, neither is he, for our supposition of his madness depends only on his being a part of us. All this is leading us further among the minefields. Perhaps Mr Simpson will write us another play to guide us out.

If he does, I hope he keeps the same cast. Alison Leggatt, George Benson, Douglas Wilmer and Graham Crowden seem to understand Mr Simpson, even if I don't.

(From: Harold Hobson, *The Sunday Times*, 27 December, 1959)

N.F. Simpson's prose hardly ever deviates into sense. It is a palimpsest of non-sequiturs, a double acrostic of crossword clues. It is also true farce in that it aims to provoke laughter by deceiving us into admitting impossible connections between improbable opposites. But with Simpson, the opposites are ideas as well as persons. He provokes the head-laugh as well as the belly-laugh. His jokes are brain-splitting as well as side-splitting. Once we have made the electric connection between the two poles of his irony, we can no longer refuse to believe in the reality of the circuit. It is the Swiftian conjuring trick performed in the manner of Feydeau.

(From: Alan Brien, *The Spectator*, 1 January, 1960)

1960

Three plays vied for public acclaim. Even today they are quick on theatre-goers' lips. Pinter survived the opprobrium delivered upon The Birthday Party and this year's The Caretaker was greeted with a great amount of applause. Wesker's I'm Talking About Jerusalem was generally regarded as being the weakest of his Trilogy, but the case of A Man for All Seasons is the most interesting of all three. It very quickly entered into that vox populi pantheon of 'great' plays like Rattigan's The Deep Blue Sea, Emlyn Williams's Night Must Fall and a host of other pieces whose fame is established less by firm critical assessment in a perspective of time than by immediate, relatively uncritical audience-response which continues to reverberate. In other words, it is an example of that old dilemma — what right has the critic to question the validity of public response? Who knows? The play was 'O' and 'A' levelled, produced ad infinitum everywhere. As usual Time has had its implacable way, which is not so much revenge as just application of one of the most important elements in the critical process — comparison and contrast. It seems now, in hindsight, to have been reckless to claim, as a number of critics did, that Bolt's play was English Brechtianism at its finest. For all Bolt's stated enthusiasm for Brecht, his play, seen in a longer, wider context, has little if any touch of Brecht in it — the use of the common man, described by some as an example of 'alienation' is no more Brechtian than the use of the Chorus in Shakespeare's Henry V. A Man for All Seasons was an above-average commercial historical documentary, neatly planned and shaped to fit the undemanding expectations of the majority of theatre-goers, with the protagonist designed skilfully to accommodate the sympathetic eccentricities of Paul Schofield's acting.

I'm Talking about Jerusalem
Arnold Wesker
April 1960   Belgrade, Coventry
June 1960   The Trilogy, at the Royal Court

Mr Wesker creates people as naturally as he breathes; at present, in the play, the ideas they embody, the passions that drive them, overlap, repeat themselves, confuse us, pall.

(J.W. Lambert, *The Sunday Times*, 10 April, 1960)

. . . a work of far less clarity and dramatic energy than its two predecessors.

(Our special correspondent, *The Times*, 5 April, 1960)

As a rule, Harold Pinter's characters live immured in a room, vaguely intimidated by the world outside, fearful of direct communication with each other, and therefore talking about everything except what most deeply concerns them. As representatives of our way of life, they precisely complement Arnold Wesker's characters, who rush out to grapple with the world, bent on communicating with each other and anyone else who will listen, and seldom talking about anything but their deepest concerns.

Yet what do they accomplish? *I'm Talking About Jerusalem*, the last instalment of Mr Wesker's trilogy, suggests that his answer is: almost nothing. The members of the Kahn family end up with their hopes baffled and their ideals defeated. The world outside has let them down; they feel alienated and rejected. No doubt they will 'carry on', but their passion for causes has abated, and they are no longer quite sure where they are going. One more disastrous adventure, you feel, and the path might well lead straight to Mr Pinter's room. Mr Wesker's conclusion, in short, is not very far from Mr Pinter's starting-point: that there is something in our society that is irrevocably hostile to the idea of human brotherhood.

At the beginning of *Chicken Soup with Barley* the Kahns, like Lincoln Steffens, 'have seen the future, and it works'. By the end of *I'm Talking About Jerusalem*, twenty-three years later, they have decided that it doesn't. Their early allegiance to Communism has long since disintegrated; and although Beatie Bryant emerges from *Roots* with a new sense of purpose and identity, we are not told exactly what she is going to do with it.

This last play deals with a frustrated attempt to translate Socialist theory into practice. Ada Kahn and her husband Dave, haters of mass production and readers of William Morris, move out of the East End into a lonely Norfolk cottage, where Dave proposes to manufacture furniture of his own design, thereby – as he hopes – reviving the tradition of pride in craftsmanship that industrialisation has stifled.

The first two acts, in which he and his wife are struggling to establish themselves, pleasantly remind us that Mr Wesker is one of the few Western dramatists who can write about political idealists without mockery or condescension. The moving-in process, accompanied by the forebodings of Ada's mother and the soaring enthusiasm of Ronnie Kahn: Dave's momentary qualms when a wartime chum turns out to have developed into a cynical 'realist': the family game wherein Ada and her young son pretend to be lumps of clay into which Dave, mimicking the Deity, solemnly breathes life – all this is lovingly observed, and lambently acted, especially by Frank Finlay as the cynic. Mr Finlay's assault on Dave's ideals – and, by extension, on his own past – is an unforgettable set piece, full of implied self-hatred; even his laughter sounds like a kind of weeping.

In the third act the dream fades. Dave's prices are too high to compete with factory products, the bank refuses him a loan, and he is forced to go back to the city, while Ronnie looks on, tearfully wondering what went wrong. Two full-blooded minor characters, Aunt Cissie and Aunt Ester, barge amusingly in; but the play as a whole tails off into something between a whimper and a shrug. An experiment in medievalism has collapsed, and everyone behaves as if it were the end of the world. Nobody points out to Dave or Ronnie that the failure of a privately owned furniture business can hardly be equated with the failure of Socialism; all that happens is that Ronnie after a bout of weeping brings down the curtain by bellowing to the fields: 'We're bloody mad to cry'. One can only agree. This final outburst of affirmation comes across as an empty gesture, utterly devoid of intellectual substance; and its effect, I am afraid, is to strengthen John Whiting's recent adimadversions on the new movement in our theatre. Mr Whiting conceded that it had a heart: 'All the throbbing emotionalism proves it . . . It is that little tiny head that worries me.'

It worries me, too. All the same, I part company with Mr Whiting when he derides Beatie Bryant (and through her, Mr Wesker) because she 'seems to see art as an educative influence, something which uplifts, does you good. Nonsense! Some of the best art teaches nothing and can do irreparable harm, if not actually deprave.' I will not embarrass Mr Whiting by asking him to give examples, but I do beg him to ponder the following remarks of John Berger's:

. . . why should an artist's way of looking at the world have any meaning for us? Why does it give us pleasure? Because, I believe, it increases our awareness of our own potentiality. . . . The important point is that a valid work of art promises in some way or another the possibility of an increase, of an improvement. Nor need the work be optimistic to achieve this; indeed, its subject may be tragic. For it is not the subject that makes the promise, it is the artist's way of viewing his subject.

Mr Wesker's view of his subject is blurred, at the end, by sentimentality and intellectual flabbiness, for which I have chided him. But he cannot legitimately be condemned for having tried to 'do us good'. I have been emotionally enlarged, and morally roused, by the experience of hearing Mr Wesker talk about Jerusalem. This is not, perhaps, what Mr Whiting means by art; but it is what most of us mean by theatre.

(Kenneth Tynan, *The Observer*, 31 July, 1960)

The Caretaker
Harold Pinter
April 1960   Arts

A wholly successful production.

(From: J.W. Lambert, *The Sunday Times*, 1 May, 1960)

Harold Pinter's latest foray into the no man's land between farce and madness is a remarkable piece of work and must take a high place among the group of 'anti-plays' now in vogue. . . .

We are here on the farcical side of no man's land: jokes based on repetition of common words, Mr Pinter's speciality, can be pure music hall, and there are some fine flights of verbal fancy ('Where were you born?' 'What do you mean?' – or 'We'd a penchant for nuts . . . Yeah . . . That's what it was, a penchant.') Yet all the time we keep touching the edge of the shadowed side: this is the comedy of those too inwardly crippled to achieve more than bare communication or, often, the rubbing together of two misunderstandings.

So far so familiar. Where Mr Pinter differs from other 'anti-dramatists' is in plunging us outright into the shadow world of madness or, as some might put it, of the state that almost wholly locks people away from communication with their kind and with the world about them. At least one of the three characters, we learn in a remarkable long speech (finely delivered by Mr Woodthorpe and to be faulted only on a point of psychiatric detail), has had a breakdown and is in fact a schizophrenic. The shadow deepens; though bursts of farce recur they are sinister (an encounter with a vacuum cleaner in the dark, for instance); the characters, each in varying degree his own mental turnkey, alternately fight and reach out to one another.

The end, of course, is deadlock. Non-communication is the world of this play; but before the end we have shared more than we expected of its terrors and its poignancy as well as of its farce.

It is a fine play, consistently carried through apart from a few puzzling but not important details (some business with a statuette of the Buddha, for instance). A particular virtue is that nowhere does Mr Pinter treat non-communication as an extraneous, rather banal 'point' to be made (compare Ionesco's *The Chairs*). It is knit with the people and the action. Yet one must still say that this plunging of audiences into the world of the shut-off mind is something that leads away from the mainstream of art – whose main business surely is with the adult relationships we painfully try to keep up and deepen. It is a fascinating byway and Mr Pinter's work literally fascinates; but one hopes he will move on.

For Donald McWhinnie's production and for the acting I have nothing but praise. This is controlled playing of a high order – watch Mr Pleasence's hands, Mr Woodthorpe's stillness, Mr Bates's machine-gun speech. Altogether an unmistakable hit.

(From: John Rosselli, *The Guardian*, 29 April, 1960)

. . . dazed and pleasurable confusion.

(From: unsigned review, *The Times*, 28 April, 1960)

'To be honest, I've made out how he came to be my uncle's brother. I've often thought that maybe it was the other way round. I mean that my uncle was his brother and he was my uncle. But I never called him uncle. As a matter of fact I called him Sid. My mother called him Sid too. It was a funny business. Your spitting image he was. Married a Chinaman and went to Jamaica. . . . I hope you slept well last night.'

This is an absolutely typical snatch of the dialogue in the year's most successful play, *The Caretaker* by Harold Pinter. And by 'successful' one means triumphant with the critics as well as with the public.

Is it literature? Obviously not. Is it dramatic – in the old sense whereby each sentence carries on the action? No. But is it dramatic – in the new sense whereby each sentence or half-sentence reveals the character of the speaker? Yes, it *is* rather. But the person to whom this tramp called Davies is speaking at such length now interrupts with: 'Listen! I don't know who you are!'

Some of the audience read deep and subtle meanings into *The Caretaker*. It is a play about three men in a shapeless and charmless room who cannot communicate with each other at all. Alternatively it is a play about three men who would not communicate with each other, even if they had the desire. It is all about nothing, and all about everything. Or is it a play about a man who is dead already – the tramp – and two other men who don't want to have anything to do with him because they are still alive?

Mr Pinter then confounded us all on the radio by saying that it was not this, or that, or any other thing – but just a *play*. He just sat down to it and it wrote itself. It is just as much without symbolism as it is without life or action. It is all just talk and pauses – especially pauses. It is most certainly a strange, fascinating, bizarre business.

> (From: Alan Dent, *Plays and Players*, January, 1961)

Excessively derivative [of Godot].
> (From: Patrick Gibbs, *The Daily Telegraph*, 28 April, 1960)

The trouble is that Pinter repeats himself from play to play. He is concerned always with the same human derelicts who, as they continually say, 'don't stand a chance'. He is, of course, mining a vein of Beckett's, and I don't believe Beckett, who writes out of his martyrdom to his own limitations, is rich enough to stand so extensive a working. After a certain point (and this is the fourth Pinter I've seen in a few months), the controlled inconsequentiality seems more mannered than funny and the unspoken terrors are too easily implied. But in Aston's long speech the terrors are at last spoken. If only Pinter would go on from there and not just lapse back into what he has already done better in other plays!
> (From: A. Alvarez, *New Statesman*, 7 May, 1960)

With *The Caretaker* Harold Pinter has begun to fulfil the promise that I signally failed to see in *The Birthday Party* two years ago. . . .

Now it may very well be that there are symbols here. The two brothers may represent the bifurcated halves of a schizoid personality; alternatively, the landlord may stand for the Super-Ego, the tenant for the Ego, and the tramp for the Id. Either way, I am not particularly concerned. What holds one, theatrically, is Mr Pinter's bizarre use (some would call it abuse) of dramatic technique, his skill in evoking atmosphere, and his encyclopaedic command of contemporary idiom.

To take these qualities in order: where most playwrights devote their technical efforts to making us wonder what will happen *next*, Mr Pinter forces our wonder on what is happening *now*. Who are these people? How did they meet, and why? Mr Pinter delays these disclosures until the last tenable moment; he teases us without boring us, which is quite a rare achievement. It is reinforced by his mastery of atmosphere. There is a special belt of English suburbia, spectral in its dusty shabbiness, that exists in no other Anglo–Saxon country. America has tenement drama, penthouse drama and drama set in the exurbanite strongholds of the middle class; but London is unique in the *déclassé* decrepitude of its Western suburbs, with their floating population, their indoor dustbins, their desolate bed-sitters, their prevalent dry rot – moral as well as structural – and their frequent, casual suicides. Mr Pinter captures all this with the most chilling economy.

We come finally to his verbal gifts; and it is here that cracks of doubt begin to appear in the façade of my enthusiasm. Time and again, without the least departure from authenticity, Mr Pinter exposes the vague, repetitive silliness of lower-class conversation. One laughs in recognition; but one's laughter is tinged with snobbism. Towards the end of the evening I found myself recalling an experimental play I had seen some ten years before. Its origins were Dutch, and it took place in a snowbound hut on top of a mountain; the *dramatis personae* were The Mother, The Daughter and Fate, who emerged from a wardrobe in the second act and delivered a baleful tirade about death. Rain, meanwhile, splashed into a bucket through a hole in the roof. When the harangue was done, the Mother lifted her eyes and said, more aptly than perhaps she knew: 'Only the drip speaks'.

Mr Pinter's play likewise has a bucket and a leaky roof, and it occurred to me, as the curtain fell, that what I had been watching was nothing more than an old-fashioned *avant-garde* exercise, galvanised into a semblance of novelty by the author's miraculous ear for colloquial eccentricities. Instead of The Brother, The Other Brother and Everyman, the characters were called Aston, Mick and Davies; and instead of declaiming, they chatted.

Yet the quality of the chat is consistently high. Mr Pinter is a superb manipulator of language, which he sees not as a bridge that brings people together but as a barrier that keeps them apart. Ideas and emotions, in the larger sense, are not his province; he plays with words, and he plays on our nerves, and it is thus that he grips us. Three remarkable actors embody his vision. Donald Pleasance, as the wild Welsh tramp, has the showiest part and gives the most spectacular performance; but I felt that he was carried, like a drunk between two policemen, by the muscular playing of his colleagues – Alan Bates, as the heartless, garrulous brother, and Peter Woodthorpe, as the stolid, pathetic one. The direction, an object lesson in the organisation of nuances, is by Donald McWhinnie.

(From: Kenneth Tynan, *The Observer*, 5 June, 1960, when the play moved to the Duchess Theatre)

A Man for All Seasons
Robert Bolt
July 1960   Globe

With all these virtues, it is disconcerting that *A Man For All Seasons* is not more theatrically gripping than it is.

(From: Harold Hobson, *The Sunday Times*, 3 July, 1960)

Robert Bolt, who wrote *Flowering Cherry*, is not the first dramatist to take a play out of the long drawn resistance and final martyrdom of Sir Thomas More. Others have perhaps made the attempt on a richer theatrical swell of emotion. But that is not the way with Mr Bolt, who checks emotion with the more fashionable tricks of a comic chorus master-cum-scene-shifter who plays many minor-roles, winks at the audience, and in the current cant, 'alienates' the drama for us.

The task is very happily done by Leo McKern. Nor could the author wish a better choice than Paul Scofield to play the quiet, obstinate scholar whose way to the block was no quick, noble run to the martyr's crown, but a long, subtle, silent, self-justification. This is finely brought out, especially in the speeches at the trial when More resists the perhaps overvehemently put arguments of Thomas Cromwell. Mr Scofield's long suffering has a beautiful, simple sincerity.

There is also the domestic background, the deep affection between father and daughter, the imperious and worldly wife who cannot understand what seems to her a wilful self-immolation of her husband's part. But here Mr Bolt makes do with rather fragmentary writing. The family life does not illuminate the central figure much. Enough perhaps that we should receive some intimation of the greatness of More's mind and heart, and in this author and actor are successful.

But they are intimations only. The piece, so well imagined and neatly contrived, remains a decent, modern example of the historical costume play and never moves even momentarily into the greater field of tragedy. We are left feeling that it ought to have so moved. But it is distinguished, respectable, worth the watchful attention it continuously exacts from its audience.

Noel Williams produces economically, in simple, imaginative settings by Motley. Alongside the performance by Mr Scofield and Mr McKern, Andrew Keir as Cromwell and Geoffrey Dunn as the Spanish ambassador were successful.

(Philip Hope-Wallace, *The Guardian*, 2 July, 1960)

Robert Bolt's *A Man For All Seasons* bears a remarkable resemblance in atmosphere and intention to Brecht's *Galileo*. Both are

attempting to superimpose an historical parallel on a contemporary dilemma, thus thawing the past into life so that we can feel its
muscles ripple yet simultaneously freezing the present so that we
can analyse its flow. Both use the now familiar disillusioning
devices of epic theatre to frustrate simple identification with the
hero, to provide commentary and explanation, and to by-pass the
easy pleasures of narrative tension. Even the key phrase which
sums up the action is almost identical – both protagonists are
martyred while ironically praising, in Bolt's words, 'the happy
land that needs no heroes'. The first act of *A Man For All Seasons* is
never clotted with boredom like the first half of *Galileo*. Mr Bolt
scatters his mind like buckshot over a variety of characters and
keeps the eye and ear leaping to follow his aim. He never makes
Brecht's mistake of underestimating the willingness of a modern
audience to digest a single satirical point. Yet the final impression
of *A Man For All Seasons* is of a worthy, intelligent, highly literate,
graduate-school lecture-drama. It is almost as if Mr Bolt had
pushed Brecht's theories farther than Brecht's practice ever
attempted to stretch. The alienation is too successful and we end
up being too detached from the mimic battle of the stage. We are
more interested in the ideas than in the men, we think more about
the interpretation than we feel about the execution.

(From: Alan Brien, *The Spectator*, 8 July, 1960)

. . . There's no point in being fooled by the Brecht mannerisms
into comparing Mr Bolt with the Master. Brecht's innovations
have changed theatrical style a little and now are there for anyone
to use, without automatically setting himself up in competition
with the old firm. Anyway, Mr Bolt's Brecht is only skin deep. A
little tinkering would convert the play into a plain historical
drama.

But that's it. For all the intelligent, crisp writing, the play never
quite got away from the world of historical romance, that land of
make-believe where everybody's suburban worries swagger
around in fancy dress. For period costume is a substitute for
depth of analysis. Provided you dress the actors up, you can get
away with types instead of people. In a costume play you can tell a
man's morals by the cut of his gown. Why, for example, were we
never given the reason for Cromwell's savage hounding of More?
'But look,' you say, 'it's plain he's an evil man. Look at his sneer,
his red gown and his stoop. He's a clear case of motiveless
malignity.' But then, by the same standard, More suffered a
motiveless martyrdom. There was not enough weight of human
truth in his make-up to endow him with more than a pointless
good. That is why Scofield, for all his efforts, never quite got away
from the small, dry, donnish note, and why despite all the talk of

politics, diplomacy and corruption, the plot seemed more
appropriate to C.P. Snow's Cambridge than Wolsey's England.
There is something a little cosy about historical romance. It
flatters your preconceptions and you come out feeling, in the
moral sense, good. Real art, on the other hand, is unsettling and
not at all jolly. Tragedy purges the emotions through pity and
fear, but historical romance, however tragic and well done, ends
simply by cheering you up.

(From: A. Alvarez, New Statesman, 9 July, 1960)

1961

Two of the most talked-of plays of this year – utterly different as they are in every respect – neatly represent an abiding critical dilemma. With John Whiting's The Devils *the problem was not so much the quality of the play (it had, on this score, high praise) as what it meant. Critics wavered about whether it would be designated Christian, or anti-religious, or 'psychological'. Interestingly, time has done little to unscramble the dilemma.*

With Livings's Big Soft Nellie, *the problem was, so to speak, less philosophically inclined. In brief, was it rubbish or a refreshing 'breakthrough' in dramatic technique? It must be remembered that by 1961 critics were having to cope with what at the time seemed an anarchic approach to the actual writing of plays, and, of all the younger dramatists, Livings was most prone to cock a snook at traditional and conventional techniques. As John Russell Taylor (*Anger and After, *p. 134) says: 'He seeks first to show people together, interacting, existing . . . he writes in terms of a total stage action rather than simply in words . . . often an apparently completely random exchange in a sequence of non sequiturs makes sense only when we see the actors together and understand the relationship between them at that particular point.' In this theatrical flux, the old stalwarts of plot, character-development, psychological truth, dramatic language, as an impersonation of 'real' speech, are dissolved. A good deal of reliance is placed on actor and director to reveal a dramatic logic which Livings's supporters claimed was there to be uncovered. Most critics realised that the development of this 'anarchy' in a number of dramatists was to a large extent influenced by the breezily permissive, energetic work of Joan Littlewood at Stratford East.*

The Devils
John Whiting
February 1961   Aldwych

I do not remember in 20 years of reviewing plays ever before having been tempted to use the word masterpiece about a new

English play. But about Mr John Whiting's *The Devils of Loudon*, the first new play to be presented by the Stratford company at the Aldwych, I am so tempted, and I shall not resist the temptation.

Mr Whiting's play is on the truly grand scale. It has a grand sweep, and a no less grand simplicity. It takes us, as all great plays do, to the very heart of the human predicament, to the point where evil is triumphant and man can only endure. There is no message. *The Devils* is as uncommitted as *King Lear*. Like *Lear* it is a terrible experience which we must go through and when we come through it we have faced some of the worst and some of the best of the human condition.

(From: T.C. Worsley, *Financial Times*, 22 February, 1961)

Much was expected; more was fulfilled. From Aldous Huxley's *The Devils of Loudon*, John Whiting (a new play at last!) has fashioned a powerful dramatic spectacle, a play of depth, force, terror, and beauty.

With consummate craftsmanship, he has distilled the essence of Huxley's detailed and relentless reconstruction of one of history's more ghastly moments: the mass 'possession' of a group of nuns in a seventeenth century priory.

The effect is of a Jacobean dramatist writing a contemporary tragedy (for which he would surely himself have been put to death as a devil) equipped with a miraculous foreknowledge of Freud.

(From: Robert Muller, *Daily Mail*, 21 February, 1961)

The Devils has, if you look for it, a beautiful Christian architecture of temptation, fall and taking up. It chips away at the old block of faith and morals. I admit that I have now no predisposition towards the Christian drama; I'd as soon see a play about murder under the mistletoe as I would about murder in a cathedral. But for all this, his nuns and priest and nun's priests, Mr Whiting has not written a play primarily about religion. The religious life is present as an immense situation; the characters stand in their vows, but exist in themselves; they are enclosed, cautioned by confessors, shown visions, but they learn man to man. Their prayers are superb soliloquies. It is as though the play were being put together by a process of addition, scene to scene; then somebody falls on his knees and everything is multiplied.

Nor is *The Devils* a psychological play, though much of it is revealed by insights or, superficially, by home truths, even such a simple one as a nun picking up a stick. As I recount it – making a nun pick up sticks – it sounds cheap and sniggery; as the nun recounts it it is profound and moving. It is poetry. Indeed only through poetry will you understand *The Devils*. *The Devils* grapples with the complexity of human experience on a level that is neither simply religious nor simply psychological. It is in its nature metaphysical. It crosses the human passion with the passion of Christ: the priest who lived by his senses offers his senses to God, not sucking at meat or tasting women, but his senses under torture: 'Offer God pain, convulsion and disgust'.

The Devils has the indirection of great art. As a play before an audience, every moment is brilliantly comprehensible; it is illumined; you can see the heart by it. But though you comprehend and become perceptive, you will not find an explanation. Because there is none. Sister Jeanne is a mystery, the priest is a mystery. The measure of Whiting's integrity is that he has not come out with an answer as if he were a cat with a mouse in his mouth. He has ended his play still staring at the hole. What, for instance, is the meaning of the last words spoken? Grandier, the priest, is dead, burnt; Sister Jeanne is alone; a few minutes before she had been searching for God in the street gutters. Whiting might have given his play a conclusion in religion with two words. 'God, God.' But he didn't. He had his nun cry out in pain and loneliness two other words. 'Grandier. Grandier.' Thereby Mr Whiting ennobled his wonderful play with a continuation of wonder. Ambiguous to the end. And we cannot see the Christ without the thieves.

Mr Whiting's construction of *The Devils* is also of deep cunning. It is made up of many short scenes that sometimes follow, sometimes overlap, and sometimes climb over each other. A word at the end of one scene may prompt the next, or dab its meaning. This gives the kind of fluidity that avoids the stilting of historical style. Peter Wood's employment of stage, his groupings, timings of speech, backing and advancing were in great spirit. ·

Sean Kenny's art has now reached such dimensions that he not only frees the playwright but releases himself to make his statement: the great crosses and gibbets, the height of the town walls, the violence of his Christ in stained glass, the fragility of the nuns' cloister, were thrilling illuminations of Mr Whiting's play – and more. They were works of intense individuality.

Dorothy Tutin, lopsided, managed to put the pain of her hump into her eyes. She comes to us, each play, with new powers. Her Viola is actress perfect: her Sister Jeanne is actress superior. Richard Johnson played Grandier with handsome gravity, the right instrument for his early lines. Then he's thrown at us as a thing; but he isn't, he is a tortured man of tragedy. Mr Johnson plays him so.

(From: H.A.L. Craig, *New Statesman*, 24 February, 1961)

1961
Big Soft Nellie
Henry Livings
September 1961   Theatre Royal, Stratford East

Big Soft Nellie typifies the best and the worst of Theatre
Workshop. Joan Littlewood's influence has usually been a boon to
her actors and a disaster for her writers. She gives actors a comic
style which enables them to turn almost any drivel into an
entertaining evening, but at the same time she reduces her
authors to turning out stuff which needs precisely this salvaging
quality from the actors. The deterioration is plain even in her best
writers, Brendan Behan and Shelagh Delaney. Their first plays,
The Quare Fellow and *A Taste of Honey*, had a unifying theme, a
consistency, a genuine seriousness. In their second efforts, *The
Hostage* and *The Lion in Love*, everything was sacrificed for
entertainment; no joke was too extraneous, no gag too old to be
included. Before anyone writes to tell me so, let me say that I
know *The Hostage* was written (in Irish) before *The Quare Fellow*;
but it was translated and re-written after Behan had begun
working with Joan Littlewood. The symptoms show.
      (From: Bamber Gascoigne, *The Spectator*, 8 December, 1961)

The thing – it seems perverse to call it a play – makes a weak soft
impact like a sponge full of tepid water dropped into sawdust.
(From: Philip Hope-Wallace, *The Guardian*, 29 November, 1961)

Mr Kinnear is apparently forced over the thin line between farce
and desperation.
      (From: S. D-L, *The Daily Telegraph*, 29 November, 1961)

Is he funny? He is. As Mr Kinnear strutted up and down with a
guardsman's stride, wheeling with perfect precision, throwing up
his imaginary baton, standing immobile as it rises and then falls,
and catching it at the last moment with electric speed and
certainty, the tears rolled down my cheeks.
      This is not merely a pastiche of great cleverness: it is also a feat
of acting. For Mr Kinnear not only performs his turn; at the same
time, he persuades us that it is Mr Marris who is doing it, a little
shapeless fellow, hot, nervous, flustered, who yet controls his
feelings, masters his apprehensions of failure, and deprecatingly
accepts the dutiful applause of his workpeople.
                    *   *   *
So, after all, Mr Livings can claim some credit for this delicious
and heartwarming scene; for it is he who has conceived the
character that Mr Kinnear plays. It is he who has conceived the
entire world in which Mr Marris lives: a world as absurd, as

106

illogical, as foolish as the real world we live in, but much more likeable, much more kind . . .

Big Soft Nellie is a committed play, a play committed to the proposition that if the meek do not inherit the earth it does not really matter, because in the process of being meek people they have a very jolly time. They may have the police after them, but if they do, the policeman turns out to be a shrewd fellow longing to be bamboozled; Lotharios say the tactful thing at moments of crisis; and even fights are only hilariously amiable misunderstandings. Mr Livings's world is not the real world. But that is the world's fault, not his. Perhaps man really did make a mistake when he started being clever.

The success of this play is the universe it establishes, and the comic invention which, especially in the second act, is unflagging. Less satisfactory is the failure in taste which allows in two jokes that would be admirable in a revue but which have no meaning in a play whose triumph is guilelessness.

(From: Harold Hobson, *The Sunday Times*, 3 December 1961)

1962

Curiously, indeed not without some poignancy, the three dramatists whose work aroused a great deal of comment at this time have, to a degree, not fulfilled their early praise. When Wesker wrote **Chips With Everything** in 1962 he was still passionately fired by the theatrical success of his trilogy. But this play signalled important changes in Wesker's approach to drama, and his subsequent failure to reproduce the excited, honest, caring, imaginative exercises of his first plays may well be the result of these changes or, even, because he so slavishly announced the changes, seemed self-conscious of them, as if he were both creative dramatist and compiler of a History of English Drama to which he had contributed a critique on his own work. Indeed, some of his remarks (see **The Transatlantic Review**) about his transmogrification are embarrassingly naive: 'Art is the re-creation of experience not the copying of it. . . . Some writers use naturalistic means to re-create experience, others non-naturalistic.' 'If I develop, it might be away from naturalism.' In a confused and, assuredly, an unconsciously portentous way, it is as if he were saying, 'I was a prose dramatist, now I'm going to be poetic.' **Chips With Everything** is the first and by far the best of his new dispensation owing, perhaps indirectly, much to the growing exasperation (shown by **Livings** at its most sensational) with traditional ways and means.

David Rudkin's **Afore Night Come** provided a prodigious talking point. Aficionados hinted darkly about a theatre of cruelty, others pondered much on Rudkin's intellectuality; critics almost, but not quite, to a man, exhibited that very English suspicion of the egg-head, the academic — labels which, as time went on, were liberally stuck on to Rudkin's plays. Critical response often shows its collective slips and, while it is true that the range of reference and allusion in Rudkin became progressively more formidable, critical opinion on the whole feared it rather than tried to understand it. Few critics seem to have realised that, in quite different ways, Wesker and Rudkin suffer from the same flaw — an inability to see the wood for the trees; or, more to the point, they both become side-tracked from the job of making drama by a nagging preoccupation with the minutiae thrown .up by their imaginations, consciences and intentions, which often have more to do with the problems of society than the requirements of art; society after all, on the evidence, benefits more from *caring people, thinking people, feeling people who can create, than would-be creators who crucify their art with polemical thought, partisan feeling and selective compassion.*

Wesker's and Rudkin's subsequent loss of dramatic force (albeit comparative) is a shallow declination compared with David Turner's rapid eclipse as a dramatist. He was one of our first and best television dramatists, and seemed set fair for a successful career as a stage dramatist when it was announced that the usually discerning Olivier had agreed to play in Semi-Detached. *However, the result was a succession of unfavourable notices for both the play and Olivier himself. Although Turner wrote several other plays, his muse never seemed wholly to recover from this early rebuff.*

Chips With Everything
Arnold Wesker
April 1962   Royal Court/Sheffield Playhouse/Glasgow Citizens (same first night)

This is a play that nobody remotely interested in the best in modern drama can afford to miss. It has imperfections but these are dwarfed by its achievements.

    (From: Peter Roberts, *Plays and Players*, July 1962, Royal Court)

... possibly the greatest post-war play in English ...

    (From: Eric Chapman, *Plays and Players*, July 1962, Sheffield Playhouse)

But don't look for faith in Arnold Wesker's *Chips With Everything* (Royal Court), a play about the RAF. There is, in fact, hatred and a furious, concentrated, eloquent passion. I may be permitted to observe that without the RAF in 1940 Mr Wesker would be in an even worse position today than I should myself, but *Chips with Everything* is not the first anathema directed by a man against what has saved him, his religion and his race.

What an anathema it is! In construction, superb; in writing, imaginative and touching; in symbolism, reverent and moving; in irony, corrosive and overwhelming. For the reason I have indicated I view with ambiguity the play's ending, in which the panoply and music of military glory are used in ironic triumph to celebrate the imminent death of two souls, one rich and educated, one stupid and poor, each the sacrificial victim of the officer class, the privileged, the rulers.

As a member of the Athenaeum and MCC, I view it with

misgiving; as a dramatic critic, I will cheer till I am hoarse and black in the face. This is the Left-wing drama's first real breakthrough, the first anti-Establishment play of which the Establishment has cause to be afraid. If there is a better play in London I haven't seen it. This is something to be discussed and re-discussed, admired, feared.

(From: Harold Hobson, *The Sunday Times*, 29 April, 1962)

Arnold Wesker's dialogue has taken on a relaxed eloquence which is stylised and yet natural. So in its impact on eye and ear, *Chips With Everything* is a stunning theatrical experience which widens the range of modern dramatic method.

Yet, as with *The Kitchen*, I felt a continual, distracting strain between the image and the slogan, the story and the moral. The narrative has not the documentary truth of a slice of life. The allegory has been blunted and coarsened to fit the events on stage. Only under a Fascist dictatorship could such precise parallels be drawn between the conscript and the employee as pawns in a top people's conspiracy.

Despite the assertions of those who have not seen his plays, Arnold Wesker has never romanticised the working class. His most satisfying work, *Roots*, is a sustained condemnation of their refusal to choose the highest when they see it.

Chips With Everything no longer shows him feeding on the fat of his own past. Ronnie, the self-pitying, self-dramatising Jewish hero of the trilogy has vanished. Instead we have Pip, the snobbish, inhibited, public schoolboy. But where Ronnie's defeats were never final, Pip's desertion leaves his followers with no hope. *Chips* presents a vision of the future which is Orwellian in the bleakness of its pessimism.

It seems to envisage a society forever divided into conscious exploiters and unconscious victims by some such talisman as the Queen's commission. It reveals a vein of priggishness in Mr Wesker's philosophy which holds that the pop ballad cannot co-exist with the folk song. It displays a strand of Jacobite fatalism in his temperament by the hunger for a well-born leader on a white horse.

Chips remains the most outspoken and explicit challenge so far from a young left-wing playwright to our assumptions about social progress. I think he underrates the fluidity of the system and the resilience of the ordinary man while he overrates the rigidity of class barriers and the cunning of the Establishment. I hope, for all our consciences, that I am right and he is wrong.

(From: Alan Brien, *The Sunday Telegraph*, 6 May, 1962)

I could fill a short book in describing why Arnold Wesker's *Chips with Everything* is a bad play. But, to be brief, its central fault is that Wesker has started with a wide-ranging dossier of conclusions about our class-ridden society and has then laboriously built them into a familiar setting, an RAF training camp, which is quite incapable of accommodating them. Aesthetically the result is that his gobbets of significance stand out as uncomfortably as undigested mouthfuls spaced along the length of a snake; and politically the effect of the clash between content and context is to make Wesker's already over-simplified sociology appear quite grotesque. It is one of the problems of serious artists in our self-conscious age that they are too aware of the need to build 'significance' into their work; but it remains their responsibility to make it fit so snugly that it *seems* to arise naturally. . . .

I increasingly find myself on a one-man crusade against contemporary settings being stretched beyond their limits and against plays in which the author's intentions stick through a thin hide of naturalism like the bones of a sick cow. The fullest possible use of contemporary naturalism was made by Arthur Miller in *Death of a Salesman*. The emphasis was all on the particular story of Willy Loman, which rang completely true in its own context. The wider applications were left implicit – Miller relied on our own knowledge of our modern society forcing us, unaided, to recognise the play's full relevance. When a playwright specifically wants to paint the wider picture he achieves far more freedom by setting his play in another time or country. This is not mere escapism, nor a desire for the theatre to be cosy and remote entertainment. Miller could never have achieved such a sane picture of mass hysteria had he set *The Crucible* in contemporary witch-hunting America. None of Brecht's major plays are set in modern Germany. And, with specific reference to *Chips*, I believe that a far better account of the battle between the Establishment and the rebel was given in John Osborne's *Luther* and of the nature of militant leadership in John Arden's *Sergeant* [sic] *Musgrave's Dance*. Neither could have achieved its wide sweep of truth in a contemporary setting.

The expressionistic plays of the Twenties were full of thinly veiled Messianic figures appearing to the workers and assuring them 'you are men, men and women unqualified, free men and women' (from Ernst Toller, this). I am all for the message, but God save us from a return to that way of expressing it.

(From: Bamber Gascoigne, *The Spectator*, 11 May, 1962)

1962

Afore Night Come
David Rudkin
June 1962   Arts

... intellectually one-celled and rhythmically monotonous. ...
smouldered interestingly ...
(From: Charles Marowitz, Plays and Players, August, 1962)

Shouts of 'quiet' from the audience almost drowned the noise of a
fainted spectator being slapped back into consciousness on the
first night of *Afore Night Come* at the Arts, while on stage the
severed head of an old tramp, ritually sacrificed on a rubbish
dump behind a pear tree, was slowly rolled in a furry ball towards
the footlights.

This atmosphere of hysteria would have roasted the heart of
the French inventor of 'the Theatre of Cruelty', Antonin Artaud.
Surrealist, poet, playwright, critic, actor, producer, failure and
madman, Artaud died at the age of 52 in 1948 after nine years in
a lunatic asylum. He was the propagandist of myth, magic and
mania in drama and summed up his creed in the cry:

> the theatre will never find itself again except by furnishing the
> watcher with the truthful precipitate of dreams in which his taste for
> crime, his erotic obsessions, his savagery, his chimeras, his utopian
> sense of life and matter, even his cannibalism, pour out.

In this first play by David Rudkin, a 25-year-old Birmingham
schoolmaster, Artaud's runaway horses of the Apocalypse have
found a British jockey. Whether he reaches the winning post still
in the saddle may be a matter for dispute. But throughout the
race – a race which at times freezes into such slow-motion that it
seems to be running backwards – the audience along the track is
held by the hair roots. Then its nose is brutally rubbed in images
of blood and poison and decay and insanity.
(From: Alan Brien, The Sunday Telegraph, 10 June, 1962)

Connoisseurs of the stock responses of Uncle Edgar (Aunt Edna's
critical spouse) will have savoured nostalgic moments last Friday
on reading the notices of *Afore Night Come* (Arts) a new play by a
25-year-old Birmingham schoolmaster called David Rudkin.
There, in most of the dailies, was the unmistakable mixture of
baffled fury and bored disgust which Edgar reserves for the
arrival of original talents in the theatre: remember Whiting's
Saint's Day and Pinter's *Birthday Party*? The same phrases are
brandished – 'meaningless violence', 'tedious bestiality'. And once
again Edgar's instinct is correct, for David Rudkin is a born
playwright and a poet, and his imagination, like that of many

112

young poets in the past, is often grisly as well as beautiful.
(From: Roger Gellert, *New Statesman*, 15 June, 1962)

In a week of high fashion from Peter Hall's companies his team at the Arts has produced a first play by David Rudkin, *Afore Night Come*, which combines two of the main elements of the drama of the moment. These are the cut and thrust of dialect – in this case Black Country, but with the usual sprinkling of foreign voices from Ireland, Wales and elsewhere – and a crescendo of mysterious violence. The first is not sufficient to make a play and the second, when used as gratuitously and heavy-handedly as this, is quite enough to ruin it.

A dilapidated but talkative Irishman arrives to pick pears in a large orchard. The other labourers mock and resent him. In the first act the hints of violence come from small actions, such as their jostling him with their pear baskets. These moments are real and frightening, but by the time the rustics were hacking off Paddy's head behind a pear tree while an aeroplane sprayed them all with insecticide my reaction had become one of sceptical merriment. The most extraordinary and gruesome events can have effective point when there is a central character, as in Kafka or Ionesco, through whose eyes the action is seen; unmotivated violence then becomes a projection of the character's fantasies. But *Afore Night Come* is a public play. The story is told from outside; the Irishman, far from being a central character, is offstage for most of the play; and there is a student working in the orchard who, we are told, might just as easily have been the victim. In spite of a great deal of confused biblical symbolism the play demands to be taken primarily as a picture of a contemporary ritual murder. As such it would be fascinating in a very well authenticated anthropological footnote. But in the theatre it is meaningless.
(From: Bamber Gascoigne, *The Spectator*, 15 June, 1962)

Semi-Detached
David Turner
December 1962 Saville (formerly at Belgrade, Coventry)

David Turner is a talented writer, Tony Richardson is a talented director, Sir Laurence Olivier is . . . our greatest actor by quite a clear margin. I make this profession of faith before going on to profess my contempt for the results of their combined efforts.
(From: Roger Gellert, *New Statesman*, 14 December, 1962)

Much of the play's pleasure derives from the Jonsonian theme of a central character gulling everyone in sight ... brilliantly complicated plot ... a satire on two motives – money and prestige.

(From: Bamber Gascoigne, *The Spectator*, 14 December, 1962)

David Turner's *Semi-Detached* is a far from harmless little play that genuinely means ill. There is something almost Jonsonian in its bile, as also in its monstrous gusto; and although its flights of verbal extravagances are dwarfed by Jonson's, the flavour it leaves behind – floridly bitter, uproariously sour – is that of authentic satire on the classical model. It should thus be welcomed, if only as a rarity.

A respected colleague strangely remarks: 'London is already over-full of coarse, not very well observed and patronising comedies of family life'. In the first place, London is nothing of the sort (apart from *Come Blow Your Horn* and *Goodnight, Mrs Puffin*, I can't think of a single contender); and in any case, Mr Turner's play belongs to a different order of comedy.

Certainly it deals with family life; but its method is one of deliberate exaggeration and *grotesquerie*, bursting through the crust of verisimilitude to expose the raging obsessions that lie beneath. The language is part realistic, part stylised. Brand-names and local references co-exist with soliloquies. In short, this is a comedy of humours. ...

Patsy Rowlands is fine as Fred's plump and weepy younger daughter, but I was more impressed by the Black Country pallor, sinewy determination and unsurprised cynicism of Eileen Atkins as her lanky elder sister. Both, needless to say, are callously exploited by Dad, who is Laurence Olivier, leering, balding, and equipped with a filthily accurate Birmingham accent. Miscasting, I fear, undoes the great man; he presses too hard, delivers too many syllables at the glib, unvarying speed of a machine-gun, and resorts too often to mischievous tricks – the lower lip retracted in bafflement, the tongue literally in cheek.

What the part needs is someone more limited; an aggressive professional comedian with a flair for timing and some residue of innocence. The innocence is vital: Fred's allegiance to his 'humour', his faith in the *mystique* of status, must be simple and total, so that even when he extols 'this basic limited company of ours, the family', we do not suspect him of making a joke, but feel instead that the author has put a few words of Brechtian comment into the mouth of a devoted capitalist crusader.

(From: Kenneth Tynan, *The Observer*, 9 December, 1962)

It was done at the Belgrade Theatre in Coventry in the summer and would have done better to be content with that. London is already overfull of coarse, not very well observed and patronising comedies of family life, the scream and caution school.

Sir Laurence works like a Trojan at his study of a dreadful, boyish, cock-sure family tryant, full of saws and instances and the pathetic detritus of self-education. He has to say things like 'I have been 'it by a piece of Eureka' and he comes as near as a fine actor can to a dismal failure with the part, which might have been a good deal less tiresome in the hands of some relatively ungifted actor who was more happily cast to type. Sir Laurence gives it every trick imaginable but only some of these really go home; the accent, costive, Midland and cockney all at once, is a terrible amalgam and rings constantly false, giving the actor trouble all night.

Happier are Mona Washbourne and Patsy Rowlands as the mother and one of the troublesome daughters. Also Newton Blick makes a late entry which is not without merit. But the play slowly capsizes. It is poor stuff in a poor school and the presence of great talent only underlines the deficiencies. Tony Richardson's production is unflinching. It was we who flinched.

(From: Philip Hope-Wallace, *The Guardian*, 6 December, 1962)

Like Ben Jonson, he is funny, and very ingenious. *Semi-Detached* is directed by Tony Richardson, and may well have the blessing of all the kitchen sink school of dramatists. However that may be, Scribe would have been dazzled by its close, interlocking plot, its plethora of coincidences, its unity of time, place, and mood, its unremitting, swift progression of incident. It all happens in a flashy lounge on a Sunday morning: and it happens without pause or cessation. . . .

The dialogue is amusing. Mr Turner has two principal jokes, which consist of discussing every domestic issue in terms either of insurance policies or of steam transport. This would become wearisome were it not for Sir Laurence's resilient invention and zest. This greatest of actors talks of steam cocks and endowments with lyrical enthusiasm and bronchial fervour. He distils from them an ignoble but vital philosophy and the air of ostentatious nonchalance with which he flicks open a particularly revolting gilt cigarette container of about the size of a coffee pot is the status symbol of a performance so rich in comedy and creative in observation that we come to admire the accuracy of Fred's aim more than we despise the meanness of its target. I suspect that this is not exactly what Mr Turner intended.

(From: Harold Hobson, *The Sunday Times*, 9 December, 1962)

1963

The authors of two plays whose production rescues 1963 from relative theatrical oblivion have never, so to speak, settled into an accepted critical status. John Arden (The Workhouse Donkey) and James Saunders (Next Time I'll Sing to You) in different senses, are wild cards in the pack. Every play of Saunders has received careful and often lengthy notices, but no success seems to have established his acceptance into the modern pantheon. For a time he was regarded as one of our leading dramatists but – to put it bluntly – who now, outside critical or intellectual circles, ever heard of James Saunders? Arden, however, seems always to have unnerved the critical world, whose individual citizens veer wildly in their estimates of his work. It is difficult to account for the relative mistiness of the prospect of Saunders but, in the case of Arden, it is perhaps his brash-seeming personality, which has led him into several extra-mural contentions with various institutions in the world of theatre, which has occasioned the wariness which is so often generated by his plays.

Next Time I'll Sing to You
James Saunders
February 1963   Arts

... may well prove to be the most exciting play of 1963.
       (From: Roger Gellert, *New Statesman*, 1 February 1963)

If anyone has turned to these columns in the hope of finding a balanced judgment of James Saunders' new and much-lauded play, he had better pass on. On this subject, I find myself incapable of being either restrained or rational. I squirmed and wriggled through its agonising longueurs and feel the need to revenge myself.

The play connects solidly with my most inflexible prejudices: *viz* literary theatre, discursive hokum, de-animated action, verbal rather than spatial imagery, and no matter what virtues I may glean from the text, my overriding conviction is that the theatre

116

should not be used this way. That gaping cavity which yawns between the proscenium walls is not intended to confine a spray of whimsical, philosophical, metaphysical verbalism. It can, and does, convey whimsy, philosophy and metaphysics, but when it tries to do so exclusively through parlance, it does violence to its own nature and might just as well be a book, a radio-play or a lecture.

From a purely literary standpoint (one is forced to take this standpoint), Saunders' work is moderately impressive. It is spiced with sharp, swift images that snap, pop and crackle through two slack and discursive acts. It is intelligent; it is sensitively-conceived and felicitously expressed. It finds in the self-imposed hermitage of one man, a kind of symbol for the ungetatableness of all of us. It emulates (wrongly, I think) a withdrawal from life as a kind of pious negation of the mundane, and explores the subject of identity in a diffusely philosophic way which is portentous without being profound, and casual without being particularly funny.

On a stylistic level, it chips together all the fashionable anti-illusionist devices Brecht and the New Drama bequeathed us. Although its pessimism smacks of Beckett and its intellectual overlay reminds one of Pirandello, it has none of Beckett's centrifugal intensity and isn't one whit as thought-out as Pirandello. It is all charged, flippant or poetic phrasemaking. The ultimate effect is of language gone on a spree – and although it is consistently spontaneous, it doesn't cleave to any thematic discipline of its own.

The play is just opaque and intelligent enough to be taken as a serious statement on something-or-other whereas for me, it is simply a kind of diarrhoea of the cerebrum and when one begins to discern the spiritual overtones, it positively palls. It is as if Saunders took for his subject the whole prolix world of Ideas, and tried to dramatise it. Not only is it a task for which Saunders' intellect is inadequate but the sort of objective no dramatist – barring Beckett (who wouldn't do it anyway) – should ever consciously set for himself.

(From: Charles Marowitz, *Plays and Players*, March, 1963)

Next Time I'll Sing to You is suggested by a theme in Raleigh Trevelyan's *A Hermit Disclosed*. The hermit in question is Jimmy Mason, who, physically filthy and ignored by the world, lived for the last forty years of his existence in a barricaded hovel in Great Canfield, Essex, where he died in 1942. On the unexplained solitude of this wretched man Mr Saunders has written a play bursting with wit and humour, and almost incredibly touching and sad.

117

There is no obvious plot in it, yet it propounds a problem for whose solution the audience waits in a condition of more than ordinary awareness. This solution is stated in the first five minutes of the play, without at all impairing our sense of astonishment, and pleasure, and grief. The play seems completely wayward, but its construction is in fact masterly. *Next Time I'll Sing to You* is not only profound and poetic and uproariously ribald and funny: it is also a conjuring trick of considerable virtuosity.

This virtuosity, before I realised what emotions it at first concealed, irritated me, and I watched the opening quarter of an hour with admiration for the players, Michael Caine, Barry Foster, and Liz Fraser, but without sympathy for the author. On a stage bare except for a slightly raised platform and a conventionalised rubbled wall, Mr Caine (brashly music hall), Mr Foster (flippantly philosophic), and Miss Fraser (dame-dumb) expressed contempt for the play, complained that they had not only to say the same lines every night but that every night they had to complain that they had to say the same lines every night, gave the audience leave to shift their bottoms (Mr Saunder's word, not mine) when they felt bored, talked to us, winked at us, insulted us, and generally made it clear, however fed up we might become, that they were stuck with the play, and had to get on with it.

*   *   *

I won't say I didn't laugh at some of this, but it is very old stuff. The tricks that were new when Bruant, Beckett, and Brecht first thought of them are now the routine property of any hack dramatist. This amorphous joking about the methods of presenting a play which as yet has not (apparently) begun to exist is nowadays the first resort of the dramatist who hopes to conceal the fact that he has nothing to say with more or less amusing comments on his way of saying it.

Then Michael Bryant came on, and bowled an imaginary cricket ball which Mr Foster clouted with an imaginary bat. The action, as absurd as any dialogue that had preceded it, changed the temper of the entertainment. For Mr Bryant was neither brash nor flippant nor dumb. With him, with his set face, with his voice that scoops upwards in amazed protest against injustice, a new element entered into the play: sorrow.

It was at this point that I recognised that *Next Time I'll Sing to You* was probably going to be a remarkable play. For this new element was not only important in itself, but it altered the values of all that had gone before. The jokes about the impotence of the players ceased to be merely a conventional way of passing the time: they were instead a statement of the play's main theme, that man is not free, that he works out a destiny which has been prepared for him ineluctably.

Yet the play is more than a dramatic demonstration of determinism. For Mr Saunders has an attitude towards determinism. He is angry with it, he is rebellious, he is grieved. He would, with all his strength of being and feeling, that things were not so. It is in this emotion that the play lives.

In the girl, who re-states the theme in the opening passage of the second act – a passage which again seems irrelevant, but is actually rigidly required by the play's structure – determinism or the powerlessness to resist, is accepted, for she actually confuses it with freedom. Mr Foster and Mr Caine, from two different points of view, make brilliant fun of it. And it tears the heart of Mr Bryant in pieces.

It is in the person of the hermit that this problem of freedom is centred; why had he grown old, neglected, and unhappy, and poor, and alone? The flesh and the intellect more or less make peace with this condition. Only the heart revolts against it, until in a retort apparently flippant, Mr Bryant indicates its surrender. Do you believe in free love? asks the girl; and Mr Bryant replies, What do you mean? That it exists? There lies the whole anguish of this magnificent play, and its pity.

(From: Harold Hobson, *The Sunday Times*, 27 January, 1963)

The Workhouse Donkey
John Arden
July 1963   Festival Theatre, Chichester

The reason why Mr Arden's work is rarely appreciated properly at a first hearing is that what Brecht pretended to do, Mr Arden actually does. The admirers of Brecht claim that his plays cause audiences to think for themselves. Instead of indulging in an orgy of emotional sympathy with certain characters and their viewpoints, Brecht, it is said, induces periods of cool and rational consideration. But the freedom of thought given by Brecht is, of course, illusory. By his employment of alienation he instructs his audience to think: but he clearly indicates to them what conclusion their thought should reach. This is why he is such a reassuring dramatist. He asks the question, and supplies the answer.

There are no answers in Mr Arden's work, and this is the quality in it which is difficult to get used to. The human mind is hot for certainty; it likes to be told that this man is good and that bad, this is the right course of action, and that the wrong. To this type of universal craving Mr Arden has nothing whatever to say, except that the audience must work out the problem for itself. He leaves one in a position of ambiguity, and removes any signpost that may show which way he has gone himself . . .

[He] sets the audience a real exercise. He leaves them with *his* facts to be tackled by *their* brains. People are always saying that they like authors who make them think. If they really mean this – and not merely that they like authors who make them think they are thinking – then Mr Arden is their man.

(From: Harold Hobson, *The Sunday Times*, 11 July, 1963)

The Workhouse Donkey is an ambitious work mixing and muddling many styles and influences and written too often in language of perversely impenetrable opacity. Mostly it is brutal Jonsonian comedy full of caricatured gulls and gallants and confidence tricksters. Occasionally it draws on snatches and snippets of Shakespeare. But, unfortunately, the major influence seems to be not English but German – Bertolt Brecht at his most pretentiously slapdash.

Much of the effort to copy 'epic theatre' goes to waste and clogs the action. The interpolated songs are neither catchy nor pointed enough. The attempt to characterise opposing groups by counterpointing pseudo-blank verse against alliterative ballad rhymes continually interposes a screen between us and the meaning.

As an early and partisan admirer of *Serjeant Musgrave's Dance* I approach any new work of John Arden's with lively respect. But it is useless to pretend that *The Workhouse Donkey* is anything except a theatrical folly, an enormous rambling warren of dead ends and blank walls without any architectural merit. The ending towers over the rest of the play like a monumental arch over a caravan site.

(From: Alan Brien, *The Sunday Telegraph*, 14 July, 1963)

As a play written by an author there is really nothing printable to be said about *The Workhouse Donkey*. But it is possible to praise Stuart Burge's production and the honest endeavours of a highly skilled cast to cover up its lamentable deficiencies.

Stuart Burge has indeed put on a Festival Show with all the ingredients I have mentioned. He keeps the action, such as it sadly and obviously is, spinning along at least up to the last quarter, where even he is defeated. He gets the frequent changes of place slickly done and he holds up to us scene after scene that seems to have the potentiality of turning out to be something at last, and it is not his fault if time after time it turns out to be empty.

So, too, with the actors. Frank Finlay is the rogue donkey of the Labour section and works like anything to make something of a part that is only dimly sketched. Mr Arden's idea of Labour politicians in conference depends a great deal upon polysyllabic humour and malapropisms. Then for good measure he throws in some rough rhymes which are meant to be pathetic and are only, as we used to say shudderingly shy-making. Mr Finlay plunges nobly on.

I felt sorriest for the admirable Anthony Nicholls as the newly-appointed Chief Constable sent in to clear up the corruption in the town. He is floated on the gas of the Higher Significance, and awful it is. But he dared us to laugh at the pomposities of his lines so hard that we actually didn't. Norman Rossington as a spiv doctor, Alison Leggatt as the brewer's lady, and Mary Miller as the doctor's natural daughter were others who coped manfully with hair-raising parts; while Jeremy Brett, in the first part, showed a delightful gift for comedy.

Mr Arden has been hawked round by his young admirers as a leading British playwright on the strength of one failure and two rather interesting muck-ups. Now he has added an ambitious piece that is both a downright failure and a muck-up and is far, far from interesting. Perhaps his young fans will now stop ruining his chance of a career as a dramatist, by turning off the praise until he has earned it.

(From: T.C. Worsley, *The Financial Times*, 10 July, 1963)

Mr Arden's finished text is far removed from a straightforward comedy of humours. It is not simply that he makes extensive use of song and dance, and allows himself to switch freely between farce and declamatory earnestness. Very often, indeed, these extensions are brilliantly expressive – especially in the ludicrously exaggerated night-club scene with balloon-clad girls inciting the customers to assault them with pins, and the mock-heroic change to capitalist Shakespearian melodrama for villainous soliloquies.

The objection is simply that elaboration all but obscures the line of the action. The language repeatedly falls into literary artifice which is both out of character and conceals meaning instead of illuminating it; and the proliferation of incident is so free that it swamps the basic narrative; it becomes progressively more difficult to distinguish between essential development and the peripheral flourishes.

All the same there are many passages in Stuart Burge's production that light up like a flame, and the Chichester cast put over the play with great panache. Robert Stephens's grafting police superintendent, Norman Rossington's shady GP, and Anthony Nicholls as the incorruptible chief constable skate over the text as if there were no thin ice. And Frank Finlay as the Donkey, adopting a gait of gnome-like virility and blustering his

1963

way irrepressibly through every awkward situation, rules the
roost as masterfully as he was meant to.

(From: Our Dramatic Critic, *The Times*, 9 July, 1963)

1964

In this year one outstanding talent appeared, blazed like a meteor and, by 1967, was brutally extinguished. The career of Joe Orton resembles Christopher Marlowe's in its irridescent brevity, and his work, like Marlowe's, has a virile innovative kind of brashness which, nevertheless, and perhaps paradoxically (considering what we know or infer about the temperaments of the two men), was far from devoid of consciously applied artistic discipline. But if Marlowe was a lyrical, tragic moralist, Orton was a prose comic moralist. 'Black comedy' is too restricted a term to describe Orton's work, though some critics could not see beyond the mordant laughter. He was, perhaps, again like Marlow, a sceptical, even, at times, a despairing perfectionist, and ridiculed mankind for not being better than it was. Critically, Entertaining Mr. Sloane was greeted with incredulity tinged with surprise and wariness, though with little disposition to underrate its radical flavour. In fact, it was less a new departure than a twentieth-century version of the verbally outrageous, theatrically unpredictable, morally ambiguous drama of the late Jacobean period. For one reason or another, Orton has the strongest affiliations with a theatrical 'Jacobethan' world – he would have been happier, perhaps, in its obviously dangerous, opportunistic, excitedly experimental atmosphere, and in its later manifestations of a profound, fantastic cynicism.

Shaffer's The Royal Hunt of the Sun, like Bolt's A Man For All Seasons, has received the unfortunate accolade of becoming a public examination text – unfortunate, in that it tends, in the minds of many, to give such plays a false status. They are 'safe'; they are 'manageable' by the young; they have 'something to say' that can easily be extracted and tossed about for discussion; they contain no moral or verbal offence. The reviews hint at the misapprehension of the play by its contemporaries and public examiners but do not get at the root of the matter – the play relies, almost entirely, on spectacular production, while the unwary assume it is expressing something of deep significance. It gives every indication now of fading like the Dodo – once arresting to the eyes, now an ungainly anachronism.

Livings, in 1964, continued his somewhat anarchic way with plot, theme and expression in Eh!, a play notable for having attracted to it one of the most popular new young actors of the time – David Warner.

123

This year, in fact, is in the nature of a warning year for critics – not to be so overwhelmed by a theatrical experience (whether offered by director or actor) that the play that is inside trying to get out is happily ignored.

Entertaining Mr. Sloane
Joe Orton
May 1964   Arts

. . . not for a long time have I disliked a play so much as I disliked Joe Orton's *Entertaining Mr Sloane*. . . . In a backhanded way this is a compliment. If an equally nasty play had been ineptly written or ineffectively acted I should have been able to dismiss it with contempt. But I can't despise this one because it comes to life; I feel as if snakes had been writhing round my feet.

(From: W.A. Darlington, *The Daily Telegraph*, 7 May, 1964)

Is this the world as Mr Orton sees it, an interesting pattern of personal relationships he wished to study or a darkly comical account of sides of human nature he detests? There is sufficient natural theatricality about his first play to encourage belief that we shall soon find his activities less obscure . . . his jokes are either rudely outspoken or depend upon a sudden elevation of conversational style into what Mr Ivor Brown some years ago christened 'Jargantuan'.

(From: unsigned review, *The Times*, 7 May, 1964)

Joe Orton, the 25-year-old author of *Entertaining Mr Sloane* at the New Arts, has been described as a primitive. This suggests an innocent and simple-minded vision of a complex and evil world – the knee-high eye view of a bright child in which unimportant details glow with a ghastly clarity and familiar gestures take on a fearful strangeness. . . .

Mr Orton is more than a primitive. Throughout this extraordinary second play he seems to be writing off the cuff and hitting out at random. Yet the language is a highly organised *collage* of juvenile slang, adman's jargon and soap opera clichés which can be simultaneously funny and sickening. And the action was cunningly enough organised to make one first-nighter cry out 'Oh no!' at a twist in the plot with all the absorbed naivety of a child at a Saturday morning film show.

Along with Charles Wood and David Rudkin (both introduced to a theatre-going public at the Arts Theatre) Mr Orton is one of those rare dramatists who create their own world in their own idiom. A new generation is treading on the heels of those grand old men of the Fifties, Harold Pinter and John Osborne.

There are many moments in *Entertaining Mr. Sloane* when the tone of voice of the actor is disturbingly at variance with the words he speaks. For instance, when Peter Vaughan looks at the sexy ruffian who has made his sister pregnant and murdered his father, and says with smiling menace: 'Your youth pleads for leniency and, by God, I'm going to give it to you.' Few non-English-speaking foreigners could grasp the deliberate incongruity of this simply by listening to the line literally translated and flatly spoken through an ear phone.

(From: Alan Brien, *The Sunday Telegraph*, 10 May, 1964)

I hope I shall not be misunderstood if I say that the English author of whom Joe Orton, in *Entertaining Mr Sloane* (Arts), reminds me most vividly is Jane Austen. Miss Austen had a keen eye for the absurdities of the fashionable fiction of her day; and so has Mr Orton. His *Entertaining Mr Sloane*, all proportions kept, is the *Northanger Abbey* of our contemporary stage. *Entertaining Mr Sloane* has most of the horrors and perversions; murder, sadism, nymphomania, and homosexuality. At one time I suspected incest as well, but in this I turned out to be mistaken. Madge Ryan in the difficult opening scene – difficult but rewarding, if it is well played, and at the Arts it *is* well played – has the task of setting the tone of the play. She does it with extreme skill: her simple-minded middle-aged nymphomaniac is just that little bit too blonde and forthcoming to be real. The rest of the company has the same exact degree of exaggeration; Dudley Sutton's murderer is just too coolly quiet to be natural, Charles Lamb's old man just too persistent, and Peter Vaughan's smartly dressed, powerful and deformed pervert just too good to be true. The calculation is close, and the satire very funny.

Entertaining Mr Sloane begins as a joke about moral horror; and as such a joke should it goes on to develop a horror of its own. It becomes a British counterpart of *Who's Afraid of Virginia Woolf?*, and its third act does not succumb to the sentimentality that spoils Mr Albee's play. It is a vision of total evil, and it is possible to perceive its merit without approving it. It might be a coterie success: a *Wrong Box*, a *South Wind*, a Beauvoir-Wences. I should not call it promising. It seems more like an end than a beginning.

(Harold Hobson, *The Times*, 10 May, 1964)

The Royal Hunt of the Sun
Peter Shaffer
July 1964   Festival Theatre, Chichester

Peter Shaffer's new play is mightily ambitious. As vast in intention
as the Andes mountains, in which his Inca Indians wait for their
Spaniards, and the Spaniards shiver at them and the snow. Not
only does he deal with colonialism; not only with the Church and
civilisation; he deals with personal values, with time, with God,
with Resurrection. Even Shakespeare didn't attempt all this in one
play, and Mr Shaffer's shoulders are, frankly, too slim.

Theatrically, the National Theatre's production feels its three
and a half hours' length; there are blotches of tedium, digres-
sions, repetition, and a general feeling of muddle. More importantly, there seems to be some essential hollowness.

A pattern of ideas can be traced from the conflict and chaos of
the story. Western civilisation, based on merchants and poverty,
confronts Inca civilisation, with its developed organisation for the
general good and its prizes for old-age pensioners. Christianity,
with its emphasis on suffering, confronts Inca religion, which
hallows happiness. The Church, with its hypocrisies and its rigid
certainties, faces the high priest of the Incas, with his own
certainty. There is nowhere any common ground.

More hopefully, Pizarro, the Spanish explorer, and Atahualpa,
the so-called Sun God, face each other and find shared personal
emotions and a personal liking for each other. The obstacle – one
frequently mooted by Mr Shaffer with cold despair and cloggy
relish – is death. The answer perhaps is the sun religion, itself a
recognition of rebirth and renewal. Or perhaps personal relationships (the old, old solution) are enough.

So much. Why then does one emerge with a sense of having
absorbed so much of lasting value? It seems to me that there is no
particular originality in Mr Shaffer's ideas, and no particular
feeling for the characters except as projection of ideas. *The Royal
Hunt of the Sun* is too consciously 'about things'. As theology or
philosophy, it is not much more searching than a decent
undergraduate discussion, and cleverly wielded dramatic images
cannot make it otherwise. Colin Blakely plays Pizarro, the only
really interesting character, with a rasping voice and much sweat;
and manages to give him an appearance of the depth that one
suspects Mr Shaffer has denied him.

Ultimately, it has to rely on its appeal as a spectacle. And, yes, it
is often good to look at: plenty of keening Indians, plenty of
bellowing Spaniards, plenty of colour and movement. John
Dexter directs as imaginatively as one would expect, but excursions into mime don't always succeed. The marching Spaniards

look as if they are doing a soft-shoe shuffle; a slaughter of Indians reminds me of a display of exotic dancing for tourists I once saw in a pseudo-Indian camp at Disneyland, USA.

(Benedict Nightingale, *The Guardian*, 8 July, 1964)

Peter Shaffer's *The Royal Hunt of the Sun* is an intellectual spectacular, a de Mille epic for educated audiences, an eye-dazzling ear-buzzing, button-holing blend of *Ben Hur*, *The King and I* and *The Devils*.

Mr Shaffer has baked a giant layer cake, with theology, sociology, history and philosophy all spread together under a pink icing of popular entertainment. He has put the gilt back on the gingerbread and in the course of this wide-screen re-creation of one of the world's great crimes created a new theatrical form which should be called Sinerama.

In the early sixteenth century, 167 gold-crazed Spanish cut-throats, their crosses sharpened to swords, set out to conquer a nation of millions and a country stretching a thousand miles. Led by Pizarro, these whippers-in of a Catholic God and picadors for a Royal corrida, hunt down the Inca Atahuallpa, Son of the Sun, to melt his empire into ingots.

Visually and aurally, in its physical investment and domination of Chichester's great flight deck of stage, the production is stunning. The two directors, John Dexter for the invaders and Desmond O'Donovan for the natives, seem able to mould both space and time: so that the rusting army marches for miles along the deserted roads without ever moving a step forward, and they stand motionless in the empty city square for ten hours which lasts as many minutes.

Without any scenery or props, in blinding light against a wooden wall, Pizarro's men mime the climb of a mountain of ice which is as exhausting and exhilarating as any Hollywood sequence filmed by cameras hanging over the edge of a real precipice. The butchery of the 3,000 unarmed and blinkered Peruvians by the grubby white gods from beyond the ocean is enacted in slow motion by a score of actors like a ritual dance of death. Almost all the incidents are choreographed with simple, stylised movements, often to the dissonant rhythms of Marc Wilkinson's music punctuated by weird harsh bird cries, which are far more effective than the most photographic realism.

*   *   *

The sets and costumes of Michael Annals also work miracles especially in two moments which remain stamped on the retina. The first appearance of the Inca when the great rosette of Spain embossed on the back wall of the stage suddenly breaks open and turns the Christian cross into the flaming pagan sun. And the

127

final tableau of the almost naked Atahuallpa surrounded by his priests whose immobile masks, oddly impressed with the Steinberg faces of American businessmen, change before our eyes from awe to amazement, through resentment to despair, as they realise their immortal emperor will not rise from the dead. . . .

(From: Alan Brien, *The Sunday Telegraph*, 12 July, 1964)

The triumphant humanist affirmation which ends Peter Shaffer's *Royal Hunt of the Sun*, at Chichester, has sent various of my colleagues out into the Sussex night vibrating like gongs about 'the greatest play of our generation'. Old Forsterian that I am, and sucker for such sentiments, I'd gladly have gone along with them. But one of those accidents of theatrical unplanning which are enough to make BBC-2's current Sunday programme of 'related theme' dramas look haphazard, took me the following night to the Aldwych revival of Samuel Beckett's *endgame*. I can't take Beckett's theatre any more seriously than his e.e. cummings typographical larks, and as a thinker he seems to me as modish and sentimental in his St Germain gloom as Mr Shaffer, in his hard-won hopefulness, is conscientiously racked. But, midway through the listless exchanges of Hamm and Clov, Jack MacGowran's spastic clown of a servant peered through a slit in the fungoid wall of their dungeon at an empty grey sea, and turned back snarling to his blind, crippled master. 'What all is?' he echoed bitterly. 'In a word? Is that what you want to know? *Corpsed*. Well? Content?' At that moment Mr Shaffer, whom I'd enjoyed and agreed with, lost. Beckett's word, for all its arch, punning portentousness, was alive. Shaffer's were dead.

The superb spectacle at Chichester is what you'd expect of the author of *Five-Finger Exercise*. That was a good, conventional drawing-room bout of family cannibalism, distinguished by some fresh and well-written speeches. *The Royal Hunt of the Sun* is a good, conventional chronicle play, in the vein of *Richard of Bordeaux* and *Adventure Story*, distinguished by some heartfelt flights of historical imagination, a stunning production and the best acting the National Theatre juniors have shown us so far. It's several ambitious strides ahead of what Shaffer's done before, but it's not the work of a poet and when it tries for poetry gives itself away. . . .

Still, as I say, I enjoyed the spectacle enormously and would urge its sheer theatrical pleasure on all who, like myself, feel starved, in our bare post-Pinter theatre of word and emblem, of the living amplitude of a good fat novel or even old Drury Lane melodrama.

(From: Ronald Bryden, *New Statesman*, 17 July, 1964)

Eh?
Henry Livings
October 1964   Aldwych

Mr Livings's way is simply to establish a community of hardy characters and then to string a series of wild inventions on it until he feels we have had enough, when he whoops up one last splendid set-piece and stops. It's the world of Harold Lloyd and Buster Keaton, but with the extra ingredient that it refers to the world in which we live and work today.

(From: B.A. Young, *The Financial Times*, 31 October, 1964)

Because Ionesco, Beckett, Pinter and Donleavy are often obscure writers, it is tacitly accepted that Mr Livings, who shares something of their outlook, must also be an obscure writer. As a matter of fact, he is an exceptionally clear writer. In *Eh?* for example, ten minutes after the curtain rises, he tells the audiences exactly what he is going to do, and then proceeds systematically to do it. It is quite in accordance with the natural perversity of things that an author who acts in this frank and logical manner should immediately be thought to be a man who slaps on to the stage a series of disconnected music-hall sketches.

(From: Harold Hobson, *The Sunday Times*, 1 November, 1964)

The fact that farce is an artificial genre, largely independent of social or psychological truth, has led to a widely-held belief that a good farce must be perfectly engineered, as neat and intricate as the inside of a watch. . . . The new Aldwych has found its own *farceur*, Monsewer Henry Livings. And the objections to his latest piece, *Eh?*, have centred on the undeniable fact that it is chaotic, the very opposite of the beautifully meshing situation-machines of Travers and Feydeau.

But to demand order of the anarchist Livings is like asking a giraffe to lay an exquisitely rounded egg. It is a psychological irrelevance. I suspect that it is equally vain to expect Livings' plays to get better. They have never been so good; but they are wonderful. The talent is not unlike Spike Milligan's as a performer. Milligan does everything badly. He bungles his jokes, gets helpless giggles, is paralysed with nervous mistiming – and yet the final result is far funnier than if a perfect comedian had put it over. That's how it is in a Livings farce. The jokes are often terrible (though usually better than Travers'), the situations apparently meaningless, the dialogues positively retrograde – and yet there is a logic to it, though not the logic of traditional farce. There is even reality: the reality of nightmare. . . .

But the greatest joy in this chaos of nightmare felicities (which

129

I've hardly begun to touch on) is that Mr Livings, who produced such banal literature when trying to write impressively in *Kelly's Eye*, should show himself once more capable of writing richly and beautifully in his true and I hope inexhaustible vein of neo-farce.

(From: John Holmstrom, *Plays and Players*, December 1964)

1965

Pinter's The Homecoming *in June and Bond's* Saved *in November provided more than enough fuel to keep the passions and curiosities of the critics and theatregoers burning. All other theatrical endeavours paled into insignificance beside these two* causes célèbres.

Pinter's play became notorious for its explicit depiction of a morally disgusting household and its delineation of a female both sexually exploited and, equally, aware of the power her subjection gives her. It encouraged one famous playwright to declare it the most degrading play he had ever seen — 'like masturbating in public'.

Saved achieved a sensational status through a scene in which a baby in a pram is stoned to death by four louts. Appraisal of the play in many critical comments had to give place to expressions of outrage and revulsion at the explicit cruelty, but some tried to explain it away on quasi-moral, quasi-sociological grounds. The scene quickly became a kind of sounding-board of opinion as the evidence for and against theatre censorship began to increase in size and volume until censorship was abolished on September 26, 1968.

The Homecoming
Harold Pinter
June, 1965   Aldwych

The play blithely plumbs the depths of human degradation and is assuredly not for all tastes.
(From: Eric Shorter, *The Daily Telegraph*, 4 June, 1965)

Mr Pinter is one of the few playwrights who are able to establish a place as a state of mind.
(From: Anthony Curtis, *The Sunday Telegraph*, 6 June, 1965)

Mr Pinter isn't to my way of thinking an *important* playwright, in the sense that he has any message to offer us or any trail-blazing innovation in technique (Ed: Who has?). But he has this enormous capacity for generating attention among his characters in which the audience becomes irresistibly involved.

(From: B.A. Young, *The Financial Times*, 5 June, 1965)

Of the playwrights who came out of the Fifties, Pinter is undeniably the master-technician. He uses the stage as an acrobat his trampoline; as a wrestler exploits the ropes, he converts its limitations into strength. His construction is tight and polished as marquetry; despite its appearance of studied irrelevance, his dialogue is the sparest in the theatre today – each calculated wamble steers toward a line which pivots the whole play, on a sixpence, in a new direction. This has been wholesomely infectious. But historically, as much has been true of many minor influences. A Shakespeare or Ibsen takes decades to sink in. It is the Beaumonts, Fletchers, Sardous, Anouilhs, Rattigans, who fasten their tone, manner and craftsmanship on their periods. Will Pinter turn out to be more than a theatrical trend-setter? Or is he merely the Sardou of the Absurd?

His new full-length play *The Homecoming*, at the Aldwych, provides a fair test. It is the most he has done so far: funniest, best-constructed, most characteristic, most explicit. The last may sound a presumptuous claim after all the reports of angry and baffled patrons stalking out of the theatres where, on a swing round the provinces, Peter Hall honed his production to its present razor-sharpness. Possibly they were more angry than baffled; had discerned the intention some of London's sophisticated symbol-hunters seem to have missed. At the interval in last Friday's performance, an indignant lady stalked into the foyer behind me, fuming: 'They're exactly like animals!' She obviously considered that she had missed the point. In fact, she had encapsulated it in four words.

Pinter's characters have always had an animal instinct for 'territory', spatial possession. The strength of his stagecraft is that their obscure warfare, however verbalised, is over the stage itself: for possession of the actual area on which they battle. To have the last word coincides with dominating the stage; the actor who ends upstaging the rest has established his barnyard dominion over them like a cock on a dunghill. In *The Birthday Party* and *The Caretaker*, this manoeuvring is implicit. It is flesh and bone of *The Homecoming*. The whole point, structure and joke of the play is its gradual disclosure that what these actors, with their modern clothes and slightly Golders Green accents, are unfurling is most readily and recognisably described in the language of a zoologist reporting the mating-customs of fighting seals on the beaches of Sakhalin.

Two elderly males, offspring of the same mother, share a lair on the northern scarp of the Thames valley – Kilburn, perhaps, or Camden Town. One, the feebler, has grown neuter with age and been forced to wait upon his stronger sibling. He, a mangy, widowed old bull, is failing too, but still powerful enough to provide food and occasionally to savage the two young bulls of his engendering who also use the lair. Snarling, they recognise his mastery to the extent that they do not bring females there. A third male offspring, however, after several seasons' absence on the east coast of America, returns to the family breeding-ground with a mate: a meek young female of tantalising sleekness. The household of deprived males gang jealously against him. One of the young bulls makes a mating-display to the female; when she responds, the younger and stronger mounts her. She, foreseeing greater sexual freedom and comfort with a multiplicity of providers, acquiesces in the rape. Her mate, recognising defeat, retreats whence he came with an unconvincing show of dignity.

Pinter translates this zoo story to human dress with considerable wit and, ultimately, some cold power. He's helped by a production tuned like a racing-car: every line has been pointed, every silence charged. Paul Rogers, as the father, and Ian Holm, as the peacocking son, deal beautifully with their scenes of surly cohabitation, established in Pinter's best vein of bickering non-sequitur, flowering when a woman arrives into baroquely genteel fantasy. Sentimentally, Rogers recalls how he promised his wife 'a dress in pale corded blue silk, heavily encrusted with pearls, and for casual wear a pair of pantaloons in lilac flowered taffeta'. Michael Bryant makes the returning son's hectoring of his wife a brilliant amalgam of human and animal nervousness, and Vivien Merchant, in a part mainly requiring enigmatic passivity, is wonderfully apt at riveting attention on each crossing and uncrossing of her legs.

The gradual shift of emphasis to animality is achieved deftly. There's a shock of poetry in the fact that the wife's only statement about America contains nothing human:

It's all rock. And sand. It stretches . . . so far . . . everywhere you look. And there's lots of insects there. (Pause) And there's lots of insects there.

The final metamorphosis, too, comes with gruesome force. Before her husband's eyes, the wife and her brutish brother-in-law roll, locked together, from the sofa to the floor. As the curtain falls, the father, crawling like an old beast, thrusts his white head up at her, bellowing desperately for a kiss. But something has gone wrong in this second half, and the failure tells much about what's lacking in Pinter.

The shape of the play is the unfolding of a metaphor. It should show the gradual convergence of two separate logics, animal and human. But in fact it works the other way round. It is the early scenes, where the characters growl and sniff around each other like dogs on a corner, which, while funny, seem truthful. The further they lapse into zoology, the more the logics diverge. Either you can claim seriously that men are at bottom animals (one can imagine O'Neill carrying through such a demonstration) or you can present the notion as a surrealist whimsy, like David Garnett in *Lady into Fox*. It is Coleridge's distinction between imagination and fancy. Choosing humour and shock, Pinter has chosen the lesser of the two. In spite of some superficial philosophising about people and 'objects', he has elected to exploit his metaphor's exoticism. He has written a stylish entertainment, but not much more. All that remains at the end is a flavour. Still, it is a strong, individual one. Perhaps it is enough for him that, like the beasts which fascinate him, he has staked out a territory with his personal odour.

(From: Ronald Bryden, *New Statesman*, 11 June, 1965)

At first and even into the second, sadder half, the relentless ribaldry and poker-faced outrageousness of Harold Pinter's new enigmatic parable (*The Homecoming* at the Aldwych) was relished by the first night audience – or most of them. Gleeful squeals of joy greeted the unvarnished home-truths exchanged by Cockney brothers in a widower's home, welcoming back a brother from America and his ex-model suburban British wife with a view to inducing her to go on the streets and keep them in comfort. But by the end I sensed some disappointment and shared it. The thing is perfectly turned, but to what end?

No doubt that is the wrong question to ask. These Pinter pieces, variously amusing according to taste and often fraught with that fashionable commodity, menace, are not really 'about' anything. This play is not 'about' a moral exposé as is Lenormad's *Les Ratés* for example. The pieces are quadrilles, stylishly danced, or like the arabesques and whorls in paint to be seen on the easels of *avante* [sic] *garde* art dealers: superbly executed doodles.

Boredom can set in fairly early with the rationalist. I enjoy myself the outrageousness and am quite happy with the baffling message of motiveless evil lurking in wait. But to me (and to me only it may be) Mr Pinter reverses the chief pleasure in the theatre: which is to sit with fellow humans (the audience) either fully in-the-know or in keen curiosity as the general state of affairs and then to see the players, probably not in full knowledge or in misguided expectation makes [sic] a mess of or redeem events through their 'own' devices and character. In Pinter the thing is the other way up. It is *we* who are in total ignorance: the actors who are exchanging wreathed smiles and knowing nods of complicity.

Why, for instance, does the chauffeur uncle have a heart attack? He was such a nice fellow and his boring anecdotes and self-regarding patter are beautifully managed by John Normington. Was it because he didn't have the courage to stand out against the arrangement whereby his niece-in-law was to be set up in prostitution? Arguably Paul Rogers the hectoring old widower also has a heart attack but doesn't die. His whine 'I'm not an old man' addressed to the enigmatic and only too willing daughter-in-law (Vivien Merchant, all poise and polish) finally brings down the curtain.

Most enigmatic of all is Michael Bryant's Teddy (the homecomer) who remains a complete blank and makes off to America again without protest or visible sign of relief at being rid of a tiresome wife. Ian Holm, with enormous gusto and volume, bounces us into feelings of interest for Lenny, the cock sparrow brother with the most enterprise. Peter Hall produces with a splendid sense of what can be got out of the veiled innuendo and non sequitur. The result is often very comic in a wry way. The grey and black horror of a living room designed by John Bury is not the least of the ingredients. But it leaves us feeling cheated.

(Philip Hope-Wallace, *The Guardian*, 4 June, 1965)

Saved
Edward Bond
November 1965   Royal Court

I wonder what William Gaskill thinks he's up to, producing such stuff. But you'll see, there'll be people who think it quite wonderful.
(From: W.A. Darlington, *The Daily Telegraph*, 4 November, 1965)

The hope that Edward Bond's play might live up to its title and redeem the so far disastrous new season at the Royal Court was woefully shattered last night.

The two previous productions have been distressing enough, but at least they were the work of Royal Court regulars to whom the theatre must have felt a certain loyalty. The new production raises the question of play selection in a more disturbing form. Mr Bond, a newcomer to the theatre (with one Sunday night production to his credit), has written a work which will supply valuable ammunition to those who attack modern drama as half-baked, gratuitously violent, and squalid. Why on earth did the theatre accept it?

Saved, which concerns the liaison between a spaniel-like South London boy and a vixenish good-time girl who spends most of the evening trying to get rid of him, is a blockishly naturalistic piece, full of dead domestic longueurs and slavishly literal bawdry. It contains the ugliest scene I have ever seen on any stage – where a teenage gang daub a baby with excrement and stone it to death.

One can no longer take cover behind the phrase 'bad taste' in the face of such material. But one has a right to demand what purpose it fulfils. In a recent interview Mr Bond said that his aim was to 'illuminate' violence. One would hardly have guessed this from the play itself which does nothing to lay bare the motives for violence and appeals to no emotions beyond those aroused by the act itself. According to one's proclivities these may be horror, sadistic relish, or amusement; a fair proportion of last night's audience fell into the third category.

The most charitable interpretation of the play would be as a counterblast to theatrical fashion, stripping off the glamour to show that cruelty *is* disgusting and that domestic naturalism *is* boring. But the writing itself, with its self-admiring jokes and gloating approach to moments of brutality and erotic humiliation, does not support this view. In so far as the claustrophobically private action has any larger repercussions, it amounts to a systematic degradation of the human animal.

(From: Our Drama Critic, *The Times*, 4 November, 1965)

I don't say *Saved* is a great play – it doesn't have to be. But it's accurate and it's honest, presenting its violence not as some neo-Gothic testimony to the cruel absurdity of the universe and human nature, but as a social deformity crying for correction. It seems to me the best new play of its kind since *Roots*. With his finer ear and stronger rein on language, Mr Bond might yet become the playwright Wesker promised then.

(From: Ronald Bryden, *New Statesman*, 12 November, 1965)

It appears that British audiences and critics can stomach unlimited helpings of torture, sadism, perversion, murder and bestiality when perpetrated by foreigners upon foreigners in the past. But that was in another country, they say, like Marlowe's *Jew of Malta*, and besides the stench is dead.

The catalogue of Hunnish horrors in the Aldwych late-night reading of *The Investigation* was bravely faced and nobly endured. But when Edward Bond in *Saved* at the Royal Court shows us London youth, here and now, beating and defiling a bastard baby, spitting on its nakedness and rubbing its face in its own excrement, before stoning it to death in its pram, then the cry goes up to ban and boycott such criminal libels on our national character.

Is it thought that such things cannot happen in this gentle and civilised land? Art and life have a way of reflecting each other in an eternity of mirrors and there is nothing that can be pictured even in the most grotesque of imaginations that has not been done by somebody somewhere sometime.

When David Rudkin's *Afore Night Come* was in rehearsal at the Arts, with its ritual murder of a helpless old tramp, just such a ceremonial execution of a derelict was performed by unknown butchers in a deserted house near the Elephant and Castle.

Saved has been unfavourably compared to another play about twisted sex and casual brutality, Fred Watson's *Infanticide in the House of Fred Ginger*, where a coven of louts also destroyed a neglected infant. Mr Watson's corner boys had at least the thin excuse of being drunk and of putting the baby to the gin bottle as a feeble-minded boozer's joke. Mr Bond's hooligans are presented as monsters of amorality who inflict pain simply to reassure themselves that they cannot feel another being's suffering. Yet, of the two crimes, the second is the characteristic, motiveless enormity of our age.

Mr Bond is no more a social-realist than Dostoyevsky, whose characters appear here domesticated and suburbanised in the guise of South London working people. The theme, far more carefully orchestrated than seems to have been noticed, is the uncanny, dangerous way that fantasy has of being transmuted into fact among people whose lives have no centre and no meaning.

The young Raskolnikov of the snack bars and the canals boasts of the imaginary manslaughter of a boy in a street accident – once the legend is created, it is a small step to making it true with the baby in the pram. The Prince Mishkin of the labour exchange and the back alleys, whose unfocused love weakens and corrupts all whom it touches, swears to his slippery girl that they will never become apathetic automatons like her parents – yet at the end he is chained to her family and drugged by their boredom. The chorus of street-corner roughs snigger about the sexiness of his plump, plain middle-aged mother-in-law to be – one night in the empty house, while he mends the ladder in her stocking, the dirty joke almost becomes a dirty reality.

Mr Bond has a fluent command of the gutter poetry of popular speech with its outrageous metaphors, its powerful clichés, its rhetorical repetitions. Even those who hate and despise his people cannot deny their physical solidity and psychological reality on stage as acted by this dedicated ensemble led by John Castle, Ronald Pickup, Tony Selby, Barbara Ferris and Gwen Nelson.

William Gaskill is an ascetic and a martinet among directors. His audiences are expected to obey his rules and he never softens the impact with an easy laugh, a sentimental gesture, a stagey flourish. His actors perform in a hard, clean, direct style which is impossible to watch except with eyes wide open and ears strained.

Saved, like Harold Pinter's *The Homecoming*, is a frontal attack on the concept of the family. The home is the centre of love, security and peace, but it can also be the centre of incest, danger and struggle. The action tests out Blake's epigram – 'Sooner murder an infant in its cradle than nurse unacted desires' – by carrying it to its extreme. What if that desire is to murder an infant, or only to drop litter in the street? How does a human life weigh in the balance against egotistical satisfaction?

He gives no answers. From the general reception of his play, few people can bear even hearing the question. *Saved* makes an unsympathetic, disturbing, wearing, sometimes boring evening in the theatre. But I believe it fulfils one of the basic functions of the drama far better than *The Investigation* – that of making us remember the monster behind the mask on every one of us.

(Alan Brien, *The Sunday Telegraph*, 7 November, 1965)

The play begins in the living-room of a working-class house, inhabited by a night-worker and his wife, who have not spoken for many years, and their daughter, a blonde little layabout. She enters with Len, whom she has just picked up. Pausing only so that she can blow her nose, they prepare half-heartedly to copulate on the sofa. So far Mr Bond has demonstrated – and continues to demonstrate throughout the play – a superb ear for contemporary *argot*; this kind of dialogue could well contribute to a worthwhile naturalistic comment on the half-world of metropolitan slum-suburbs. But now comes the first false note, arousing suspicion of the play's real purpose. As this pair writhe and fumble on the sofa, for far too long, we begin to wonder if we are not merely being titillated, and what interruption will be contrived. The interruption duly arrives; but then the whole groping business starts again.

There follows a succession of scenes in a confusing time-sequence establishing varying degrees of brutality, fecklessness and aimlessness, which might hold up if supported by the quick cuts of film or television; in the theatre, separated by long waits while shadows bump about the stage shifting the exiguous scenery, they are exposed as thin jottings from life as essentially vacuous as the characters they sketch.

Then comes the filthy scenes already described. Even amidst its horror further doubts arise. Why does the baby, which has previously howled for a quarter of an hour at a stretch, utter no sound? For practical reasons, obviously – and a perfunctory reference to its having been dosed with aspirin only underlines the contrivance. And after the killing, when the reluctant mother, Pam, returns, how are we to believe in her sudden concern for the child? How even more are we to accept that she never so much as glances into the pram to notice the mangled little corpse? Again, a perfunctory statement that 'I can't bear to look at you' only underlines the contrivance. It begins to be impossible not to think that whole scene of the killing is contrived. Cruelty and viciousness, on stage, are no strangers to the theatre. But was there ever a psychopathic exercise so lovingly dwelt on as this, spun out with such apparent relish and refinement of detail?

Here is the crux for modern drama. It is becoming more sharply and urgently associated with contemporary life than it has been for centuries, if ever. Things as horrible as this baby-killing, and worse, happen every day; but it is not enough merely to enact them. Without the shaping hand of art in the writing the result is only reporting. And when to reporting is added the intensification of stagecraft and powerful acting, and the prolongation of sadistic antics far beyond the time needed to make a valid point, in circumstances carelessly rigged, the conclusion is inescapable: that we are being offered not a keenly understanding, and therefore implicitly compassionate, study of deprived and unfortunate people, but a concocted opportunity for vicarious beastliness – still, I naively suppose, a minority taste.

I have attacked *Afore Night Come* and *The Marat/Sade* on similar grounds. I can't regret having done so, though both are masterpieces of intellectual coherence and emotional validity compared with *Saved*. Others might include *Infanticide in the House of Fred Ginger* and *Entertaining Mr Sloane* in the arraignment. All are perhaps tarred with the same brush; but there comes a point when both life and art are irretrievably debased, and Edward Bond's play in this production is well past that point.

(From: J.W. Lambert, *The Sunday Times*, 7 November, 1965)

In his play of marvellously observed dialogue and first-rate dramatic form, Edward Bond places his act of violence in the first half, as is done in *Macbeth*, *Julius Caesar*, etc. Unfortunately the extreme horror of this scene, though no more lurid than many an accustomed fact to which English railway toilets give testimony, has run away with most dramatic criticism and blinded it to the rare qualities shown in the rest of the play, which from time to time achieves astonishing heights of dramatic prowess and containing a last scene of which Chekhov himself would have purred his approval, a scene lasting how many minutes? (time stood still for me) with its one singular utterance of three words. . . .

By all means let us protect our children from such evils – and incidentally *Saved* is a club performance, which is the nearest approximation we in the theatre can make to the X certificate. But as facts of life they are as indigenous to our natures, and to be as capably apprehended and understood as the accepted stot – and for the same reasons, because the non-apprehension or non-understanding of our natures is going to make a mess of things, and cause appalling horrors to be perpetrated under the name of justice or even sanctimony.

The first time a school-master ordered me to take my trousers down I knew it was not from any doubt that he could punish me efficiently enough with them up. The theatre is concerned, whether in the deepest tragedy of the lightest comedy, with the teaching of the human heart the knowledge of itself, and sometimes, when it is necessary – and we are obviously going through such a time – with the study, understanding and recognition of that most dreaded and dangerous eccentricity in the human design, the tripartite conspiracy between the sexual, the excretal and the cruel.

As I have said, *Saved* is not for children but it is for grown-ups, and the grown-ups of this country should have the courage to look at it; and if we do not find precisely the mirror held up to nature in which we can see ourselves, then at least we can experience the sacramental catharsis of a very chastening look at the sort of ground we have prepared for the next lot.

(From a letter written to *The Observer*, reprinted in *Plays and Players*, January 1966, Sir Laurence Olivier)

1966

There is an unreal quality about many of the critical reviews of this year. It is as if, after the traumas of kitchen-sinkery and what followed, the critics were anxiously treading water while they looked around for signs of safety where the landmarks were the old and familiar ones. The words 'classical' and 'tragic' and 'poetic' appear again in the reviewer's vocabulary but often with a recklessness which suggests panic in the briny. Harold Hobson breathes easier when he concludes that Little Malcolm *is an unexpected respite for the Right-wing from the enfilading Left-wingery of the previous decade. He rhapsodises about what he considers to be John McGrath's achievement of 'the accent of veritable tragedy' in* Events While Guarding the Bofors Gun, *comparing it to the end of* Ghosts. *Jeremy Rundall finds the same play 'a subtle and intelligent classical drama'. Hobson, by now prepared for lyricism, judges* Belcher's Luck *to be 'essentially and beautifully a poem to the burgeoning fecundity of the fertile earth. It is filled with the ceaseless murmur of countless bees, with ripening fruit, with teeming trees'. His transports here, having moved him into rhyme, seem to have blunted his usually superb ability to avoid the jejune, even the ridiculous: for he adds, 'the text is thick with images of procreation, and the truest-feeling character in the play is pregnant'.*

Meanwhile B.A. Young was declaring Little Malcolm *to be a 'masterpiece' – but he did not define his terms. Truly, 1966 was a year of critical wobble and uncertainty to the end, with some critics so apparently discommoded as to worry whether the success of Charles Dyer's* Staircase *was attributable to the performances of Paul Scofield and Patrick Magee or the skill of Dyer.*

Little Malcolm and His Struggle Against the Eunuchs
David Halliwell
February 1966   Garrick

Where do you suppose that David Halliwell, the author of *Little Malcolm and his Struggle against the Eunuchs* (Garrick), got his first job after leaving RADA? Why, in Nottingham, of course, in this week's capital of culture, barbarism and *haute couture*. But his play is set in Huddersfield, and cast among the students of an art school. One of them is expelled, and begins to form a revolutionary party. In the grime and grease of his unappetising lodgings, the hero and his friends go through hilarious charades of incipient totalitarianism, and there is a horrific moment when what seems like a game becomes something else. There is another when a girl is beaten up.

Mr Halliwell has an effortless mastery of rich verbal expression; his humour is at times side-splitting. Brilliantly acted by John Hurt, Tim Preece, Kenneth Colley, Rodney Bewes and Susan Hayworth, the play is, in its boring ending, directed too slowly by Patrick Dromgoole. When Mr Hurt asks, 'What shall I do?' there should be no time for a voice from the gallery to reply, 'Poison the author'. That way 'Young England' lies.

Little Malcolm is a swinging [sic] Right-wing attack on what Mr Halliwell represents as the incompetent, sadistic, discontented, grant-aided, self-important, revolutionary young, and the best of all the jokes about it is that its first production was given by Unity Theatre. But perhaps, as the *Daily Worker*'s amiable comments on Graham Greene suggest, there has been a change of policy on the Left, and in future Jimmy Porter is to be seen through sour glasses.

(From: Harold Hobson, *The Sunday Times*, 6 February, 1966)

I saw this play at the Dublin Festival last year and came home bubbling with enthusiasm for it. I thought there were faults, both in construction and production, that could easily be eradicated; and I have to confess that in the London production they haven't been. But a flawed masterpiece is still a masterpiece, and if ever a play deserved that name it is this one of David Halliwell's.

It deals with the nine-day career of the Dynamic Insurrectionist party, which exists mostly in the head of its leader, Malcolm Scrawdyke, a failed art student at Huddersfield Tech. Malcolm is perpetually hypnotised by the sound of his own voice, and when he is talking he can devise wonderful schemes and even carry his friends along with him. But he is fatally weak-willed; he is the kind of man who has to give himself a count-down before making any kind of move, and then as likely as not, he won't make the move anyway. So the party's first *putsch* gets as far as the door of the attic studio where it has been hatched, and there it suddenly and finally stops.

The play's importance lies in the light that it throws on all fascistic movements. The party is begun almost as a game, a reaction against fancied persecution by the Principal of the Tech.

Then a mock trial is held of one of the party's four members, and it becomes clear that power has gone to the heads of the other three. From that moment on they are incipient Nazis. If Malcolm had been a strong leader instead of a weak one, the movement could have gone from strength to strength. But his weakness becomes apparent, and it collapses.

(From: B.A. Young, *The Financial Times*, 4 February, 1966)

The only reason for interesting oneself in the theatre is that it still offers intelligent young writers a halfway house between the minority-form of the novel, where they can fail cheaply on their own terms, and the mass market of films and television. But since the uprush of new talent in the Fifties the supply has fallen off: the successors to Osborne, Pinter and Arden seemed to prefer either the obscurer integrity of fiction or the quick money of TV. Now at last we've a swallow to suggest that a second generation may be following in the footsteps of the Fifties playwrights. David Halliwell's *Little Malcolm and his Struggle against the Eunuchs* at the Garrick is the brightest debut since Arden's. . . .

With its surrealist excursions into pure subjectivity, it could easily have emerged, like *Billy Liar* and *The Ginger Man*, as an acted novel. The wonder is that, once past a fumbling opening, it unfolds with a sure theatricality, in a mixture of harsh comic fantasy and real cruelty as heady as *Who's Afraid of Virginia Woolf?* It's upheld by the ambiguous power of its imagery: the icy attic, a wintry orange skylight lending its leprous paint the richness of impasto (Tim O'Brien's set is a stunning visual invention); the rebel's uniform of nonconformity, jeans, duffles and frowsy manes; the Hitlerian echoes, only half-parodied – the conspirators hail each other with a claw-salute at once wryly Goonish and evocative of Nazidom.

Above all there's John Hurt, superb as Malcolm: trotting back and forth round his cage in a flapping, Leninesque greatcoat, looking under his shock of auburn hair like a small, ill-tempered Christ. It's a performance of exhausting energy, full of tension and pathos. In the midst of venomous delirium he can suddenly fall quiet, to listen curiously as a sick child to the thunderous sex-fantasies of his gangling follower Nipple, 'the greatest sucker of them all', played almost as impressively by Tim Preece. Perhaps the play's finest achievement is the way it sustains the balance between its vision of madness and a parental compassion for its outcast adolescents. Patrick Dromgoole's direction emphasises two faults in the writing – twice, the audience is allowed to take a physical collapse for death – but on the whole is admirable.

(From: Ronald Bryden, *New Statesman*, 11 February, 1966)

1966

Events While Guarding the Bofors Gun
John McGrath
April 1966   Hampstead Theatre Club

There is precedent for keeping the best wine till the end; which justifies me in mentioning last, of the week's English language entertainments, John McGrath's *Events While Guarding the Bofors Gun* (Hampstead). Lance-Bombardier Evans is in charge of an unruly mob of British soldiers stationed in Germany. He is intelligent, kind and good, but he stands for nothing except his own natural virtue; and natural virtue, says Mr McGrath, is not enough. As in Mr Coward's 'A Song at Twilight', the action does not begin till the last line before the interval. After that the comparison is wholly in favour of Mr McGrath. There is not, of course, the attraction of mannered phrases and Molyneux dresses; Mr McGrath's characters are national servicemen and their language has a crudity which would make the older dramatist elegantly wince. What Mr McGrath achieves is the accent of veritable tragedy. The ending of absolute defeat is both shattering and sublime, like the ending of *Ghosts*, like the ending of the Sicilian Expedition. The performances of James Bolam, Patrick O'Connell, Brian Murphy and David McKail in particular, as well as the direction of Ronald Eyre, rise to the play's great height.

(From: Harold Hobson, *The Sunday Times*, 17 April, 1966)

The smell is authentic. The army *is* like that. Anyone who has seen service – and especially National Service – as the schoolboy in a bunch of disillusioned swaddies, the amateur among professionals, the idealist in a closed society whose members have long ceased to believe in anything less tangible than a pint of bitter, a Woodbine and the bunk next to the stove – will recognise John McGrath's picket guard for the real thing. He has recaptured so faithfully the idiom of barrack life, with no more than a veneer of stylisation, that the long first act of his play could be taken for documentary – which I imagine is the last thing he wants.

Events While . . . is in fact a subtle and intelligent classical drama. Superficially it invites comparison with *Chips with Everything*, but McGrath has more to say than Wesker about human beings and has produced a finished, properly constructed piece of work instead of an open-ended tract.

(From: Jeremy Rundall, *Plays and Players*, June, 1966)

Staircase
Charles Dyer
November 1966   Aldwych

... nothing to add to what has been done as well in a thousand books and plays ... downright trite ...
(From: Hilary Spurling, *The Spectator*, 11 November, 1966)

Toward the end of *Staircase*, Charles, once in the dear, dead days a chorus boy, now a middle-aged dresser of hair behind Brixton Market decides to walk out on his partner Harry. Silver curls quivering with irritation, mouth pursed in 20 years' accumulated peeve, he starts throwing into a suitcase the contents of his barber's cabinet – brushes, pomades, a folded newspaper. I doubt if the detail registered beyond the front stalls, but it's one of the evening's best: the paper is *The Stage*, folded at the artists' advertisements page.

It's been a long time since that sort of detail counted for much on the Aldwych stage, or anywhere else. Naturalism of that kind – the open, three-walled doll's house complete with real doorknobs, spoons and chamber pots – is out of fashion, and will recede even further when the splendid new Barbican auditorium, unveiled by Peter Hall last week, is built for the RSC in 1971.

Yet it would be a pity if the new Elizabethanism of our theatre ruled out entirely plays like Charles Dyer's new comedy – I hope its choice by the RSC signals recognition of this. The naked stage has a built-in tendency to produce a drama of existential choice, of metaphysical freedom unconditioned by history and society. It tends to exclude a whole subject-matter whose importance the queen of Existentialism herself, Simone de Beauvoir, has acknowledged in the title to one of her volumes of autobiography – *la force des choses*, the power of things.

Its importance emerges if you try to imagine *Staircase* staged, as it easily could be, without props or scenery, like a Beckett duologue. It would become an amusing but slight psychological study of a marriage: of the boredom and strains mutual dependence imposes, the difficulty of committing oneself wholly to one's partner, of loving oneself, let alone someone else.

Partly that is what *Staircase* is: and someday, in a better society, it may become nothing more. But that leaves out two things which, as matters stand, are the most important about the play. It's set in England now, under present English law; and the marriage it depicts is that of two male homosexuals.

Suspended irony
Largely, as I say, it could be any marriage – that's the point.

145

Charlie and Harry reminisce about the early days when they dreamed of transforming the shop with electro-hydraulic chairs, shell-shaped basins, of moving to Bond Street. They bicker about mothers-in-law, who left the teapot dirty, who cut his toenails in the kitchen? It's ordinary as a seaside postcard, save for the one irony which hangs over the evening, making it funny, tragic and enraging. . . .

(From: Ronald Bryden, *The Observer*, 6 November, 1966)

It is calculated with almost uncanny precision to hit precisely that place in the spectrum of public taste where essentially square, conservative audiences can be pleasantly, superficially outraged and go out of the theatre with all their original received ideas comfortingly re-affirmed but feeling that they have had an evening of pretty hot, daring stuff.

(From: J.R. Taylor, *Plays and Players*, January 1967)

Patrick Magee composes a memorable figure wonderfully unlike himself, with wide hips, sagging stomach, and a voice perpetually moaning the loss of the good looks he had when he was young. This Harry Leeds needs sympathy, and is constantly wounded by humiliation. There is something both ludicrous and moving in the way he broods over the distresses he suffered as a scout-master. The mothers of young boys used to say to him with accusing voices, 'Aren't you married, Mr Leeds?' It is he who is invariably put upon; it is he who makes the tea for Mr Scofield's Charles Dyer, the woman of the partnership, prissy, pampered, pomaded, still wonderfully handsome, a ruined god, and at this moment frightened out of his wits. For he is awaiting a summons for indecent behaviour, for, in fact, having masqueraded as a woman at a public house.

In his sudden bursts of panic, in his vain boastings of a largely imaginary past as a pantomime dame, in his irritability, and in his readiness, in his own terror, to wound his pitiably vulnerable companion, Mr Scofield's performance as Charles Dyer is riveting, revolting, and masterly. I wish, however, that Mr Scofield would cease from inventing new voices for himself. As in *The Government Inspector*, Mr Scofield here builds up a voice that is a marvel of composition but is monstrously difficult to understand. This is not of the first importance. It is the character and its development that matter, and Mr Scofield holds these in an exact grip.

(From: Harold Hobson, *The Sunday Times*, 6 November, 1966)

Belcher's Luck
David Mercer
November 1966   Aldwych

[Dialogue] outlandish; [plot] grotesque; [stagecraft] gummy.
What the Royal Shakespeare Company is doing with this kind of
meretricious rubbish I cannot imagine.
(From: Hilary Spurling, *The Spectator*, 25 November, 1966)

In David Mercer's *Belcher's Luck* (Royal Shakespeare Company:
Aldwych) a smouldering aristocrat, Sir Gerald Catesby, the last of
his line, wanders mumbling round his corrupted estate, of which
the walls are crumbling and most of the rooms in the great manor
house are shut up. The estate is run, or, to speak more exactly,
run down, by his old batman, Harry Belcher, with whom and on
whom Catesby has lived for forty years with a harmless and
imbecile affection.

Belcher, strong, virile, ambitious, has no more idea how to
make an estate productive than his master has. Of crops and
cattle, of arable and pasture he knows nothing. He wastes what
little resources are left on breeding horses. Horses, and getting
girls, any girls, anywhere, with child, are all he cares for. These
two figures, Sir Gerald and Belcher, are sharply contrasted: the
one a shaking, exhausted, puritan virgin, the other throbbing
with life: decaying owner and perhaps natural heir; but both
alike, equally in their supineness or vitality, wholly, entirely,
unrelievedly engaged in ruining a splendid heritage. Polo ground
or bingo hall, they both come to the same thing in the end.

Belcher's Luck is rich in incident, story, character, and theme.
The arrival at the mildewed old house of Belcher's bastard son,
Victor, whom Sir Gerald has expensively educated to the point of
mental breakdown (there is nothing to be hoped for from our
universities;) and of Sir Gerald's cool, immaculate-eyed niece, Mrs
Rawston, produces a crisis that does not so much finish with
murder as begin with it. There is class war and war between the
generations, and surprisingly in neither case are Mr Mercer's
sympathies altogether on one side. There is a great deal of
comedy, and enough raw language to maintain the Royal
Shakespeare Company's reputation. It would be easy, but
short-sighted, to write of this fine and memorable play as if it
were merely an old-fashioned though exciting melodrama about
the struggle for a rapidly vanishing but still desirable inheritance.
But it is more than this, even if we add to such a description an
acknowledgement of the now admired social and political
implications.

It is in fact essentially and beautifully a poem to the burgeoning fecundity of the fertile earth. It is filled with the ceaseless murmur of countless bees, with ripening fruit, with teeming trees. The text is thick with images of procreation, and the truest-feeling character in the play is pregnant. The theme of life bursting out all over is as conscious in Sir Gerald and Victor, in whom it is sterile, as it is in Belcher and the farm girl Lucy. They cannot rid themselves of a preoccupation with it either by prayer or by fantasy, and Sir Gerald's pleading with God is as useless as Victor's visions of dead philosophers.

The play is as much a celebration of the luxuriant fruitfulness of a harvest world as was Marcel Aymé's *La Jument verte*. But it is in a graver, a more wary key. For *Belcher's Luck* is, among many other things, a play about the survival of the fittest, and the fittest to survive are not necessarily the most admirable. The last victory goes to those who, without generosity and without passion, use fecundity as a controlled instrument of war.

(From: Harold Hobson, *The Sunday Times*, 20 November, 1966)

1967

Tom Stoppard, author of one of the three arguably outstanding plays of 1967, Rosencrantz and Guildenstern Are Dead, *later became a cult figure; Peter Terson's* Zigger Zagger *came to be regarded as the quintessential example of a genre to be found dotted about the theatrical history of the sixties and seventies, and becoming thicker on the ground in the eighties – plays concerned with the intention of a sport, its participants and its society; Charles Wood's* Dingo, *too, was pigeon-holed as a major representative of another genre, examples of which proliferated as the eighties approached – the denigration of popular heroes such as Churchill and Montgomery. Between the early sixties and the present day more and more began to be published about Lloyd George's post-coital breakfasts, Churchill's material appetites, Eisenhower's taste in females and so on. Both in film and in the theatre sensational revelations abounded, but it was plays like* Dingo *and Hochhuth's* Soldiers *which exploited them to support left-wing, anti-authoritarian art. The beginnings of the new 'political' (i.e. largely left-wing) drama are to be found in the late sixties. But even so the old principle that explicit proselytising is less effective than the indirect persuasiveness of disciplined art, holds its truth.* Dingo *and its ilk dated quickly, and perhaps their most interesting feature now is the extent to which they acted as a catalyst for critics to reveal their own political colouring.*

Rosencrantz and Guildenstern is one of the most popular plays in amateur repertoire today – difficult though it is to manage – and it has had, and continues to have, a respectable amount of professional revival. Since its first production Zigger Zagger *has been seldom seen on stage, despite its sensitive, topical and authentic depiction of football mobs.*

Rosencrantz and Guildenstern Are Dead
Tom Stoppard
April 1967   National Theatre at the Old Vic

... nothing if not bland ... in both [*Rosencrantz and Guildenstern*

149

Are Dead and *The Royal Hunt of the Sun*] a single idea is developed without imagination and in language of tedious brutality.
(From: Hilary Spurling, *The Spectator*, 21 April, 1967)

. . . the most important event in the British professional theatre of the last nine years.
(From: Harold Hobson, *The Sunday Times*, 16 April, 1967)

I had a sensation that a fairly pithy and witty theatrical trick was being elongated merely to make an evening of it. Tedium, even kept at bay, made itself felt.
(From: Philip Hope-Wallace, *The Guardian*, 12 April, 1967)

What do Rosencrantz and Guildenstern do when they are not taking part in the play of *Hamlet*? It's a fair question, and there might be quite an interesting answer to it even if it were asked and answered in conditions of straight realism.

But that wouldn't do at all for Tom Stoppard, whose *Rosencrantz and Guildenstern are Dead* opened at the Old Vic last night under the production of Derek Goldby.

He does not regard them as human beings at all, and he says they are dead even before his play begins because for him they have never been alive, and are scarcely alive even to themselves.

Except when they are taking their parts in Shakespeare's play – and even so they never fully understand what they are up to – they live in a sort of dreadful limbo, apparently an anteroom in the castle, where they pass the time tossing coins and nattering.

Occasionally they are silent and unnoticed spectators at bits of the play in which they do not themselves appear. For example the scene between Hamlet and Ophelia which she describes to Polonius is enacted in dumb show before them.

They make nothing of it, however, or of anything else that happens. Rosencrantz's complaint that half of what Hamlet says means something else, and the other half means nothing at all just about sums up their attitude.

They have no communication with the court. Indeed, the only character with whom they ever talk is the Player King, who is a mysterious being endowed with some kind of powers of divination.

Well, it is all very clever, I dare say, but it happens to be the kind of play that I don't enjoy and would in fact much rather read than see on the stage. It is the kind of play, too, that one might enjoy more at a second hearing, if only the first time through hadn't left such a strong feeling that once is enough.

John Stride (Rosencrantz) and Edward Petherbridge (Guildenstern) carry the play firmly on their shoulders and are funny when they get the chance (which happens quite often). Graham Crowden is impressive as the Player, and John McEnery gives an effective impression of Hamlet.

(W.A. Darlington, *The Daily Telegraph*, 12 April, 1967)

I know of no theatrical precedent for it, but among other things it might be called a piece of literary detection. From the labyrinthine picture of Elsinore Mr Stoppard has blown up a single detail and wrenched enough material from it to create a drama.

The shadowy history of Rosencrantz and Guildenstern always sticks in the mind as a classic instance of the fate that befalls little men who are swept into great events. Much is said against them in the course of *Hamlet*, but they hardly deserve it: they are too insignificant to escape anonymous servitude.

For most of Mr Stoppard's play they are shown in private – abandoned in an ante-chamber of the palace waiting for the next call, spinning coins and playing word games, desperately latching on to the First Player as the only character who will speak to them.

From time to time the court sweeps on to conduct its incomprehensible business and sweeps out again leaving the interchangeable nonentities stranded like driftwood on the beach.

What emerges is a compound of Shakespearian criticism, Beckett-like cross-talk, and the mathematical nonsense comedy which befits a nonsensical situation involving two cyphers. The couple have no memory of the past, no understanding of the present, and no idea where they are going.

All they have is words, and the endless word games they play represent both a way of passing the time and an indefatigable attempt to make sense of their predicament.

Mr Stoppard manages to relate the material to the Shakespearian action – as where a quickfire question game (as exciting as a tennis match) is used as a preparation for an interview with the prince, who promptly wins the game and set (' "We were sent for", you said. I didn't know where to put myself').

But his real triumph is in relating the partners' preoccupation with free will to the players, whose profession insists on fixed destiny and who stage a rehearsal of the *Gonzago* prologue forecasting the fatal voyage. Mr Stoppard secures an existential conclusion in which the partners discover their death warrant and choose to deliver it so as to emerge, if only for a second, into lives of their own.

There are times when the author, like his characters, seems to be casting about for what to say next. But for most of the time he walks his chosen tight-rope with absolute security.

In its origin this is a highly literary play with frank debts to Pirandello and Beckett: but in Derek Goldby's production, these

151

sources prove a route towards technical brilliance and powerful feeling.

Edward Petherbridge and John Stride manage to develop a touching sense of mutual need between the partners while preserving their blank outlines intact.

Marc Wilkinson's defunctive music contributes superbly to the atmosphere; and Desmond Heeley's sets – a sepulchral palace and a ghost ship under a slack rotting sail – exactly catch the specification for the action 'within and around the action of *Hamlet*'.

(From: Irving Wardle, *The Times*, 12 April, 1967)

Zigger Zagger
Peter Terson
August 1967   Jeanetta Cochrane

It leaves the back of one's neck in no doubt that something very big and happy indeed, in the person of Peter Terson, is about to happen to the British theatre.

(From: Ronald Bryden, *The Observer*, 3 September, 1967)

Out of a rowdy and rudely devoted football crowd Peter Terson has fashioned for the National Youth Theatre an exciting new play about youth.

Zigger Zagger at the Jeanetta Cochrane Theatre is the most clearly observed and honest study I remember of young people since Ann Jellicoe's *The Knack*.

Not that it has very much to do with sex. That is a subject which it takes in its stride. Mr Terson is after bigger dramatic game. A purpose in life, no less.

And though his play doesn't press the theme at first, it leaves us wondering and impressed. It leaves us wondering about the values and vigour of young people who make of football a god. It leaves us wondering about how Terson, the resident playwright at the Victoria Theatre, Stoke-on-Trent, should have found such an effectively theatrical form (vaudeville) for his urgent content.

And if it begs the question why a young man should not be apprenticed to some trade as well as following football madly, the incidental comments and social satire cleverly disguise a certain wobbliness of theme.

Against incessant and highly choral background of football supporters chanting, rattling and roaring from their terrace those traditional twisted songs and slogans, Mr Terson shows a boy who leaves school at 15 and wonders how to spend his life.

Shall he give all to football and only live for Saturdays? Or settle down and become apprenticed to a trade?

He lacks a father, and his mother is hopelessly promiscuous. His sister's husband is always nagging him about the virtues of a safe domestic life. And there is Zigger, the club supporters' leader, who stands for the free, somewhat hooliganised life which recognises no authority but its feelings.

Michael Croft's production punchily sympathises with the football crowd.

There may be nothing new actually said in the play but it comes over with remarkable freshness.

(From: Eric Shorter, *The Daily Telegraph*, 22 August, 1967)

Dingo
Charles Wood
April 1967   Bristol Arts Centre

Mr Wood is perhaps a poet first and a dramatist second.

(From: Alan Brien, *The Sunday Telegraph*, 30 April, 1967)

Charles Wood's *Dingo* is the play which the Lord Chamberlain is supposed to have considered too outspoken for the National Theatre to produce last year.

(From: Eric Shorter, *The Daily Telegraph*, 29 April, 1967)

Charles Wood's devastatingly sardonic sermon on war is meant to hurt, and it does. It would hurt much more if he had as much control over his material as he has over his language, for he allows the play to drag on so much in its second act that all our pent-up indignation soaks away while he nags on and on about first one point, then another, ending with a somewhat puerile conclusion to the effect (if I got him right) that the Second World War was fought not to destroy Fascism but to amuse Sir Winston Churchill.

No one has ever had Mr Wood's ability to transmute the language of the private soldier into poetry, and he has never done it so well as he does in parts of *Dingo*. But all this business of laughing at heroism, laughing at Field Marshal Montgomery, laughing at patriotism, laughing at officers and the Military Police, laughing at loyalty and discipline and sentiment – isn't it all beginning to wear thin?

It's so often been done before, often worse, but sometimes much better; and the ones who did it better were men like Wilfred

Owen and Siegfried Sassoon, whose disgust with warfare stem-
med from their participation in it, an advantage not shared by Mr
Wood during his regular service as a cavalry trooper. So Owen
and Sassoon do not, like Mr Wood, throw out every noble instinct
as worthless. When you take a cold look at it, *Dingo* boils down to
little more than a long succession of sneers. Nothing is found for
admiration at all.

The play is full of what are usually regarded as obscenities
(though they've always been a part of the soldier's small talk) and
contains some very real horrors. It is imaginatively directed by
Geoffrey Reeves and very well performed indeed by a cast led by
Tom Kempinski, Leon Lissek, Mark Jones and Henry Woolf. I
found it nauseating, but it confirms the high opinion I already
have of Charles Wood's capabilities.

(B.A. Young, *The Financial Times*, 29 April, 1967)

'The set is the Second World War – all of it,' claims the author.
Not quite: he doesn't show Auschwitz or Dresden. The second act
is in a German stalag – its barriers represented by boxing-ring
ropes – where POW officers, tarted up as Gwendolen and Cecily,
are acting scenes from Oscar Wilde to cover an escape attempt;
the first act is in the Western Desert, where Schweik-like old
sweats are masturbating among mine-fields, tanks and hideously
savaged corpses, occasionally interrupted by a bemused officer on
a bicycle and, more to their taste, by an entertainer who combines
the 'Aythengyow!' of Arthur Askey with well-mimicked extracts
from Churchill and Montgomery. (He *becomes* Montgomery
during the play's course.) This is very much a tankies' play.
Ex-trooper Wood knows more about the spirit of an armoured
regiment (in peace-time) than Simon Raven, say, will ever learn. A
very high level of foul-mouthed wit and self-denigration accom-
panies the tunes of glory, the Desert Rat flashes and battle
honours.

The entertainer is excellently played by Henry Woolf, a
chubby, versatile young man who looks like Dudley Moore. But
really it's a part for Olivier, in his Archie Rice mood. Lord
Chandos's National Theatre board would never allow him to play
it. Nor would the Lord Chamberlain. You might think such
matters of state as the validity of World War II and the national
idolatry of the Unknown Warrior are just what a national theatre
should deal with. But, according to Jo Grimond in the *Guardian*,
'one of the main functions of any state is to stop nonconformity',
and Lord Chandos's justifiable powers of censorship support the
argument that 'the State may do more harm than good to the
living arts'. Yet a more democratic state once sponsored Aris-
tophanes's serious lampoon on General Lamachus – as serious as

Wood's own Montgomery – before the whole citizenry. Nowadays *Dingo* must be tucked away in Bristol Arts Centre where it will do no harm, performed for a sophisticated club membership by skilful *US* veterans from the Royal Shakespeare Company, assisted by Lord Goodman's Arts Council. Rightly; but this play is too big to be judged by a handful of journalists. The other-rank survivors should see it, on TV.

Exciting, serious, comic and healthy though it is, I found the play foul in both senses – revolting and not fair. Because of sick motivation, like the very natural desire for glory and triumph shared by Churchill and Montgomery and countless others, World War II is exposed as a racket. Big questions are dodged: 'What about the Jews? What about the Camps?' The only answer is the Groucho-Marxist line: 'We don't know about that yet.' The Desert Rats may not have known the full truth about their enemy; but, surely, they knew enough. Another ranker put the charge more fairly, Williams in *Henry V*, when asked whether the cause was just, the quarrel honourable:

> That's more than we know. But if the cause be not good, the king himself has a heavy reckoning to make, when all those legs and arms and heads, chopped off in a battle, shall join together at the latter day and cry all: 'We died at such a place.'

Surely Montgomery and Churchill's friends can face this reckoning without needing the protection of noble censors? The honours the war-chiefs earned cannot be easily removed, any more than Muhammad Ali can really be stripped of his title. (Now, *there's* a drama for you: a man who's channelled his violent instincts more effectively than any man alive and can make world news from his refusal to serve in an unjust war.)

(From: D.A.N. Jones, *New Statesman*, 5 May, 1967)

1968

Few critics would agree with the contention expressed by some that Bond's Narrow Road to the Deep North *has deserved a place of far higher status than is usually given it. It was not greeted, in June 1968, with that somewhat frenzied anticipation and wild surmise which Bond's later plays invited. Indeed, it semed not to have the very qualities which later gave Bond the position of a kind of gangland Godfather in the world of British theatre. It lacked his serrated moral thrusts, his crevasses and dangerously raw language, his most prevalent mood in which the slightest hint of sentiment, optimism, the tenderer affections were quelled by anger, cynicism, even violence. With the large majority of Bond's plays one has to make an act of profound faith to accept that, basically, he is a man who cares, and that his plays are, perhaps unbelievably, about the need for a kind of loving. He seems to do his best to disabuse you of any disposition to think the best of him − except in* Narrow Road *where language, character, theme, are all in a less strident key, where the reflective dominates and in which the felicity of the craftsmanship is not drowned in spectacles of blood, tears, toil and sweat. It is not typical Bond − perhaps, ironically, that is why it is not generally regarded as among the best of Bond.*

In October 1968, as now, the currents of critical comment on Alan Bennett (Forty Years On) did not flow in one direction. What was, and is, he − buffoon or serious dramatist? In his earlier career he did not help one to resolve the question: his personal television appearances in which he revealed a fine grasp of the clown's art, occurred in parallel with his writing of plays like this one where, as Benedict Nightingale declares, in a well-turned phrase which does credit to the craft of criticism, 'Escapism rarely comes as civilised as this'.

Few doubts were expressed about the serious intent of Peter Barnes's The Ruling Class, *comic though it was in spirit. Its reception by and large was favourable but, more pointedly, the 'heavier' critics, such as Martin Esslin, found in it 'a solid core of significance'. This was its social comment, its commitment to a bitingly satirical attack on the establishment and, through it, the insensitivity of that kind of privileged human being who puts benevolent feelings into aspic. The play was another harbinger of the coming tidal wave of social drama, and some critics sensed it.*

Arguably, in this process, a good deal of perception of other kinds was either blunted, ignored or killed at birth, as the role of art in general came more and more to be regarded as a mirror of social injustice and/or as an active element in quests for radical social change.

Narrow Road to the Deep North
Edward Bond
June 1968   Belgrade, Coventry

... the work of a playwright with a confident method and an unmistakable voice.

(From: Irving Wardle, *The Times*, 25 June, 1968)

As usual there is a remarkable lack of construction in the formal sense of preparing the audience for what is to come or making it care for what has gone.

(From: Eric Shorter, *The Daily Telegraph*, 25 June, 1968)

This is far the best of the three plays by Edward Bond that I have seen. It is the most coherent, and built to a better pattern with the climaxes falling effectually. The deliberately simple style makes anything in the way of deep characterisation impossible, just as it prevents the actors from doing much more than speak their lines without adding any personal element to them. But this is clearly the effect intended, and it is often remarkably poignant.

But what has Mr Bond to tell us? Only that Colonialism was bad (a generalisation that won't always stand up to close inspection); that tolerance is better than imposed doctrine; that peace is preferable to violence. With all respect, we knew these things before, and Mr Bond has not yet offered us any alternative system to live by.

All the same, there is no doubt that his simple call to universal brotherhood went down well with the characteristically young and intelligent Coventry audience. It chimes effectually with the current student movement against outmoded systems of control. Like this movement, however, it leaves us wondering where we are to go when the existing authority has been overthrown.

(From: B.A. Young, *The Financial Times*, 25 June, 1968)

Edward Bond's new play *Narrow Road to the Deep North* was commissioned as part of an international conference on people and cities. Its world première at the Belgrade, Coventry, had interest for other reasons. Would Bond strike again? Would the censor lift his horrid eyebrows while permissive men ran to court screaming about the freedom of the playwright? The questions are irrelevant. This is not only Bond's best play, but its depth of dramatic perception drowns all overt thoughts of sin, sex, and censor. He has written a parable which goes something like this: the history of the world is the history of cruelty where what is needed is love. There is nothing tendentious, though it is occasionally wordy, in the communication. He gives us the story of the growth of an empire (Bible-supported guns), of the dirty untruth of politics (bravado-supported lies), of the pathetic illusions of individualism (hope-supported despair). Mr Bond shoots it out with an effective visual simplicity and with verbal subtlety – a combination of epigrammatic haiku wit and sizzling contemporary idiom. He has learned much from Brecht's economic use of narrative incident, but he still has to learn where that fine line between satire and mere sensational retort is drawn.

The play is produced with taut, nervous energy, and all the acting responds magnificently to this astounding exercise in controlled anger. Susan Williamson, Edward Peel, Paul Howes, Nigel Hawthorne, and Gordon Reid must accept the general credits on behalf of all the company. Peter Needham takes the laurel. It is not merely that he acts with superb timing and physical delicacy, but that he also gives a point of objective rest (like a kind of Tiresias) which enables the audience to realise that Mr Bond is not shooting in the air, but to kill – our apathy about the mess we have made.

(Gareth Lloyd Evans, *The Guardian*, 25 June, 1968)

Forty Years On
Alan Bennett
October, 1968   Apollo

... the effect of Mr Bennett's text is deeply dispiriting ... the quality of this endless bludgeoning nostalgia, as sapping as a dose of bromide, which somehow reduces everything – the small youth of Flanders, Bloomsbury, Chamberlain, the blitz – to a deathly sameness ... a common insipidity.

(From: Hilary Spurling, *Spectator*, 8 November, 1968)

It's a nice coincidence that *40 Years On*, which seems to regard succeeding generations of nobs and rulers as a procession of amiable old nannies, should open in the same week as the first major revival of *Look Back in Anger*, which sees daggers in their smiles and would regard, let's say, a shooting stick as a sort of cattle-prod designed for the humiliation of the lower orders. Have we advanced so much? Can we condescend from afar, like historians? I don't think Jimmy Porter would be convinced. Class-distinctions may be fuzzier than they were in 1956, but two per cent of the people own 55 per cent of the private wealth and the next government will surely be packed to mental suffocation with graduates of *those* playing fields. Indeed, Alan Bennett's 'comedy review' might make a latter-day Porter bubble with impotent exasperation; he might even accuse it of a disingenuous crypto–Toryism. Porter: 'Auntie Alan at his tales again, smickering over the claret in the senior common room and doing his damnedest to make light of the death-watch beetle behind the founder's portrait . . .' Cliff: 'That's right, boyo, destroying the walls – and when will the whole rotten lot fall, eh?' Porter (despondent): 'By God, it's a slow eater, that beetle. Old Alan will be laughing for another century at this rate.'

As satire, *40 Years On* – at the Apollo – is certainly nearer kiss than curse. It's an affectionate lampoon of a random array of well-bred dummies: T.E. Lawrence, Baldwin, Bulldog Drummond, Wilde, public schoolmasters, Bloomsbury, even the English nanny herself. 'If you go out without your wellies you'll go blind', declares one of these platitudinous monsters. 'That's why St Paul went blind, walking to Damascus without his wellies.' As we know from *On the Margin*, Bennett has a mean ear for cliché and the verbal ingenuity to twist it into appealingly absurd shapes. 'They're rolling up the maps all over Europe', says a spoof Asquith. 'They'll not be lit again in our life time.' Patterns of speech interest him much more than patterns of behaviour – and not necessarily as guides to character but as ends in themselves. Whoever the mouthpiece, Bennett could never resist the pun about Sheikh Hands (who seduced Lawrence) or the prayer which ends, 'that seekers may be finders, and finders – keepers'. I don't mean to imply that he fails to discriminate between particular types of character – he knows his prigs, pedants and emotional derelicts, he catches the leaden facetiousness of school masters – but I do think that his interest in them is that of a dabbler, a collector of historical curios with a taste for unexpected ornamentation. His Virginia Woolf, 'elegant and quizzical, her great nostrils quivering', is a very camp conception; so perhaps is the 'review' as a whole, absurdly camp, grotesquely irrelevant, peculiarly original, rather like a theatrical St Pancras Station.

The temptation to accept it as such is very great. If one isn't over-impressed by the pretence of the action being an end-of-term entertainment at 'Albion House', and stops bothering to regard it as a paradigm of Establishment history; if one sees it as a series of prettily turned sketches and submits to that abundant verbal wit, one may pass an unusually buoyant evening. Escapism rarely comes as civilised as this; acting and direction (by Patrick Garland) rarely as self-assured. John Gielgud plays Albion's headmaster, a fastidious, maudlin old spinster, and is at his most elegant, attenuated and mellow, like a Stradivarius playing Mozart. You couldn't recommend their efforts to implacable revolutionaries, who wouldn't tolerate the moral vacuum, or to foreigners, who would rightly be nauseated by the sight of the English indulging that over-rated national pastime of 'laughing at themselves'; but I can't deny that I, at least, laughed myself silly. (From: Benedict Nightingale, *New Statesman*, 8 November, 1968)

Alan Bennett in *Forty Years On* at the Apollo last night turned up a wry, irreverent, and often wildly hilarious kind of *Cavalcade* in reverse. I found myself laughing helplessly, more often than at any time this year so far. One can in such matters only speak as one finds and I daresay a lot of people will find it in bad taste, cruel, not to say blasphemous. Certainly there are scenes in which Mr Bennett himself plays, like that chestnut about the confirmation class, which seem a bit self indulgent and prolonged. The kind of rough justice dispensed to the memories of T.E. Lawrence and Neville Chamberlain is pretty savage. But any script is welcome which gives Sir John Gielgud such a glorious canter as a clucking, prissy head-master on the point of retiring and for whose benefit the boys of 'St Albion's' stage this woebegone pageant of our half century. I have never seen him funnier.

Dorothy Reynolds too, school matron in 'real life', and many of those female parts which Mr Bennett has not himself appropriated, gives her funniest performance since the head mistress in *Miss Brodie*, crisp and lethal. Paul Eddington is the master who is credited with having devised this deplorable parable so much to the head's distress, and takes on anything from a sententious 1940 MP to a Dornford Yates or Bulldog Drummond chappie out to trounce the enemies of England.

Yet for all its witty, inventive flippance, the strange charade sometimes manages to strike a note of genuine feeling – for sad, far off victims, failed hopes and faded story. To strike a more critical note, it is inescapable that the evening tends slightly to run down in the second half.

For me, it is the funniest show of its kind since *Beyond the Fringe* and might easily become a habit. The brilliant director is Patrick Garland.

(Philip Hope-Wallace, *The Guardian*, 1 November, 1968)

The Ruling Class
Peter Barnes
November 1968   Nottingham Playhouse

Mr Barnes, however, will have to try again.
        (From: John Wardle, *The Times*, 9 November, 1968)

. . . the best new British play I've seen this year.
        (From: Ronald Bryden, *The Observer*, 17 November, 1968)

Nottingham Playhouse, on which we have come to rely for the sort of classical revival you never see in London now, plunges occasionally into the world of modern fantasy, presumably to keep up with the times.

Its latest plunge is called *The Ruling Class*, by Peter Barnes. It is a wild and woolly fantasy on the idea of an English earl who supposes himself the Deity.

He dispenses good cheer and feeble jokes, based mainly on his being who he thinks he is. The saying of grace before a meal or the taking of Our Lord's name in vain evoke a predictable response; and naturally his family are very worried about him.

The solution is to marry him off so that he shall beget an heir who can inherit the earldom while he is put away.

This makes a good scene when the girl of his dreams, Marguerite Gautier, appears to sweep into his life and sweep him off. Vivienne Martin and Derek Godfrey play it for all its revue-sketch worth.

Soon, however, he recovers his sanity and much of the fun goes out of the entertainment. Those who help him to recover it are a sort of caped King Kong and a rival claimant for divine status, dressed in kilt and raving.

Need I go on? The play does, for about an hour more than it need. Impossible to sift the significant bits from the merely silly interpolations.

There is however a final impressive scene when our hero, now quite sane – and therefore horridly Victorian and reactionary and anything but Christian – addresses the House of Lords. Its evocation in John Napier's design presents a wonderful picture of a mouldering peerage.

What is it really about? Well, if you can picture an anglicised and immature Jules Feiffer having a go at Baron Corvo's novels you may have an idea what Mr Barnes (assuming he himself knows) is up to.

He suggest that truly godly people are always thought mad and that it is only the brutal and unloving kind of reactionaries who are believed to be normal.

Some good players are mixed up in it, especially Dudley Jones as an outspoken butler, Ronald Magill as a doddering bishop and David Neal as a stock psychiatrist. But at root the humour is curiously old-fashioned and pseudo-Wildean, despite a zany surface. Director: Stuart Burge.

(Eric Shorter, *The Daily Telegraph*, 9 November, 1968)

. . . he writes with such zest, such fertility of ludicrous invention, such a power of outrageous caricature and extravagant fantastication that one can scarcely forbear to cheer . . .

(From: Harold Hobson, *The Sunday Times*, 10 November, 1968)

How history repeats itself! Whenever a playwright of major potential appears on the scene, inevitably he gets a bad reception: it happened with Pinter (with Harold Hobson as the single honourable exception); with Osborne (all against, except Tynan); with Arden. And now, as another potentially major playwright appears, it has happened again, again with Harold Hobson and Ronald Bryden alone dissenting from the universal chorus of disapproval. Well, it is not really surprising: inflexible, routine minds simply do not have the resilience and adaptability to get the point when they are confronted with something original, non-routine, challenging, requiring some attention and reflection.

That Peter Barnes presents such a challenge is beyond doubt. *The Ruling Class* may have its faults – it is much too long, even in the cut version in which it opened at Nottingham, and it may be over-emphatic – but it is an exhilaratingly talented play, the work of an exuberantly baroque, grotesque imagination lying somewhere between Hieronymus Bosch, Barbey d'Aurevilly and Aubrey Beardsley, written in a witty, dramatically viable language which instantly electrifies. And it consists of a succession of brilliantly theatrical situations, *coups de théâtre* and ironic surprises which are constantly entertaining and a joy to watch.

To top it all, behind all that brilliant surface there is a solid core of significance and indeed, depth. To dismiss such a play, as most of our critics did, with the remark that the conditions it attacks in the ruling class do not exist in reality, represents about the level of understanding which a critic might display who attacks *Hamlet* because ghosts don't *really* have to fade away when the cock crows, or *Peter Pan* because clocks don't go on ticking inside crocodiles. The grotesque family of aristocrats is, of course, anything but realistic. What is real is the basic attitude which is attacked and which is *not* just an addiction to hunting and shooting, sexual perversity, the advocacy of hanging (although these do still exist in this fair land, God wot) but the basic insensitivity and hardness of heart embodied in a society which puts good manners and the mere absence of outward friction above real feeling, openness to other people and, let's be brave and use the pooh-pooh'd word, love.

For the hero of this weird Gothic satire, the fourteenth Earl of Gurney, is considered mad while he proclaims his oceanic feeling of all-embracing love that makes him think that he is one with God, with Christ; but sane, when having been cured by confrontation with another patient who believes he is Christ, he inhibits these feelings and turns into a sado-masochistic killer who wreaks vengeance on prostitutes in the manner of Jack the Ripper by night, and holds forth on hanging in the House of Lords in the daytime.

This hero – or villain – of the piece is surrounded by a glorious gallery of grotesques: dotty bishop, chinless wonder, nymphomaniac society lady, old-world butler who in secret is a card-carrying Communist and spy, German psychiatrist, a pair of horsey county ladies, and a host of others . . .

. . . We shall hear from Peter Barnes again before long.

(Martin Esslin, *Plays and Players*, January, 1969)

1969

The earliest 'slice of life' plays of the last four decades of this century conveyed their messages about society with a good and efficient deal of comedy. Indeed the rash of what was called 'satire' – though much of it was really clear invective, scorn, farce and innuendo – which appeared on television in the 1960s, notable in That Was The Week That Was, *may well have been a potent influence on stage dramatists: it kept them, so to speak, funny while they got on with being serious. Some critics opted for the fun, while others (see B.A. Young's review) struggled hard and eloquently to resolve the dilemma posed to the critic, of the possible incomparability between entertainment and education, or, as in the case of Harold Hobson's comments, between art and social committal. It was raised with stark relevance in the critical estimates of* The National Health. *In any play in which both are attempted, must not one go to the wall? This was a question which implicitly or explicitly was to face the critic more and more as the seventies approached.*

The National Health
Peter Nichols
October 1969   Old Vic

A rewarding and amusing evening, then, but the final entry must be read: Operation successful, play dead.
(From: Frank Marcus, *The Sunday Telegraph*, 19 October, 1969)

It had a pungency that Chekhov would have envied at times and it caught me between wind and water, half in tears and half with laughter.
(From: Philip Hope-Wallace, *The Guardian*, 17 October, 1969)

The closing sections of this play are among the ugliest stretches of writing I remember.
(From: Robert Cushman, *The Spectator*, 25 October, 1969)

164

Peter Nichols has such a welcome and theatrical originality – the finale is pure music-hall delight – that I'd hate to sound churlish. His mingling of comedy and tragedy, of fact and fiction, may not yet be perfect, but it has a verve and a sting and a humanity that's missing on most of London's stages.

(From: Helen Dawson, *Plays and Players*, December, 1969)

There are plenty of aesthetic reasons for standing up and cheering this play: but, as in the case of *A Day in the Death of Joe Egg*, it makes you feel ashamed to talk about art. We are not short of good playwrights in Britain, but I know of none with Peter Nichols's power to put modern Britain on the stage and send the spectators away feeling more like members of the human race.

The National Health can only be described as a portrait of six male inmates in a hospital ward. It also amounts to a study of organization versus the individual, and to a microcosm of our society: but such themes only arise from his detailed concern for the people themselves and their response to seeing each other die.

As in *Joe Egg*, the writing combines scrupulous naturalism with music-hall turns. This is thoroughly appropriate for the macabre normality of the situation, and it allows Mr Nichols to turn the relationships around so that the balance of sympathies is constantly changing.

To begin with it angers you to see the staff treating the inmates as children and dismissing their sufferings with hearty clichés, 'HAVING FORTY WINKS ARE WE?' bawls the sister cheerfully into the ear of a sleeping old man. Then, as the nocturnal crises build up, the petty rows, the crazy tirades, the habit of interminable self-repetition, sympathy temporarily veers the other way, and the callousness of the staff seems an indispensable protective mechanism.

Mr Nichols plays this up still further by interpolating a mock-television series compounded from Dr Kildare and *Dr Finlay's Casebook*: an idiot medical romance in which the hospital staff, the fat bespectacled nurse and craggy consultant, reappear in the story of a true-love kidney transplant. It is compered by a laughing boy orderly who presides over the whole play as the master of ceremonies in a dance of death, finally appearing as a black-face coon in the pantomime finale. Part life and soul of the party ('Bring out your dead') and part sinister (as where he puts a half-cured alcoholic back on the bottle), he seems to be expressing the author's own view that 'there is something bent about the healing arts'.

His is the only position in the play's scheme that emerges ambiguously. For the rest of the way we are with common humanity, handled with a touch which Chekhov would have

165

approved. As we get to know the characters through and through, and as the ward steadily empties (after the fashion of 'Ten Green Bottles'), the play reaches a state in which any slight change exerts a delicate chain reaction throughout the company.

For instance, Robert Lang, as a frustrated would-be teacher, strikes up a friendship with a Brummagem alcoholic (a lovely seedy performance by Charles Kay): then a leatherjacket boy, briefly seen earlier on, comes back from another crash as a helpless idiot, and immediately Lang seizes on him and drops his other friend. You see prejudice giving way to human feeling; and then prejudice once more reasserting itself. That is the open-eyed, unfooled, compassionate world Mr Nichols explores; and, as in *Joe Egg*, he is superbly served by his director Michael Blakemore.

(Irving Wardle, The Times, 17 October, 1969)

The National Health (Old Vic), takes place in a hospital ward, to the accompaniment of exploding bowels and bottles of urine. I do not see why we should subsidise the National Theatre to provide us with what most people produce for themselves at least four times a day, but I cannot pretend that I feel strongly about it. What is wrong, and seriously wrong, with Mr Nichols as a dramatist is less his concern with coprology than his extreme sentimentality.

The dominating impression created by *The National Health* is that patients almost invariably leave hospital only for the graveyard or as badly crippled and humanly degraded as when they came in. The commonest observation shows that this impression is as false as that there are fairies at the bottom of the garden. It is merely the Romantic Agony in modern dress. The bustling callousness of nurses, the fantastic daydreams of surgeons, the screams of the suffering are perhaps credible. But when Mr Nichols involves a young motor cyclist in an accident that makes him a physical and mental wreck; when he ascribes this accident to the humane desire to avoid hurting a dog, and further, if I heard aright, says that it smashed up one bus load of mongols and another of old age pensioners – I no more believe it than I would if he told me that the effervescent young girl so radiantly played by Cleo Sylvestre married a duke.

Of course, both things are possible, even highly possible. But one knows that the accident is there, not because in its attendant circumstances it is likely, but because Mr Nichols is determined to have it so. It is the thirteenth stroke of the clock that discredits all that have gone before. It is as sentimental and as foolishly romantic as anything in the Finlay and Kildare stories that Mr Nichols laboriously ridicules, and a good deal less wholesome.

Mr Nichols is extraordinarily bitter in this play, and the hatred which he expresses for the medical profession almost pathological. His central character, a kind of chorus, is an orderly whom Jim Dale plays as a spritely Puck until Mr Nichols reveals that he is really Mephistopheles. This young man taunts a long-enduring and kindly homosexual, played by Robert Lang with a welcome warmth and lack of sensationalism, and tempts a cured compulsive drunkard back on to gin. He is the explicit exponent of Mr Nichols's thesis that there is 'something bent' about people who go in for healing others. The passion of Mr Nichols's apparent hatred of life is interesting, but it is saddening also. I am afraid that it is no good asking him to change his outlook. If he did so I think that there would be nothing left.

(From: Harold Hobson, *The Sunday Times*, 19 October, 1969)

Basically, what Peter Nichols has given us in his play for the National Theatre is a slice of *Emergency Ward 10*; but whereas *Emergency Ward 10* was designed to present hospital life as reassuringly as possible to a timorous public, *The National Health* seeks to draw attention to its shortcomings. The ward in which the action takes place – a horridly evocative design by Patrick Robertson – is a squalid dormitory with the usual faded brown and green paint, and of the nine or ten patients we meet there, hardly one is without either physical or social handicaps that would make his company hard to bear. The staff are appallingly over-worked, and consequently slap-dash or unfeeling or both. The routine is hospital routine at its old-fashioned worst.

Lest any corner of human misery should be overlooked, there are marginal discussions on race-prejudice, euthanasia and homosexuality. Depressing? Not for a moment. *The National Health* is as funny a play as I've seen for quite a time.

As he showed us in *A Day in the Death of Joe Egg*, Mr Nichols believes that the best way to treat suffering is to face it boldly and laugh at it. Laughing at suffering is not the same as laughing at sufferers; it is an affirmation that the human race can rise above the worst that can happen to it. No one is mocked in this play for his weakness or incapacity. But every opportunity is taken to highlight the ludicrous situations that can arise when a dozen broken-down human machines are brought for repair into a ridiculously inadequate repair-shop.

It is a commonplace that because we are all so scared of illness, we invest our doctors with a kind of superhuman glamour. Well, not our own doctors, of course, but doctors in the abstract – doctors like Kildare and Finlay and Cameron. Mr Nichols is as keen to correct this illusion as he is to give us a properly scornful attitude towards illness, and he interrupts his main day-to-day narrative of life in the surgical ward with dream sequences in which an eminent surgeon transplants a kidney from a West Indian nurse to his own doctor son, ending with a double wedding – old doctor to theatre sister, young doctor to West Indian. These bits – merciless send-ups of the romantic medical school of literature – are hilariously funny, and beautifully acted by Paul Curran, Robert Walker, Maggie Riley and Cleo Sylvestre.

Romance is allowed to send us away on a light-hearted note so we can forget about the patient who has died from cancer of the stomach, or the boy turned by a motor-bike accident into a helpless idiot. Staff and patients together line up for a cakewalk to the music of a little band at the side of the stage, and so we go out with enough euphoria to get us to the bus-stop.

And after that? After that we remember the patients, grown men crying with pain, or helplessly wetting their beds, or living in a dream from which they must continuously be awoken for the next item of hospital routine; and we remember the woman doctor so exhausted by a day-and-a-half's continuous duty that she falls asleep while attending to a sick man, and the nurses whose overwork barely gives them time to learn their charges' names, and the oxygen cylinder that is without a key because no one had time to put it away properly. Mr Nichols doesn't, as I understand him, expect us to be sorry for these matters. He wants us to see how absurd it is they should be with us in our affluent society, and perhaps – if we are in a position to – resolve to do something about it.

The National Health is directed by Michael Blakemore with imagination, wit and precision, and played admirably by all the cast.

Among the patients, Robert Lang (gastric ulcer), Charles Kay (dipsomania) and Brian Oulton (cancer) are outstanding.

Among the staff – besides those I've mentioned – there is the incomparable Jim Dale as an orderly who occasionally steps out of character to act as a chorus. I'm not sure Mr Dale isn't the best comic actor we have.

(B.A. Young, The Financial Times, 17 October, 1969)

1970

David Storey has been a consistently underrated dramatist. True, he has had a share of praise but it has only just escaped being mere grudging encouragement. His Home is one of the best examples of his work. He has always had a feeling for and ability to handle language over a wide gamut of effect which put him ahead of most of his contemporaries in verbal sensitivity. And, in Home, his concern for the individual human victims of what he takes to be an inimical society is not expressed with polemical, frenzied insistence, but with a sense of artistic tact. Indeed he goes far to reconcile 'entertainment' and social commitment. Not all the major critics, by any means, recognised this; but one, Irving Wardle, in a review of remarkable balance and lucid style, not only highlights Storey's unusual ability but, if only obliquely, picked out some of the more general implications of the prevailing tension between a beleaguered traditional view of art and the new, purposeful militancy.

If ever theatrical history produced a classic example of irony it was in July of this year when, after a long silence, Christopher Fry's name returned to the theatre billboards and his new play A Yard of Sun, was presented, not in the West End, but in Nottingham. Even the barest snippets from reviews underline the irony – 'Fry remains faithful to his earlier self' (Bryden); he still has his belief in 'inventive excess' (Bryden); 'no issue is being squarely faced' (Wardle); 'There have been times when I doubted whether I was capable of writing anything at all that would not be met by contumely' (Fry in an interview).

All this and much more in the same vein had been and was heaped upon Fry by many who had either forgotten or never knew the enormous amount of pleasure he had provided and the praise, many felt, he had earned, in the grey wartime days. But if, as a by-product, Suez, Hungary, the Welfare State and a socialist Britain nourished the seeds for kitchen-sink drama and drama of social relevance, they also withered and destroyed the reputation of any form of art, dramatic or otherwise, that wasn't prepared to storm the ramparts, wave the political flag and ravish the citadels of privilege. Wardle is final in his judgement that 'no issue is being squarely faced' by Fry. But this is to condemn a man by subjective expediency – whose and what 'issues' should Fry have faced? Indeed, what might seem 'issues' to Wardle or anyone else, were alien to Fry's muse. And there was

169

the rub, the irony. Fry persisted in his 'old-fashioned' way of writing a highly metaphorical, verbally prankish, sometimes unexpectedly mocking, set of variations on the human heart. He believed in art as a civilised agitation of the sensibilities and emotions, not as social therapy. He became the fall-guy for the huge attack on 'aesthetic' conceptions of art which had dominated western culture for many decades. Fry may be guilty of verbal excess, of over-optimism about the human condition – of course, his firm religious beliefs did not help him – and of shallow themes. These weaknesses elevated him to the status of prime target for demolition, and his strengths – delicacy of touch, a care for lyrical utterance, and a certain innocent joy – did nothing to reprieve him.

The most remarkable features of the reviews of A Yard of Sun *are, on the one hand (as in Hobson, Lloyd Evans and Trewin) the defensive, nostalgic and obstinate faith in Fry and his traditional qualities; and on the other (Bryden, Wardle, and others not included here) a hint of impatient, even supercilious, rejection.*

Home
David Storey
June 1970   Royal Court

. . . a little tedious to watch . . .
> (From: John Barber, *The Daily Telegraph*, 18 June, 1970)

. . . a literary exercise . . .
> (From: Frank Marcus, *The Sunday Telegraph*, 21 June, 1970)

. . . a sadly tedious tale . . .
> (From: Hilary Spurling, *The Spectator*, 27 June, 1970)

. . . he has an ear as acute as Pinter's and a quality more genuinely human.
> (From: J.C. Trewin, *Birmingham Post*, 18 June, 1970)

David Storey never develops a play in any way you could expect. This one he hardly develops at all. Between lunch-time and tea a faint breeze of friendship blows the four together. There are hints of what brought the two apparently respectable old chaps into the 'home'. We are given a glimpse of a pathetic ex-wrestler reduced to semi-humanity by pre-frontal leucotomy. As the lights fade at the end, Harry and Jack stand weeping uncontrollably at their inner thoughts.

I found it heartbreaking. Mr Storey has pitched on the essential

truth that the real pathos of madness lies in its incommunicabil-
ity. . . .

. . . My admiration for Mr. Storey's writing goes up with each
play I see. He has begun to work quite independently of any stage
conventions generally accepted, yet he has an instinctive knowledge of what 'comes off'. . . . *Home* does not develop but is slowly
unveiled as a whole that was whole when the house-lights first
went down; but in general Mr Storey seems to me a true original,
sensitive and poetic and constantly aware of a dramatist's
responsibility towards his audience.

(From: B.A. Young, *The Financial Times*, 18 June, 1970)

It seems to be quite a fine day as Harry first appears on the
terrace, appreciatively sniffing the air for his pre-lunch constitu-
tional, and settling down for a minute on a white garden seat to
watch the world go by. Here he is, presently, joined by Jack, also
out to take the air, and the two gentle old men draw up to the
table for a pleasant chat. Evidently they are fairly recent friends,
probing each other for life stories and diving off into inconsequential tales about their relatives. 'I had an aunt', observes Jack
weightily, 'who for a short time lived near Gloucester'. There is
something not quite right about it. Are they bowling-green
regulars, perhaps; or are they meeting in a sea-front hotel? It
takes some time before you realize that the setting is a mental
home.

Unlike the above description, David Storey's play takes no
interest in cheap surprise effects. There is no single moment of
disclosure, for the play is written from the viewpoint of the
inmates to whom the situation is habitual. What it shows, and I
have for years been waiting for a play that attempts this, is the
efforts of people whom society has put away to create a society
among themselves. Although there is only one obviously hopeless
case among the characters, we are given to understand that none
of them will ever get out again. Left to vegetate between one meal
and the next, they play out a pitiful replica of life outside.

As you get hardly any firm information about the characters
and as nothing obviously 'happens' there is a temptation to line up
the piece with other recent exercises in creating drama out of thin
air. But virtuosity of the Tom Stoppard variety is not Mr Storey's
line. If his people never reveal themselves it is because they find
their histories too painful to discuss: any unmasking of their past
actions would bring the frail edifice of respectability tumbling
down. All they can do, whenever conversation approaches the
danger zone, is to weep briefly and in silence.

And however uneventful by ordinary standards, what happens
in the delicate terms that Mr Storey lays down is certainly cruel

171

enough. The action consists of an encounter between the two men and a pair of middle-aged women patients; the point being that where Harry and Jack have adopted masks of the utmost gentility, Marjorie and Kathleen have the manners of two suspiciously prurient schoolgirls. They poison the air with slander and insult, and dissolve into helpless giggling at their own infantile vulgarities. . . .

In its muted way, this is a social tragedy, showing a defeat repeatedly suffered in the past, and certain to happen again. What saves it from appearing maudlin is Storey's flawless sense of tone: his capacity for pitching characters just short of the grotesque, so that you can go along with them for much of the route and never take refuge in labelling them as sick. The fifth character, a leucotomized boy who shambles on to perform strong-man acts with the weightless furniture, puts the others into a perspective of sanity.

The weak link in the play is its excessive economy of dialogue. On this and past showings Storey does not have the gift of placing recurring lines that grow with repetition. Even in Lindsay Anderson's production there comes a time when we have heard enough about Mona Washbourne's aching feet. However, all that can be done to extract resonance from the lines has been done. It is a production in which every detail represents a firm telling decision, from the first sight of Joceyln Herbert's chipped white chairs and the balustrade with one support knocked out. You see vividly what you are meant to see.

The production has the crowning advantage of a beautiful pair of performances from Ralph Richardson and John Gielgud, who from their first moments on stage play together, like two master instrumentalists, Richardson's oboe answering Gielgud's viola in a duet that extracts endless variety from the broken sentences, reassuring platitudes, and *Godot*-like catalogues of their scenes together. I have never seen theatrical tears shed to better effect.

(Irving Wardle, *The Times*, 18 June, 1970)

A Yard of Sun
Christopher Fry
July 1970   Nottingham Playhouse

It's not hard to see in it also a meditation on his own earlier work. Was he right or wrong, frivolous or more serious than anyone recognised?

(From: Ronald Bryden, *The Observer*, 19 July, 1970)

The younger generation cannot realise the impatience of older people awaiting the new Christopher Fry play, *A Yard of Sun*, which had its first performance at the Nottingham Playhouse on Saturday. Just after the war every new Fry play was greeted, by many, as a milestone on the return to dramatic poetry or as an affirmation of the comic spirit. It may be, in fact, that Fry's glint, bubble, and colour of words were like champagne to people grown used to wartime gruel. Some said that Fry's plays were nothing but bubble.

This new play has less verbal effervescence, but the old, curiously lovable, things are there – the cheeky hobnobbing with God, the jaunty camaraderie with Time and the Seasons, the transparent faith in man's essential goodness, the swooping flight of lyricism, the unexpected jabs of low comedy. Yet, is this play saying anything that Fry hasn't said before – that God's watching, that things are all right, but it'll be a bit dodgy till we finally breast the tape on Judgment Day?

I suspect that the play is better than Stuart Burge's slack production makes it seem. Apart from Eithne Dunne, Cherith Mellor, Michael Burrell, and Frank Middlemass, the acting is either lackadaisical or amateurish. Mr Middlemass gives splendid life to Fry's best character – a harrassed, unconsciously comic Italian called Angelino. The play is set in Siena during the Palio – and I suspect that this and the characters' names, are symbolic, but of what I'm not sure. For me, the play was a pleasant nostalgia, and I shall continue to wear my 'I like Fry' button, but what the youngsters will think I don't know.

(Gareth Lloyd Evans, *The Guardian*, 13 July, 1970)

It may now seem laughable to describe the theatrical upheaval of 1956 as a revolution, but it certainly claimed its victims, and no more glittering sacrifice was offered up than Christopher Fry – the darling of the old regime, and the outcast of the new. As he remarked in a recent interview: 'There have been times when I doubted whether I was capable of writing anything at all that would not be met by contumely.'

Since *Curtmantle* in 1962 his voice has been silent in the English theatre. And in *A Yard of Sun* he picks up the thread from 16 years ago to complete the quartet of seasonal plays that first made his name. He thus starts with a strong appeal to the British sporting instinct; and if anyone doubted it the play concerns him as a writer of iron integrity.

In *Curtmantle* he seemed to be shifting his ground to fit the Brechtian mood of the times. But now he returns to his manner of the early fifties. At that time you could have suspected him of supplying the kind of vague Christian benevolence and verbal

173

fireworks calculated to appeal to postwar audiences. No such suspicion can apply to a piece written in that vein today.

A Yard of Sun, the summer play of the quartet, concerns a series of family reunions in the immediate aftermath of the war. The setting is Siena, whose equestrian festival, the Palio, is used to extend the domestic action on to a communal-religious plane. . . .

Fry's fastidious verse strikes me, as it always has done, as the reverse of dramatic poetry: not a method of packing in more expressive content, but of disguising the lack of it. There are some neatly turned puns and clarifying encapsulations in the text. But generally the verse acts as a way of converting clichés into fanciful imagery and concealing the fact that no issue is being squarely faced.

Stuart Burge's production articulates the congested writing most persuasively, and strikes a fine compromise between Italianate verve and British sensibility, and it is beautifully framed in Robin Archer's ornately crumbling courtyard. The company hardly come together as a family; but separately John Shrapnel's baleful Roberto, Michael Burrell's naive ex-fascist, and Robert East's dapper profiteer form a gallery of sharply drawn types. And if only for the sake of Frank Middlemass's Angelino, as touchingly forlorn as an abandoned mother-hen, one wishes there could have been a real family reunion.

(From: Irving Wardle, *The Times*, 13 July, 1970)

No festival – and this is Nottingham's first – could begin with a more genuinely exciting new play than Christopher Fry's.

It is exciting for several reasons. I will name only two of them. Firstly, it completes the seasonal quartet of verse plays that Fry opened with *The Lady's Not for Burning*; one of the important achievements of our stage since the war.

Secondly, it restores to us, after too long a break, a dramatist of great humanity and gentleness, with a civilised style that nobody writing for the theatre at present has matched.

I realise that there must be prejudice, and that Fry is coming to a world of the theatre that has changed wildly; a world of anarchic experiment and often cheap and flabby dialogue. Nothing, one would say, could be more alien to a writer of Fry's generosity, his questing verbal imagination, and his incomparable sense of phrase.

His dialogue is less luxuriant than it was, which can be a theatrical advantage. His use of the verse form disciplines his expression, gives a haunting quality to every scene.

He is writing about survival and renewal. *A Yard of Sun* – the title itself is characteristic – is set in the Italian city of Siena in the year after the war and on the eve of the famous annual Palio, the horse race between the city wards.

(From: J.C. Trewin, *Birmingham Post*, 13 July, 1970)

This is a good moment for Christopher Fry, whose latest work, *A Yard of Sun* (Playhouse) has opened the Nottingham Festival, to return to the British stage. It is now fourteen or fifteen years since a group of angry and articulate young men swept into a cupboard Mr Fry's glittering verbal toys, and substituted for childish things their adult preoccupation with righteous indignation and social messages.

St Paul also, when he became a man, put away childish things, and it might have been better for Christianity and the world if he had not. Certainly today few of the rising hopes who eclipsed Mr Fry preserve their first leaping enthusiasm. This does not necessarily mean that they were wrong and Mr Fry was right. But it does mean that the time is no longer propitious for his being contemptuously rejected. In the disillusionment that has followed *Venus Observed* and *The Dark is Light Enough*, we should at least be prepared to find out what Mr Fry is saying, and not too hastily conclude that he is saying nothing at all.

A Yard of Sun is the summer play which Mr Fry has long promised would complete the famous quartet that began with *The Lady's Not for Burning*. Its setting, gorgeously realised by Robin Archer, is a shadow-steeped courtyard in Siena just after the end of the war. In the background, elegantly echoing through Mr Fry's elaborately imaged verse, is the Palio, the historic horse race through Siena's narrow streets and great Piazza that has taken place almost unchanged for several centuries. It is unchanged because it is founded in enduring things, in the adoration of the Virgin and the rivalry of men. This is expressed by Mr Fry in a bravura passage as dazzling as anything he has written; and against its constancy he puts the changing fate and character of human beings, in that sprung rhythm and baroque fancy for which he is celebrated. . . .

(From: Harold Hobson, *The Sunday Times*, 19 July, 1970)

1971

Old Times *was the outstandingly distinguished play and production of 1971. Throughout his dramatic career Pinter has invited contention and contrary opinions, and this is clearly demonstrated even in the shortest collection of reviews. Trewin has, and continues to have, doubts about the point of it all, though with his typical fairness he gives pen to his recognition of Pinter's strong grasp of dramatic technique.*

More surprising is Benedict Nightingale's virtual recantation of his former adverse opinion of Pinter. It is, again, a testimony to the inherent fairness and balance of the best critics that Nightingale should have so comprehensively announced his change of heart.

Pinter brings out eloquence in dramatic criticism, and, indeed, some of the finest reviews of the whole period were written about his work. Bryden's is a splendid example, with the bonus of his recognition of the sensitively creative part played by Peter Hall in the realisation of Pinter's plays, and to the natural intimacy that seems to exist between Pinter and the actors, possibly partly because he himself is an all-round theatre-man – actor, director and dramatist.

West of Suez *was regarded as the best of a group of plays Osborne wrote from 1966 onwards. He had been tending towards a mixture of unpleasant rancour and sentimentality in his attacks on contemporary society, but in* West of Suez *there is a harder, if more anxious, vision and assessment of the parlous state of mankind. There is in it still too much of the Empire-bashing which was to become a standard easy exercise of some younger dramatists with little of Osborne's skill or genuine if perversely expressed concern for his fellow-men, but it roused critics and audience to an excited hope that the old devil of 1956 was himself again – if a little smoother in appearance.*

Old Times
Harold Pinter
June 1971   Aldwych

There used to be puzzle-plays that depended upon the last line. Today there is Harold Pinter, almost magisterially inexplicit, and sometimes (I murmur unkindly) applauded on the principle that what is enigmatic must be wise.

What, then, of the future? Surely we ought to look forward and ask how these plays will wear. Will they be directed as ceremonial rites – as Peter Hall has directed this – or will they fade into the older times another generation will dismiss?

I have my own view; at least, I cannot deny Mr Pinter's theatrical expertise.

Why are three people, on an autumn night in the deeper country, restoring their London world of 20 years ago? Choose your answer. You may work on a theory that involves lesbianism and the supernatural, or you can decide that the intermingling of moods and minds, the apparent presence of a woman known once to both husband and wife, speaks for the haunting past from which we can never escape. Have it your own way; Pinter wishes it.

I appreciate the excellence of the playing, the delicacy with which three members of the Royal Shakespeare Company, Dorothy Tutin, Vivien Merchant, and Colin Blakely, keep to the complex rhythm of the dramatist's literate and sometimes amusing dialogue.

Mr Hall and his designer, John Bury, work nobly for their author. It is probably my fault that Pinter seldom excites me. Speaking somewhere in this play about the possible permutations of the twin beds, the man acted by Colin Blakely says: 'It's the castors that make all the difference.'

So with Pinter as he slips with theatrical guile round his problem. The castors make all the difference. Here again, no doubt, they have helped to create one of the show-pieces of the London season. But (in a whisper) is it really important?

(J.C. Trewin, *Birmingham Post*, 2 June, 1971)

The searching gravity to which Miss Tutin's smile surrenders gives her performance irresistible grace.

(From: Harold Hobson, *The Sunday Times*, 6 June, 1971)

At the end ... Miss Tutin holds the house spellbound with a surrealist narrative.

(From: John Barber, *The Daily Telegraph*, 2 June, 1971)

... Anyone with an ear for Harold Pinter's dialogue will recognise the territory on to which his new play *Old Times*, at the Aldwych, shifts with those lines. A gauntlet has been thrown down. Battle is engaged. The battleground is Kate: which of the two, Deeley or Anna, has possessed more of her? The weapons, as usual, are sex and language: the language of innuendo, cultural discomfiture, the slight verbal excess staking an emotional claim. Truth has nothing to do with it. 'More often than not'? Really? The winner will be the one who can impose his or her version of the past. Anna has made her opening thrust. Kate cooks for Deeley. With her, she read poetry.

It would make life neater for all those graduate students labouring over Pinter theses if one of them could prove that his first, favourite book had been Henry James's *Sacred Fount*, with its twin theories that, in love, there is always one who eats and one who is eaten, and that truth is a question of who offers the more stylish scenario. But *Old Times* all too clearly is simply a natural growth of his own talent.

Within the same triangular frame of memory as *Silence*, it mixes the sexual ambiguities of *The Collection* with the territorial wars of dominance which underlay *The Homecoming*. Growth seems a better word than advance. The techniques, the preoccupations are the same. There's no new departure from the ground he has made his own. But the mastery of it is more stunning than ever, the economy even more perfect. Wonderfully taut, comic and ominous, *Old Times* shows Pinter more and more himself and less like any other playwright writing today.

More clearly than before, it takes the form of a duel: a game of skill to the death. One after the other, the adversaries offer their blows to the body. Brutally, Deeley tells how he picked up Kate in a cinema showing *Odd Man Out*, walked her home and bedded her. Anna listens smiling, with no more belief than Mick in *The Caretaker* gave to Davies's story of his papers at Sidcup. Then it is her turn, and she has a double riposte. Funny how vividly you imagine what you think happened, isn't it, whether it happened or not? She has a memory – is it real? of a man who cried in Kate's bed. But of course it is unreal beside her memories of their life together: poring over the Sunday papers, rushing out to old films at suburban cinemas – like *Odd Man Out*.

It's like watching a marvellous skilled game of cricket or tennis. What kind of ball will they send over next? How will the receiver parry it? Deeley has more crude power – he is Kate's husband, isn't he? – but he flusters more easily, being Irish, and lacks Anna's patient finesse. She has the authority of money and culture (a husband and villa in Sicily, a velvet glove of good-tempered gentility to mask her steely determination), and Kate's vague, smiling passivity seems on her side. But much as Pinter enjoys games, they aren't what he writes about. As in *The Homecoming*, the final, devastating victory belongs to neither battler, but to the woman battled over. People are not prizes to be won in tournaments. They belong to themselves.

Peter Hall directs the comedy with a musician's ear for the value of each word and silence which exposes every layer of the text like the perspex levels of a three-dimensional chess-board. 'Do you drink brandy?' asks Deeley. Vivien Merchant's pause before replying that she would love some is just sufficient to remind you that, on Pinter territory, every question is an attempt to control and every answer a swift evasion. In the immaculate cast, she has the advantage of her long mastery of Pinter idiom, from the deployment of hesitations down to the crossing of strapped-over ankles. But in its way Dorothy Tutin's silent Kate is as commanding a performance, and the surprise of the evening is Colin Blakely's Deeley: funny, desperate and individual as his character roles at the National never fully revealed him.

Is there nothing to criticise? Looking wildly for some hole to pick, I can find only a small misquotation (which had to be pointed out to me) in the lyric of *Lovely to Look At*. That, and a faint disappointment that, when Kate turns over the table of the game of words in which her would-be possessors try to pin her down, she does so with the same symbolic super-articulacy as they. Instead of refusing its rules, she seems to make them her own. But it's a tiny shadow on a superb evening and achievement, worth all the six years since *Homecoming* that we've had to wait for it.

(From: Ronald Bryden, *The Observer*, 6 June, 1971)

When we left our hero, Harold Pinter, he was in a sad plight, having stumbled into as dry and tedious a desert as ever vulture ranged. I should know, I was one of the vultures. I bloodied my claws on *Landscape* and *Silence*, back there in 1969, and even dared threaten the intrepid Harold with my beak. Would he stay put, to ossify and bleach, or try to find his way out? Well, the answer is at the Aldwych: *Old Times*, a miraculous escape, firmly establishing the bespectacled, mild-mannered playwright as the Clark Kent of the British theatre.

Form has much to do with it. For some time Pinter has been moving further and further from naturalism and, it's seemed, from drama itself. *Landscape* was more like a tone-poem, in which the characters offered contradictory views of the past in monologues. Then there was *The Basement*, which took two men and illustrated their contest for the same girl with a cursory flurry of mime and verbal Pinterism. It seemed more gesture than drama,

179

more scenario than play. Indeed, it *was* a scenario, since in *Old Times*, which replaces one of the men with a cloying and possibly Lesbian woman, Pinter has given us the play proper. The bones are cloaked in flesh; but in such a way that we never lose sight of their existence. *Old Times* moves happily on a naturalistic level, and left me, at least, agog for its denouement. It has all those elements of conflict and tension apparent in his early plays, so sadly lacking in his recent ones; it also has that spareness, that sense of the essential, apparent in his recent plays and largely lacking in his early ones. Level has now been reconciled with level; archetype with character; emblem with social observation; *The Basement* with *The Homecoming*. . . .

. . .There have been times when Pinter has almost perversely withheld essential information, as if intent on mystification. Most playwrights' reputations depend on what they reveal about their characters; one has felt that his depends on what he does *not* reveal. He's told us, again and again, that the mind has chasms and the subconscious is impenetrable, and left it at that – creating an impression of depth by reporting the existence of the well. There are mysteries enough in this play, and no doubt it will cause dispute for years, not least about the ending. But they're the sort to multiply speculation, not nullify it. Enough has been suggested by the time Blakely weeps to sustain all my explanations at their various levels. In other words, Pinter's newly forged dramatic form has proved itself. Could any be more fitting for a writer abnormally aware both of the beguiling, fraudulent, social surfaces and of the fear and greed deep, deep beneath? Finally, I think, Pinter reduces life to these two elements: which may explain not only the disturbing effect of the play as a whole, but also Dorothy Tutin's obscure remark about wedding and change of scene. Neither 'matter' beside this basic, brutal truth.

Pinter is the poet of the id; and *Old Times* is an elegantly shaped, economical and loving piece of work, witty and precisely articulated. The language has none of that lyric self-consciousness which marred *Landscape*. If it seems precious at times, it's because Miss Merchant is speaking, and that's how her part is. She achieves much behind her melting refinement, Blakely behind his tense smiles; but the most impressive presence is that of Dorothy Tutin, sitting back and luxuriously watching, like an amused cat biding its moment. The acting is superb, and Peter Hall directs with the same sensitivity he's brought to Pinter's previous work: never has he, or we, been so amply rewarded by him, before.

(From: Benedict Nightingale, *New Statesman*, 11 June 1971)

West of Suez
John Osborne
August 1971   Royal Court

. . . for once the most fluently dogmatic of dramatists has run out
of ideas. What are left are opinions.
  (From: J.C. Trewin, *Birmingham Post*, 18 August, 1971)

Osborne grouped his last two plays under the title, *For the
Meantime*. It is good to feel *that* particular period is over. This is a
brave and loving play. He has dared to appear reactionary on the
surface because he is deeply troubled by the present and alarmed
at the future. With much to savour at the time, and a great deal to
digest later, *West of Suez* is a remarkable evening in the theatre.
  (From: Helen Dawson, *The Observer*, 22 August, 1971)

It is a theatre to be proud of that gives us – merely to skim the
cream – within a twelve-month or so Mercer's *After Haggerty*,
Wesker's underrated *The Friends*, Greenwood's equally underrated *Hankey Park*, Mortimer's *Voyage Round My Father*, Nichols'
Forget-Me-Not Lane, Pinter's *Old Times* and now (at the Royal
Court) Osborne's *West of Suez*. And just to clear the decks, the
answer to the question already put to me verbally a hundred
times, 'What about the new Osborne, then – is it worth seeing?' is
a loud and unequivocal Yes.

It cannot be a coincidence that all these fine plays are
backward-looking, the present a void, the future (as always) a
threat – and the past, for all its narrowness, cruelties, stupidities,
absurdities, something to be recalled not only with impatience but
with baffled affection, not only in anger but with reluctant
respect. It is a measure of all the dramatists concerned that they
are able to encompass with abrasive generosity this tragi-comic
trawl of ambiguities; and Osborne, I believe, has in *West of Suez*
taken a great bound forward.

The advance lies not in any blazing new insight into the human
condition, but in the vastly increased resonance with which *West of
Suez* expresses the disappointment at the heart of almost all
Osborne's work – and which he is still rashly inclined to equate
with despair, just as he still seems to confuse boredom with
accidie. But there is a paradoxical economy in this leisurely play
which encompasses all the sorts of anguish he has extravagantly
lashed before. . . .

  . . . Osborne himself reminds us, with a passing reference to
Trofimov the perpetual student in *The Cherry Orchard*, of Chekov;
but it is not Chekov direct that *West of Suez* recalls. Here is
Osborne's *Heartbreak House* (which Shaw called 'a comedy in the

181

Russian manner'); and Wyatt Gillman is an inverted Shotover. Shaw too, over fifty years ago, was concerned to pillory, with regret, a slow-pulsed, over-ripe civilisation; but he was still able to set up against it a rampaging old mystic with his eyes on the stars, even though by that time he had almost lost any faith in human nature. Osborne's alchemy leaves us with a man whose potential talents have been wholly exercised in constructing ironical defences; behind them he passes the time in the role-playing of total scepticism.

Sir Ralph's portrait of this man, a burnt-out case from birth, seems to me a total triumph. The big frame moves with a puppet-like angularity, plays at a babyish physical incompetence. But the head turns like an old stag's, the eyes, widening and narrowing, are always watchful – and the voice takes on a score of colours just as the phrasing, the pauses, the downright breaks are themselves a miracle of characterisation. False innocence brings in the hint of a whimper, calculated self-reproach a touch of unction; marvellously controlled, too, the voluble flood of embarrassment with which he greets his fellow-writer; and an absolute kaleidoscope, not without flashes of steel, colours his duel with the woman journalist. If this is the epitome of Western culture in decline, it is a downright dangerously irresistible image.

(From: J.W. Lambert, *The Sunday Times*, 22 August, 1971)

A couple of years ago John Osborne told an interviewer that he would like more than anything to write another *Cherry Orchard*. Coming from him, it seemed a surprising choice. Strindberg, yes. But Chekhov? However, his subsequent *The Hotel in Amsterdam* showed this to be no idle remark. And any lingering doubts are dispelled by his new play.

The connexion is unmistakably spelled out, even in the programme photograph, which shows a new Osborne, bearded like his model and gazing quizzically over a pair of steel-rimmed glasses at the characters in the consulting room. He seems made up for a character performance, but let us move on to the play. It takes place in a villa set in a former British island colony (the feeling is of the Caribbean) where an English family are holidaying under the baleful scrutiny of the natives.

Part of the interest in the first act lies in following just how much Osborne is taking from Chekhov. There are the four daughters of a famous author, all striving to have a good time in conditions of continuous boredom and a creeping sense of malaise. The villa belongs to the eldest, Robin, and her retired military husband; and the setting thus combines elements from *Uncle Vanya* and *The Cherry Orchard*.

Their time on the island is running out, but meanwhile they

talk and drink. The old brigadier, like Vanya, is neglecting the estate for the bottle; while Wyatt, the old writer, appears in the position of Serebryakov, the spoiled star of the family long used to holding the centre of attention. Also on hand are a grittily philosophizing doctor, and nihilistic external student whom Wyatt at one point explicitly likens to Trofimov.

One can see the attraction and possibilities of this for Osborne. He has almost from the start (as in *The Entertainer*) possessed a marked but insufficiently exercised gift for oblique double-density dialogue; and, starting with this known capacity, the act of writing an ensemble Chekhovian piece could serve to release him from his old strait-jacket of one-character drama. Then there are the obvious analogies between pre-Revolutionary Russia and post-Imperial Britain, in which Chekhov's affection for the moribund elements of society clearly attunes itself to Osborne's nostalgia for English tradition.

Forgetting about Chekhov for a moment, *West of Suez* does at least mark a technical development on Osborne's last two plays. Its exposition (although still loaded down with indigestible information on people we have not met) is far defter than that of *Time Present*. It contains some blistering marriage rows (for the corrosive Jill Bennett and the icy Geoffrey Palmer) where the partners face each other like armadillos, carefully measuring out half smiles and occasional unguarded tones of voice from under armour-plated shells.

Also, continuously self-regarding as it is, the dialogue crackles with an aggressive wit, never subsiding into the complaining moan of the last plays.

Osborne, finally, has written a peach of a part for Ralph Richardson in the character of Wyatt: a bewildered and cossetted old lion, with a flair for advancing outrageous opinions in tones of naive apology, and picking up other people's platitudes with a hearty appreciation that treads a delicious borderline between simple-mindedness and deadly ridicule. Thickly protected behind a coating of old-fashioned slang, he is in his way as much an armadillo as any of the others; and Richardson's capacity to turn inside aside by disarming reversals of mood, or a quick flick of that head, repeatedly earn him his central position as a master of the evasion game. In the context of the piece, what sustains the character is its ambiguity, at once an embodiment of the England Osborne is sorry to lose, and a reason for the loss.

One does not need to follow up the Chekhovian connexion to find the rest of the play deeply disappointing. First, in writing for a large cast of equal characters Osborne has only increased his one-character problem. Instead of one protagonist, there is now a stage-full of them, each hogging central position whenever a chance appears. Thus one is left yet again with the inert Osborne semi-circle surrounding a temporarily privileged egoist.

As a result, no shared atmosphere develops, no sense of the simultaneous intersecting passage of several lives. The idea of Chekhovian 'atmosphere' may be outmoded, but Osborne is clearly striving to generate it in his sections of lyrical cataloguing, where small knots of characters pile up details of the past.

Again, while nothing much needs to happen on stage in work of this kind, it is a rash writer who dispenses with a framework of inner or off-stage action. *West of Suez* possesses no such framework, so that coupled with the absence of ensemble is the lack of any sense of direction. . .

(From: Irving Wardle, *The Times*, 18 August, 1971)

1972

*Stoppard, like Pinter, is an actor's playwright, and all of his plays rely to a
great extent on the 'feel' his actors have for the intricacies (for that is what
they are) of his characterisation. In a sense, perhaps, he does not so much
create a set of developing characters as a group of highly sophisticated
mechanisms, each one with its allotted and carefully designed function in
the play.*

*Trewin, in his inspired phrase about Michael Hordern, amply confirms
Stoppard's reliance on the actors, and Peter Roberts in his comment on
Stoppard's 'ingenuity in manipulating characters we don't believe in'
confirms the curiously mechanistic process by which his characters are
bolted together. Some critics, among them Roberts, found that Stoppard
has no compassion, 'like Nichols' (Peter Roberts). This is a further piece of
evidence as to the growing concern of the critics with the 'social' content of
the new drama. They couldn't condemn Stoppard – he is too clever, too
funny, perhaps, indeed, too ambiguous – but it's as if they kept a reserve
judgement up their sleeves.*

Jumpers
Tom Stoppard
February 1972   Old Vic

My only regret is that the purpose of the exercise should have
remained so obscure. Still, it will keep people arguing: I predict
that there will be many exotic interpretations.
   (From: Frank Marcus, *The Sunday Telegraph*, 6 February, 1972)

[Michael Hordern] looks like a cross between a tired bloodhound,
a worried owl and the late Sir Alan Herbert.
        (From: J.C. Trewin, *Birmingham Post*, 3 February, 1972)

. . . one is left to admire only his ingenuity in manipulating
characters we don't believe in.
        (From: Peter Roberts, *Plays and Players*, April, 1972)

185

1972

Jumpers, says Tom Stoppard, its author, in a programme note, 'is a play with a central argument, and it becomes very quickly obvious what that argument is about.' It is in fact about the nature of God; but neither the theme nor the plot is the attribute of *Jumpers* that gives such unique pleasure. People I spoke to as I came out were less positive than I have been about its theme; indeed, it may well be about the nature of philosophy, the subject of God having been chosen merely as a basis for discussion. This is the kind of thing that happens when you tangle with philosophers. As for the plot, which involves the murder of a professor of logic by (or probably by) a retired musical comedy actress married to a professor of moral philosophy, it need not detain one at all, though as always with Mr Stoppard it is neatly contrived and provided with some cunning surprises.

What gives the play its real distinction is the quality of the conversations that bubble and glitter continuously from start to finish. Philosophy is a subject very easy to extract fun from, and Mr Stoppard, who is clearly well up in it, invents philosophical discussions with astonishing fertility of ideas and humour of expression. . . .

. . . I can't hope to do justice to the richness and sparkle of the evening's proceedings, as gay and original a farce as we have seen for years, but a farce for people who relish truly civilised wit. The jumpers of the title, I should say, seem to represent philosophers, and if the Vice-Chancellor claims to be a gymnast as well as a doctor, lawyer and philosopher, we need take this no more seriously than we do the track suits in which the chorus of jumpers (or philosophers) make their appearance. 'O, I'll leap up to my God!' said Faustus. Here are people actually doing it.

(From: B.A. Young, *The Financial Times*, 3 February, 1972)

Jumpers at the Old Vic is Tom Stoppard's first full-length play since the delightful *Rosencrantz and Guildenstern*. It is another comedy as erudite as it is dotty, with some dark philosophic meaning buried under the fantastications.

You could say it was stark raving sane.

Unlike the earlier play, it lacks the firm underpinning of a sober and powerful myth.

Here the substructure is a tortuous who-dun-it. Word games and metaphysical speculations decorate it like paper streamers on a paper gazebo. The result is inevitably flimsy.

It is set in the future, when a British astronaut is seen roving the moon on the giant TV screen in a London flat. Outside the Radical Liberals are on par-parade [*sic*] after an election victory.

On a vast white bed Diana Rigg lies half-naked, playing a ravishing pop singer who has lately collapsed at a public appearance and is now in the care of a demoniac psychiatrist.

Michael Hordern, as her husband, a philosophy professor, is next door, dictating an endless lecture on whether God exists, a Jonathan Miller-style parody of all such brilliant mumbo-jumbo. He also worries, with cause, about the psychiatrist's relationship with his wife.

Also involved – besides acrobats, a missing hare, an atheist archbishop, a hanged man, and a girl trapezist – is a detective inquiring into the murder of a professor. He was shot at a wild party which was in its last throes when the curtain went up.

The surrealist central theme, however, is less engrossing than the intellectual jokes and the whirlwind set speeches, cascades of words soaring like tailed comets. Miss Rigg, with her siren voice and long, sinuous limbs, has two of these, both stunning. Her lament over the rape of the moon is the high point of the night.

Mr Hordern, with his Felix-the-Cat lope and Gladstone-bag of a face, has never been more entertaining and Graham Crowden makes the psychiatrist a formidable Satanic dandy. Peter Wood has directed with a gusto that disguises the undoubted weakness in trumps of the hand he is playing.

(John Barber, *The Daily Telegraph*, 3 February, 1972)

1973

There is something about the very title which grips the expectations —
Equus. *It very quickly became a cult play on both sides of the Atlantic, the
more so in the United States, perhaps because of its psychiatric layers. Its
critical reception was favourable, and several shrewd interpretations of its
'message' were expressed, perhaps the most lucid being Billington's in* The
Guardian.

*Its reputation as the best play for many years grew apace, but more
recent opinion has been far less accepting and favourable. Interestingly,
what seems to have lowered its estimation is less an awareness of both the
obvious superficiality of all the characters except the psychiatrist and the
boy, and a certain clumsiness of construction, than a suspicion that it is an
elitist throw-back of the days of 'non-committed' theatre.*

Bingo *has been discussed in the Introduction. The contemporary
reviews show conclusively that most of the critics did not concern
themselves with its several categorical distortions of history and its fanciful
depiction of Shakespeare, but with its modern 'message'. Billington, so
astute about* Equus, *nevertheless committed himself with an unwonted
dewy-eyedness to the astonishing statement that it's 'the first play I've seen
to paint a credible portrait of Shakespeare'. What kind of credibility is
possible in a dramatic statement that blatantly flies in the face of the few
known facts? And what, in reading Harold Hobson's lengthy and
concentrated review, is one to make of his statement that 'Mr Bond may
condemn himself, but he is in very good company'. Whose? To what end?
Why is self-condemnation to be purged by multiple guilt?*

*What most of the critics failed to do with Bond's play was to assess it in
any other terms than that of its message for our own times. They ignored
what, arguably, later critics of this century, of equal if not in certain cases
superior sensibility, would have seized upon — Bond's outrageous
manipulation of history for his own purposes, and, even more, his bland
special pleading that the 'history' he substituted was the 'truth'. And there's
the rub.*

Equus
Peter Shaffer
July 1973   National Theatre

Freud is watching. . .
> (From: J.C. Trewin, *Birmingham Post*, 27 July, 1973)

Peter Shaffer is, in the truest sense of the word, one of our best playwrights. He would be even better if he would persuade himself that he is not a poet or a philosopher.
> (From: Frank Marcus, *The Sunday Telegraph*, 29 July, 1973)

It involves, I'm afraid, nearly everything you always knew about psychiatry, but were afraid to believe . . . with all my reservations Equus is a play to be seen, if only to be disbelieved.
> (From: Kenneth Hurren, *The Spectator*, 4 August, 1973)

Peter Shaffer is a writer of formidable intelligence and traditional stage technique whose consistent purpose has been to invoke the primal dramatic forces which would blow his own equipment sky high. In style one can never predict what kind of piece he will write next; but his theme remains constant. Whether he is opposing Christian and Aztec culture in the *Royal Hunt of the Sun*, or a philosopher and an anarchist poet in *The Battle of Shrivings*, Shaffer is repeatedly mounting a tournament between Apollo and Dionysus under various coats of arms.

The argument of these plays is lacking in sinew; but the really sad thing about them is that while they are intended to celebrate the dark gods, it is always Apollo who wins. Mr Shaffer, a Western intellectual, was born into his service; and when he tries to conjure up Dionysus all he can offer is a projection governed by the Apollonian rules of reason and control.
> (From: Irving Wardle, *The Times*, 27 July, 1973)

The scene is like a boxing ring or bull-fight arena, with the audience ranged on two sides. It represents the room of a psychiatrist, terrifyingly bare, a room professionally dedicated to the driving out of devils from the minds of patients so that – this is Mr Shaffer's frightening thesis – other devils may enter worse than those that have been expelled.

The patient in this case is a youth who has committed the horrible crime of blinding six horses. The psychiatrist who sets out to cure him is a man who is already beginning to fear that the work his profession imposes on him is in itself criminal. He has nightmares in which he sees himself as an Ancient Greek priest disembowelling children, and throwing their entrails to Zeus, a

189

god who does not exist, the parallel with his profession being that in order to cure the deranged he amputates part of their personality in the name of normality, which is a god as mythical as Zeus.

What becomes clear in the course of the play is not whether the boy can be cured, but whether he ought ever to have become ill. On these points Mr Shaffer is categorical. Any psychiatric cure, he says, is a dangerous sham. In a shattering speech at the end of the play the psychiatrist, in intense distress, admits – no, proclaims in the voice of a prophet – that the boy's cure has been effected only by a complete disembowelment of all that in him is potentially finest: that in fact, though in appearance at peace he leaves – and necessarily leaves – the hospital a human being crippled and ruined.

What has been taken from him is the capacity for worship, the realisation of the supernatural, the transcendence of material things, without which, in Mr Shaffer's Dionysiac, religious, ecstatic view, life is empty and hollow.

(From: Harold Hobson, *The Sunday Times*, 29 July, 1973)

Peter Shaffer's *Equus* is sensationally good. Like *The Royal Hunt of the Sun* and *The Battle of Shrivings*, it is based on a direct confrontation between reason and instinct. Like them also, it suggests that, though organised faith is usually based on neurosis, a life without some form of worship or belief is ultimately barren. But it's a far better play than either if only because the intellectual argument and the poetic imagery are virtually indivisible.

It deals with the psychiatric exploration of a hideous crime. A 17-year-old boy has blinded six horses with a metal spike; and we watch as the doctor patiently pieces together the evidence that will explain this act of cruelty. Gradually we learn that the boy's mother, a religious fanatic, has filled his mind with images of Biblical cruelty; that his father, a taciturn printer, cannot communicate with him about anything; that his sexual instincts have been aroused by horse-flesh and that he has come to love one particular animal as a god; that, impotent when seduced by a girl in the stables, he has wreaked a terrible revenge on the all-seeing horses around him.

A classic case-book drama then? Not at all. For, though Shaffer pieces the evidence together with an accelerating detective story tension, his real concern is with the relationship between the psychiatrist and the boy. Humane, clinical, and efficient, the doctor realises that by restoring the boy to 'normality' he is in fact killing the motivating force of his life. 'Passion', he explains, 'can be destroyed by a doctor. It cannot be created'. And the question the play asks is whether, by rooting out the brain-sickness and abnormality of individuals, we don't ultimately deny their humanity.

What makes the play so exciting is that it presents this argument in such bold, clear, vivid theatrical terms. From the opening image of the boy nuzzling another actor clad in skeletal, horse's head and hooves, we are constantly aware of his strange passion; yet the main action takes place inside a sparse rectangular room representing the orderly world of the psychiatrist. Shaffer is also shrewd enough to make the psychiatrist a complex human figure.

John Dexter's spare, lean production (notice the economy with which the actors, by a flick of the hand, suggest equine movement) also contains two outstanding performances. Alec McCowen's psychiatrist is a brilliant study of a man of reason, soured by the need to bottle up and contain his instincts; and, as always, he articulates arguments beautifully. And Peter Firth matches him admirably as the haunted, hapless, soft-featured boy.

(Michael Billington, *The Guardian*, 27 July, 1973)

Bingo
Edward Bond
November 1973   The Northcott, Exeter

In short this is another of Bond's denunciations of money and law and order. It also finds room for religious bigotry represented by a group of anti-enclosure fanatics. I do not understand their place in the scheme.

(From: Irving Wardle, *The Times*, 15 November, 1973)

Bingo (the title refers to money-grubbing) suffers from a central figure who broods on the sidelines of life and dies repeating sadly 'Was anything done?' It suffers, too, from our expectancy that his every line will be of a divine eloquence.

(From: John Barber, *The Daily Telegraph*, 16 November, 1973)

A despairing, disgusted suicide seems scarcely less historically credible than a lesbian love-affair between Queen Victoria and Florence Nightingale. And yet, whether he's writing of the treatment of vagrants in seventeenth century England or the details of Shakespeare's own dealing in Stratford, Bond consistently aims at an authenticity he never contemplates in that mad fantasy, *Early Morning*.

(From: Benedict Nightingale, *New Statesman*, 23 November, 1973)

Edward Bond is a brave man. Rushing in where Shaw, Emlyn Williams and Clemence Dane didn't exactly succeed, he has written a play about Shakespeare, *Bingo*, given its premiere at the Northcott Theatre, Exeter. I don't think it has the tragi-comic stature of his previous work, *The Sea*; but it makes a fascinating attempt to use the life of Shakespeare to explore some of Bond's recurring obsessions.

The dominant theme is the insufficiency of the creative life. The setting is Stratford in 1615–16. Shakespeare is settled in New Place but finds himself plagued by the cruelty and violence of Jacobean society, by demands for support from both local landowners and victimised tenant farmers, and by the banality, stupidity and greed of his own family. He admits to Ben Jonson (who stops off for a loan and a booze-up) that he is written out: and the question that beats in his mind as he draws towards death, alone in a cold room is 'Was anything done?' Has his life, in fact, achieved any useful purpose?

Clearly the play is not meant to be taken as a literal historical record but as a metaphor for the agony of the artist unable to cope with the brutality of his environment. And as such it has a sparse, grim, austere effectiveness: as a pensive Shakespeare broods over the hangings, whippings, bear-baitings and torturing of Jacobean society, you get a sense of the privileged, futile isolation of the successful writer. The familiar Bond theme of the conflict between justice and the tyranny of law-and-order is also ingeniously related to the battle over land enclosure in Shakespeare's Stratford. But, like every other writer, Bond falls foul of the problem of how you make Shakespeare talk: when he is taciturn, brooding and withdrawn in his New Place garden you believe in him totally, but when he sits in a snowbound field uttering lines like 'I have a wound as large as a valley' you feel Bond lapsing into indulgent phrase-making.

It is, however, the first play I've seen to paint a credible portrait of Shakespeare, and, subtitled 'Scenes of Money and Death', it constantly relates the artist's problems to economic reality.

(Michael Billington, *The Guardian*, 16 November, 1973)

Edward Bond's *Saved* and *Lear* were plays of a man without faith, and with only a small, defiant residuum of optimism, clinging desperately to the last shreds of hope. If there be a few just men in the city, then the city will be saved; if there be one just action, even if it fails, then living is not utterly vain. But in Mr Bond's latest play, *Bingo*, directed by Jane Howell at the Northcott Theatre, Exeter, the mood has become deeper and the optimism more shrunken. There is nothing in it to compare with the determination of Len, in *Saved*, trying to mend the broken chair, nor the bravery of Lear upon the wall. There is compassion, but it is a compassion that reckons itself helpless; there is the recognition of right, but it is right that there is no possibility of achieving. This is a play, memorably poetic and mysterious, in which the despair is total.

It attempts one of the most difficult things in the world, that is, the portrayal of genius, in this particular case a man generally considered transcendent, namely Shakespeare (played by Bob Peck). But it examines, not his genius, but the nature of the mistake which, in Bond's opinion, this genius made. It is possible to see very distinct stars by not looking at them directly, and the genius of Bond's Shakespeare becomes vivid for the very reason that it is never referred to.

It is possible to believe that this man, sitting gloomily silent in his garden at New Place, or beneath the shadow of a gibbet, occasionally bursting into a passionate tirade about bear-baiting, or garrulously drunk in the snow, did really write Shakespeare's plays. It is possible to believe this, because Bond never mentions them. He simply takes them for granted, and because he does so, we take them for granted, too.

The play ends with a truly terrifying scene in which the last moments of the dying Shakespeare are made hideous by the frightening, deadly and malignant battering on the bedroom door of his hated wife and daughter, whom he has locked out. Miss Howell has very finely regulated the rhythm and the force of this attack, whose effect is even greater than that of the knocking on the door in *Macbeth*. It is the climax of the total meaning of Mr Bond's play. Shakespeare at the end of his life comes back to Stratford. He is rich and secure; he has a beautiful garden, whose peace, one would imagine, would soothe the stormiest heart; he can afford, and get, domestic service which today a member of the peerage might envy. He has written, as we know, though Mr Bond does not tell us, plays that surpass the limits of human achievement as shown by any other modern dramatist, except, perhaps, Racine. But his gloom is impenetrable, and his condemnation of himself without qualification.

He has, it is obvious, failed in the elementary task of any happily successful man, which is to make his family love him. But he has failed, too, in his work; not in anything remotely resembling T.S. Eliot's argument that, for example, *Hamlet* is less than perfect, but in ever having given any time at all to writing *Hamlet*. This is Mr Bond's view, and it is unusual. It is also easy to make fun of, for if Shakespeare wasted his time by writing *Hamlet*, by what possible criterion is Mr Bond not wasting *his* by writing *Bingo*? But almost any deep feeling can be made to look ridiculous by even elementary casuistry. Mr Bond may condemn himself, but he is in very good company.

The quality of Shakespeare's self-condemnation is simple and important, and it raises issues which are urgent in society, but especially so in such an institution as that in which *Bingo* has received its first performance, the University of Exeter. It is the fashion for modern historians, of whom Fernand Braudel is the most profound example, to run down the importance of battles like Lepanto, for example. To Bond's Shakespeare in his retirement, but not when, say, he was actually writing *Hamlet*, this would have been a terrible sin. The importance of Lepanto, or any other battle, to the Shakespeare of *Bingo* is not any conceivable political consequences it may have had, but that it involved the death of many thousand men. Men are killed; women vagrants are hanged; bears are most cruelly baited. Bond's Shakespeare feels at all this repulsion and pity. But what has he actually done to stop it? He has concluded a profitable property deal with his friend Mr Combe (the agreement still exists) and written a few plays. It is not, in his opinion, enough.

It is in mine, though, But then, I do not agree with Mr Bond's argument. There are spiritual values to be considered, as well as material. We have got rid of bear-baiting and of hanging for vagrancy, though not yet of battles. Compassion is still necessary – but though necessary, not in itself sufficient. *Bingo* puts on trial all those students and professors (and me, too) who watched it on Wedsnesday night, and, perhaps without quite realising what they were doing, gave it so thunderous a reception. For it says unmistakably that the values for which Exeter University stands, and Oxford and Cambridge, and Keele, and Sussex, are wrong.

Well, as I say, I do not agree with Mr Bond. I would not have the professors sacked, nor the grants of the students withdrawn. I believe it is as inadequate to judge society and civilisation solely by the number of miners who can afford television sets, or by the percentage of the disabled who are equipped with Jaguars, as it is to judge them solely by the architecture of Wadham, or the quality of Exeter University Library. But Mr Bond asks questions that ought to be asked, and anyone who understands this play, which is not in the least what was expected of him, will brood over it uneasily for a long time.

(Harold Hobson, *The Sunday Times*, 18 November, 1973)

1974

At the beginning of the decade Harold Wilson invited the nation to march with Labour into the seventies. Perhaps even with his shrewdness he could never have forecast the extent to which the art of the decade, especially the drama, would reflect the inevitable spin-offs of his own and his followers' dedication — to both the new society which, they declared, lay just around the corner, and to the surgical thoroughness with which the old dispensations must be despatched to limbo.

In dramatic history, the 1970s is the decade when a rapidly increasing amount of creative effort was put into writing plays designed to fulfil the new commitments — the welfare of humankind in an inimical society. The drama of protest, of slogans, of militancy, of 'working class values', of vernacular language, of 'social realism', of anti-heroes and heroines, was upon us. The hearts of some critics leapt when they beheld what was increasingly presented to them in the theatre. Michael Billington, though showing some hesitation about the way in which, in David Hare's Knuckle 'the form sags under the sheer weight of what it's asked to convey', still found it 'consistently entertaining' in its attack on the 'denigration of the profit motive'. Even the most distinguished representative of the older generation — Harold Hobson — declared it to have a 'verve and freshness, a vertiginously varying pictorial imagination, rare in political drama'.

A month later, in April, Billington positively purred over David Storey's Life Class, even nuzzling close (for him unusual) to critical recklessness — 'Storey hits a fundamental truth which is that many teachers can express themselves creatively through the manipulation of their pupils'; that is, arguably, 'fundamental' but, more to the point, it is an old chestnut. He praises Storey on the curious ground that having asked, in his play, questions like 'Is art possible in an egalitarian society?' and 'Why are there so few women painters and sculptors?', he doesn't answer them — 'Many plays of ideas actually put a stop to one's own thoughts by providing gift-wrapped take-away solutions'. One would dearly like to have samples. Equally curious is his double-handed reference to Aristotle — Storey presents 'a totally credible image of life' while 'observing (like all his work) those old-fashioned Aristotelian unities'. Old? — yes but why 'old-fashioned'? This is surely a qualified form of approval.

195

Some other major critics of Life Class *neatly if unconsciously reveal their responses to the 'new' drama. Trewin, the gentle traditionalist, is regretful; Hurren (writing for the Tory* Spectator*) growls in protest; Lambert, torn, one feels, between a natural instinct to cleave to older dispensations and a not too well feigned feeling of 'duty' to his times, tries to make out a case for Storey as a traditionalist!*

For Brenton's The Churchill Play *Billington remained true to his discontent with what he calls 'plays of ideas'. He implies that its technique is less admirable than its ideas, but the suggestion is that that, perhaps, doesn't matter. But he is countered by Cushman and B.A. Young who are much less than enthusiastic. Indeed Cushman displayed throughout the seventies perhaps the most rational balance about the heady drama which intoxicated many of his colleagues.*

*Yet, almost as if to confound the neat pigeon-holing that historians are heir to, in the spring time of the year was engendered a trio of plays (*The Norman Conquests, *by Alan Ayckbourn) which, though they had their own highly individualistic vision and, indeed, criticism of society, were in many respects artistic light-years distant from much of the writing of their author's dramatic contemporaries. In form they were ingenious, in theme, like the best comedy, concerned with the eternal truths which often lurk behind contemporary values; in tone and language they enfolded a whole set of comic modes – farce, satire, pun, word-play, epigrammatic wit, sheer absurdity, and pathetic irony. And, lo and behold, their characters were drawn from that portion of the middle class which is neither gin and tonic (with ice) upper nor lager and lime nouveau lower, but an older group, more secretive, more comically potential, in a sense – the middle-earthers, for whom Babycham with a cherry goes down well.*

Perhaps it reveals how thin the critics' adhesion to the 'new' committed drama really was, or, indeed, how much they welcomed, as many theatre-goers did, some relief from the raw, often humourless puritanism of political plays, but whatever the cause, it is to the lasting credit of the critics that they (including Billington, the most faithful and lucid spokesman for political drama) recognised and welcomed Ayckbourn. The coming of Ayckbourn enabled some critics to take a breath, heave a sigh and look around. Once again the whirligig of time and talent was confounding what seemed to be a pattern.

As an addendum to the year, the emergence of Snoo Wilson should be noted. He was not the first but was perhaps the most memorable – solely by virtue of his name – of a fairly new conveyor belt of young fire-in-the-belly, militancy-in-the-eye, social-realism-in-the-heart dramatists. One after the other they came – both men and women – and one after another their plays seemed to be flung at the public.

Knuckle
David Hare
March 1974   Comedy Theatre

The writing is marked by wit, intelligence and a deepening sense of strain: the author becomes the captive of his own idea. Hollywood into Guildford is a good joke, but an imperfect equation.

(From: Robert Cushman, *The Observer*, 10 March, 1974)

On the surface, David Hare's new play appears to be a crude, melodramatic thriller in the style of the television screen-fodder of which a series called *Crane* is perhaps the most typical. . . .

Mr Hare even shapes his script like a television script. With the aid of a variety of peripatetic sets on trucks he divides his acts into innumerable short scenes that seldom contain more than two characters. This is one of a number of tactical mistakes I have to impute to him. If it were possible to flick from one scene to another as instantly as in a television play, there might be some justification for laying on a two-minute scene in which nothing happens. . . . When it involves some hard scene-shifting, there isn't.

The dialogue is another stalling place. It is written in thrillerese, either short and sharp and full of the clichés of villainous behaviour, with its occasional essays into aphorism; or it plunges into long purple passages designed for direct delivery to the house. Now the trouble with theatrical parody is that when you are imitating something bad the result must either be hilariously funny or seem as bad as the original. Most of Mr Hare's dialogue, cleverly observed though it is, just seems bad. The idea was an ingenious one, but it doesn't come off. . . .

On the deeper level, Mr Hare is telling us how desperately wicked it is to make money in the City. He clearly has a consuming hatred of the profit motive. Only the gun-runner, of all his male characters, is reasonably pure of motive. I just wish he had not been so apparently naive about it all. . . .

I sincerely wish I could have found something nicer to say about *Knuckle*; one knows its author to be talented, and his idea is a fertile one even if in practice it proves a failure.

(From: B.A. Young, *The Financial Times*, 5 March, 1974)

I hope David Hare's *Knuckle* won't get rapped for it's the kind of play I welcome on the West End stage: an attempt to use a pop format, in this case the hard-edged Mickey Spillane thriller, as a vehicle for moral comment. In the end the form sags under the sheer weight of what it's asked to convey, but the play is consistently entertaining and, with pleasing irony, uses a commercial stage to attack the degradation of the profit motive. . . .

. . . I must confess at times I was reminded of the over-zealous revolutionary in Shaw's *Misalliance* who cries 'Rome fell, Babylon fell, Hindhead's turn will come.' Moreover, the inherent melodrama of the pulp-thriller seriously undermines the attack on the genuine evils of property speculation. But the play is much subtler than it at first appears. . . . In reality the work is built round a sustained, intelligent contrast between the volubility of open protest and the discretion, elegance, and quietness of much British capitalism; and in that way it more seriously questions our allegedly 'civilised' values.

(From: Michael Billington, *The Guardian*, 5 March, 1974)

Mr Hare's imagination has little to do with any company of angels, but it is magnificently apocalyptic. No primrose by a river's brim a yellow primrose is to him: somehow or other it will turn into an appalling symbol of the City of London. Eastbourne and Guildford are not peaceful, pleasant towns: out of the darkness he sees them as visions of only too imaginable horror. Miss Nelligan's tremendous apostrophes exult, and exalt, and make one shiver.

Whenever I visit the Yvonne Arnaud Theatre in future I shall think of Guildford's steep High Street as trodden exclusively by, not red, but red-hot, stockbrokers, and infirm old men who fall down at the sight of a pretty girl so that they may grab at her legs to save them from collapse: dreadful and mournful creatures all, not unworthy of a shrinking pity. These visions of Mr Hare's are libels not devoid of sublimity on two of the most agreeable towns in England; and they are fearlessly set forth by Miss Nelligan and Mr Fox. Mr Fox and Miss Nelligan give splendid, dangerous performances; Michael Blakemore's production is taut and swift; and whether this review be considered left-wing or even High Tory propaganda, it should be noted that the deduction which the merchant banker draws from his daughter's last hate-filled remark on the Crumbles immediately before she vanishes from sight and which it would be unfair for me to reveal, is absolutely correct.

(From: Harold Hobson, *The Sunday Times*, 10 March, 1974)

Life Class
David Storey
April 1974   Royal Court

Life, as the most articulate student says, engulfs art – and that is the trouble with Mr Storey's play.
> (From: J.C. Trewin, *Birmingham Post*, 10 April, 1974)

. . . easily the most stimulating play in London.
> (From: Michael Billington, *The Guardian*, 10 April, 1974)

. . . puts in a keen entry for the Most Boring Play of the Year Award . . . it is an indolent approach to the dramatist's craft if ever there was one.
> (From: Hilary Spurling, *The Spectator*, 20 April, 1974)

The theatre is filled with the rich and confident strains of a Brandenburg Concerto, in which a rigorous classical framework flowers on springing lyrical tendrils. On the curtain, plunging vertically like an arrow of God, Blake's angel blasts its trumpet into the skull of a startled skeleton.

The ringing music dies away, the searing picture fades – and in their place comes up a bleak, dusty, damp-cold studio in some art school in the North of England. The Royal Court's stage is set (by Jocelyn Herbert) with overpowering irony for David Storey's new play, *Life Class*.

This is the second play I have seen in which the mass of the characters are students at a Northern art school, the other being David Halliwell's *Little Malcolm and his struggle against the Eunuchs*. Both, I must say, might have been written to reinforce the prejudices of those (myself among them) who cannot but feel that much public money is being wrongly used for a system of further education in which the aimlessness of the students is matched only by the disappointed incompetence of their teachers.

This is no idle, passing sneer; rather – like Mr Storey's play – a lament for missed opportunities. His students may once have shown some sign of talent, but they are never going to develop it in this helpless environment. Roustabout, genteel, hippie, prim, none of them is a mere type; isolated in their life class (another irony), each has a defence against bruised sensibility. All, in Lindsay Anderson's unforced orchestration, are subtly caught by a splendid group of young players. . . .

Cunningly – especially for a play at the Royal Court – Mr Storey has slipped his more positive notions in, so to speak, through the side door. The need for some sort of discipline is expressed by a student who is doggedly trying to turn art into science. The need

199

for something more than discipline is passionately expounded – in the clipped Mr Jingle-like phrasing which in this play replaces the iambic pentameters of *Cromwell* – by the school's head, a craggy, self-educated eccentric, presented by Brian Glover with dour conviction: 'Respect for the past, and a wholesome acceptance of the present . . . if life itself is degenerate, then art should set ideals.'

No dramatist today would dare, I suppose, to put such sentiments into the mouth of his hero or anti-hero; yet I suspect that Mr Storey does not think them altogether contemptible – a suspicion more than confirmed when, as the stage picture darkens on Mr Bates's defeated man stumping off in a flicker of belated determination, Bach's buoyant certainties well up once more to send us, too, off with a firm step.

(From: J.W. Lambert, *The Sunday Times*, 14 April, 1974)

The Churchill Play
Howard Brenton
May 1974   Nottingham Playhouse

Like most young British dramatists, Howard Brenton is obsessed with the state of the nation. . . . You come out discussing the truth of the play's ideas rather than its technique; and on this level Brenton is endlessly stimulating.

(From: Michael Billington, *The Guardian*, 10 May, 1974)

Mr Brenton's play amounts to little but a routine disapproval of authority. It is talkative but lacks any depth of thought or characterisation . . . to quote Dorothy Parker, there is less in it than meets the eye.

(From: B.A. Young *The Financial Times*, 11 May, 1974)

. . . unwieldy . . . passion declines into aggro (the distinguishing mark of most of his contemporaries) . . .

(From: Robert Cushman, *The Observer*, 2 June, 1974)

Howard Brenton has a terrifying imagination that makes his *The Churchill Play* (Nottingham Playhouse) a very disturbing experience. It is an experience one would not like to have missed, but it unsettles the foundations of the world on which England unsteadily rests. One of the few matters on which it is still generally assumed that there is a consensus of opinion is that in May, 1940, England found a man who could, and did, save her.

The haunting and alarming suggestion made in Mr Brenton's powerful play, whose effect is only partially eroded by Richard Eyre's unfocused direction, is that the man England found was the wrong man; that the war of 1939–45 was less Hitler's war than Churchill's; that the British, and especially the Scottish, people, were so demoralised by bombing that they bitterly resented Churchill's keeping them at war; and that this was the cause of our loss of empire, and the moment when our freedom went.

Now there is nothing in my experience of the war that can be squared with Mr Brenton's account of the demoralising effect of the German bombing. I was in the east, and most heavily hit, part of London during every raid but two during the entire war: I saw London burn and explode round me: but, with the exception of a couple of foreign journalists, I never heard anyone express even the smallest fear or tension. Mr Brenton was very young at the time, and there is much evidence in his play that he has listened to, and been impressed by, some very lurid stories: stories no doubt factually true, but not because of that necessarily universally truthful. I do not therefore accept as valid his attack on Churchill for allegedly hounding into battle a nation whose spirit was broken. What I do accept is that *The Churchill Play* is a work of great aesthetic and intellectual power, a work as impregnably self-defended and ambiguous as was Sartre's when Sartre was at the height of his creative power.

For it is defended, and it is ambiguous. The portrait of Churchill in *The Churchill Play* is drawn in such a manner that Mr Brenton could himself repudiate it. *The Churchill Play* is set in 1984, when England has become a country of concentration camps. A gentle, bewildered, liberal officer in this camp, Dr Thompson (Julian Curry), thinks it therapeutic for the internees to write and present a play of their own. His commanding officer is doubtful about the wisdom of this, but allows it to go forward. An NCO, Sergeant Baxter (Dave Hill), takes it to be a sign of contemptible weakness, and makes no secret of his view that the internees should be shot like mad dogs. But they are not shot. They act their play before a Parliamentary delegation, and it is in this play that the attack on Churchill is made.

It is perfectly possible to maintain that the attack is only what one would expect from political prisoners. But there is no suggestion of a counter-case. The furthest the play will go in defence of the class from which Churchill came is a passage in which Mr Brenton shows, in speaking of the shining youth of Lord Randolph Churchill before he was stricken with syphilis, that he is not indifferent to the grace of an English aristocrat who has been to a great public school. . . .

Our two most arresting political dramatists are Brenton and

David Storey, because beneath the politics of their work there is a mysterious spirit of poetry. In Storey there are Wordsworthian quietness and regret: in Brenton the wild strangeness of the best scenes in Wilkie Collins's *The Woman in White*. This strangeness, in the frantic walk of Captain Thompson, or the inexplicable tale of an incident on an unidentifiable plain told by a Welsh internee (James Warrior), is what makes a Brenton play memorable. The wind is malign, and ever so slightly the bones are ill at ease in their sockets.

(From: Harold Hobson, *The Sunday Times*, 2 June, 1974)

The Norman Conquests
Alan Ayckbourn
May/June 1974   Greenwich

Table Manners

Here, let us be grateful, is the week's happy ending. After the futilities of *That Championship Season*, the feeble obscenities of *The Bewitched*, and the mediocrity of *Who Saw Him Die?* we have found – out at Greenwich – another of those domestic comedies that show Alan Ayckbourn to be our most expert dramatist in an often abused genre.

(From: J.C. Trewin, *Birmingham Post*, 10 May, 1974)

In his use of obsession, Ayckbourn is like Feydeau.

(From: Charles Lewsen, *The Times*, 11 May, 1974)

Alan Ayckbourn is an unpredictable writer; the only thing you can forecast safely about any play of his is that it will be hilariously, and never cheaply, funny. It may have a plot of hair-raising complications; it may have hardly any plot at all. *Table Manners*, which is the first play of a trilogy, *The Norman Conquests*, has a plot of the utmost conventionality, a story of multiple seduction that might date from the seventeenth century.

The scene is a country house in which Annie, played by Felicity Kendal with a fine blend of comedy and pathos, is looking after widowed mother. Annie has arranged to spend a dirty weekend with her sister Ruth's husband Norman, and for this reason, suitably disguised, has asked her elder brother Reg and his wife Sarah to mind the house for her. As it happens, the seduction never occurs. Norman, and subsequently Ruth, join the family party and an even sextet is completed by the presence of Tom, an amiable but extremely thick vet practising nearby.

The action all takes place around the table in the dining room of Alan Pickford's pleasant cottage set; it rises to a climax at supper in the first scene of Act 2 that is as funny as anything Mr Ayckbourn has written.

So much for story. How dull it might have been in other hands! But in this writer's it provokes an almost unbroken obligato of laughter. He is our greatest master of situation comedy today. There are not many actual jokes in the play, certainly nothing like an epigram; but Mr. Ayckbourn has such a precise knowledge of how we behave that he can always present it to us at once familiar and mistreated, so that a conventional line of action leads to a ludicrous consequence.

(From: B.A. Young, *The Financial Times*, 10 May, 1974)

Living Together

. . . offers a far more honest, accurate picture of British family life than many a touted work by so-called serious writers.
(From: Michael Billington, *The Guardian*, 22 May, 1974)

This is a complete play on its own.
(From: B.A. Young, *The Financial Times*, 22 May, 1974)

'Ho,' said an eager young voice behind me, just before the play started, 'is that the famous hearthrug?' Indeed it was, and that hearthrug is soon likely to be much more famous.

It is the centrepiece of the second of Alan Ayckbourn's *The Norman Conquests*, three plays embracing the events of Saturday afternoon to Monday morning in a shabby Victorian house in the country upon which assorted members of a middle-middle-class family stressfully converge.

One play, *Table Manners*, is set in the dining-room, another, *Round and Round The Garden* (due in a fortnight), is indeed set in the overgrown garden, this week's uproarious entrant, *Living Together*, in the sitting-room. On the strength of the first two, and the evidence of new-come acquaintances, each play does indeed stand on its own feet, and all three could as Mr Ayckbourn claims, be seen in any order; their action is not consecutive but, as the structuralists would say, synchronic.

If this were all, such skill would be grounds enough for admiration. But of course it is not all. From *Relatively Speaking* on it has been clear that Mr Ayckbourn's dazzling comic gift also pierces to the heart. Whether *The Norman Conquests* as a whole will sound the resonances which underlie the gentleness of *Time and Time Again* and the cruelty of *Absurd Person Singular* remains to be seen. What is already clear is that *Table Manners* and *Living Together*, crammed with brilliant human observation, springing explosions of laughter with unquenchable dramatic resource, are symphonies of transmuted pain, exhilarating peaks of comic catharsis.

I make this confident claim, of course, on the strength of the performances now being given at Greenwich. Alan Pickford's designs, of both sets and clothes, seem to me to catch exactly the sense of running-down in the house, the temperament and aspirations (or lack of them) in its people. As for Eric Thompson's direction – well, except in pure director's theatre we can never precisely know all a director has contributed; but we can admiringly note the pacing of the piece, the establishing of a basic rhythm which carries the audience with it and builds a cumulative response. Here, as in his other Ayckbourn productions (and for that matter in Theatre 69's *Journey's End*) Mr Thompson's touch seems to me impeccable.

In *Time and Time Again* Tom Courtenay played a misfiring provincial schoolmaster whose involvement in other people's lives always brought some sort of disaster. Now Mr Courtenay plays a rather similar character: an assistant librarian who feels wasted at work and put down at home, blundering amorously along, spicing his own bewilderment with mischief behind a protective hedge of beard, sulking, coaxing, slumping – but I see I am describing a man, not a performance. Praise enough, perhaps.

He has too a sort of alter ego, a local vet of slow and stolid demeanour, whose persistence in hanging round the daughter of the house and failure to propose to her, coupled with hints of a sharper wit elsewhere, give him the air of a vacant Lopakhin. His embodiment by Michael Gambon is a near-miracle of perfect passive timing in one social mishap after another. And how cleverly and sadly Mark Kingston reveals a lost boy beneath an exuberantly extrovert, tolerantly henpecked husband. All three men, in fact, are lost, stumbling along, staving off in their various ways the onset of total inertia.

Not so the women: Felicity Kendal, tiny, wistful, a dogged and incompetent little house-keeper, nursing the awful old mother who broods upstairs, waiting for the proposal which never comes from a man she doesn't want to marry; Penelope Wilton, dark, briskly beautiful, a career woman wonderfully crumbling into the caresses of her impossible husband; and, most pitiful, Penelope Keith, as a wife whose whole world has contracted into an obsessive concern for domestic trivia – see her fold napkins, insist on an unnecessary *place à table*, nearly come to blows over the coffee – and see this poor neurotic woman flower for a moment when awful Norman turns to her. Here – indeed throughout the plays – we laugh until we cry: and there is in these lives much to cry about.

(From: J.W. Lambert, *The Sunday Times*, 26 May, 1974)

Round and Round the Garden

Briefer than *The Oresteia*, funnier than *The Wars of the Roses*, Alan Ayckbourn's exhilarating trilogy, *The Norman Conquests*, looks set for a place in theatrical history ... [they] are about something important.

(From: Michael Billington, *The Guardian*, 7 June, 1974)

Round and Round the Garden takes a third look at the amorous affairs of Norman, Tom, Sarah, Annie, Reg and Ruth, this time from the garden we have only glimpsed before through an open door. The overall plot remains the same, of course, but some of the incidental detail is quite unexpected, notably Tom's assault on Ruth, whom he believes has been leading him on when she has only been advising him on a proper approach to Annie. There are comic climaxes as good as any in the other plays – Sarah's half-hearted resistance to Norman's first approach, Penelope Keith at her best, snapping a diminuendo refrain of 'That's enough!' as she fails to fight him off; the game of catch, devised by Reg, that leads only to one successful and one unsuccessful clinch.

No need to repeat my admiration for the company. Tom Courtenay, Penelope Wilton, Michael Gambon, Felicity Kendal, Mark Kingston and Penelope Keith; and for their director, Eric Thompson, the designer Alan Pickford, the lighting man, Nick Chelton. But it is interesting to consider the value of the plays more closely before leaving them for the West End transfer that must inevitably await them.

The fact that they fit together so ingeniously that they could, given enough room and enough stagehands, be played simultaneously by a single cast is more than a mere curiosity. Though each piece is a perfect work of art, the three form a serial of an original kind, in which the entire story is presented not in three consecutive instalments but in three instalments that show the same sequence of events from different angles, and by doing so add something each time to our knowledge of the characters and their motives.

Mr Ayckbourn's choice of middle-class domestic trivia for his experiment doesn't mean that there is anything unimportant about it. The domestic trivia of his middle-class families are material as valid as the trivia of Molière's middle-class families, or Congreve's, and the observation of family ties in *The Norman Conquests* seems to be no less important (or funny) than that in *George Dandin* or *L'Ecole des maris*.

Comedy rivals tragedy throughout the history of drama (and indeed Mr Hovhannes Pilikian wants us to believe that Sophocles' and Euripides' tragedies were really meant to be played as farces). When serious social commentary is involved, comedy is frequently the chosen medium, as in *The Recruiting Officer* or *The Inspector General*. Social commentary is not as it happens a major factor in Ayckbourn, but it is clear from *Time and Time Again* and *Absurd Person Singular* that it could be if he wanted it.

Mr Ayckbourn's dramatic technique in his chosen field is unrivalled at the moment. As is generally known by now, the three *Norman Conquests* plays were composed together, the three scripts laid out side by side. In *How the Other Half Loves* Mr Ayckbourn out-Goldoni's Goldoni by presenting simultaneously two scenes taking place at different times. His scripts are as full of scrupulously detailed specification as Feydeau's. They use few of the clichés of farce, they do not depend on seasoning with epigrams, they do not call for star performances.

They are situation comedy of the highest and most valuable quality, and some of our theatrical whizz-kids, with their apparent belief that audiences must defer to them, not they to the audience, would do well to study them. But if all this suggests that Mr Ayckbourn's work is intellectual, let me say as plainly as I can that his plays, among which *The Norman Conquests* rate very highly, are as accessible and enjoyable as any I can think of over the last 20 years.

(From: B.A. Young, *The Financial Times*, 7 June, 1974)

The Trilogy

The three comedies that constitute Alan Ayckbourn's remarkable trilogy can, according to their author's programme note, 'be seen in any order since, like a three-ended ball of string, it doesn't really matter where you start to unravel'. I wish he hadn't said that. I was beguiled into a reckless belief in the impossible.

Ayckbourn's accomplishment, in making three separate hilarious entertainments from precisely the same set of events and circumstances, is masterly enough without his contention that there is any such thing as a three-ended ball of string. There is a fourth end in there somewhere, the last to come to light. Ayckbourn produces it in the last scene of the third play, *Round and Round the Garden*, and I suspect that it does matter, very much, that this play (which goes on slightly beyond the time when *Table Manners* and *Living Together* have finished) should not be seen before the other two. For one thing there is its small but vital extension of the events with which all three are concerned; and for another, its opening scenes are really not very funny in themselves but only become so through foreknowledge of the characters involved in them. Anyone lacking this foreknowledge might well be as confused as you unquestionably are by this review which, as a sort of demonstration, I have begun at the wrong end.

I thus appreciate your difficulty, not really quite grasping the idea of this unique trilogy. John Hopkins, I believe, wrote a highly acclaimed set of plays for television in which the same situation was explored, successively, from the viewpoint of each of the people who figured in it. That, however, is an approach with far more scope, allowing variations in such matters as motive, characterisation and dramatic development. Ayckbourn varies none of these elements, but only the settings – successively, the dining room, living room and garden of a modest, vicarage-type house in the country – in which the situation reveals and resolves itself; and in his thrice-told tale he allows himself, making his feat the more astonishing, a minimum of complications. . . .

There isn't a happy ending in sight for anyone. Emotionally, the plays, like love, are a package deal of pleasure and pain, but no one is left actually bleeding and it is the pleasure that lingers in memory, along with the perfection of the ensemble playing under Eric Thompson's direction (I would not easily forgive a single change in the cast when the plays move, as they must, to the West End), and the joy of savouring Ayckbourn's comic craftsmanship.

(From: Kenneth Hurren, *The Spectator*, 15 June, 1974)

Alan Ayckbourn's *Absurd Person Singular* was set in three separate kitchens on three successive Christmas Eves; and his leading lady, no less an authority on comedy than Sheila Hancock, nicely declared the other day that a bathroom or even a bathroom cupboard wouldn't constrain a writer of his resourcefulness. Well, he hasn't taken his dramatic hide-and-seek that far in *The Norman Conquests*, but he's getting warmer. The first play of the trilogy is, so to speak, narrated by the dining room, the second by the sitting room, and the third (which we've yet to see) by the garden porch; and all cover the same fraught but funny weekend. Let me quickly make the necessary introductions. Annie (Felicity Kendal), Reg (Mark Kingston) and Ruth (Penelope Wilton) are siblings: Annie looks after their aged, nasty and so far invisible mother, and is tweedily courted by tongue-tied Tom (Michael Gambon); Reg is married to bossy Sarah (Penelope Keith), Ruth to feckless Norman (Tom Courtenay). What turns this from a family tree into a play, and from one play into three, is Norman's attempt to lure Annie away for a dirty weekend in East Grinstead. Sarah, who fancies Norman herself, talks Annie out of the trip with a fine show of moral indignation; and the clan is left to contemplate its treacheries, jealousies and half-recognised ennui over the coffee cups and home-made wine.

There's discomfort in the farce, though it feels less prickly than *Absurd Person Singular*, which showed a petit-bourgeois property speculator achieving wealth and status while more educated and genteel people gradually lost both, hitting both the bottle and the bottom by the final curtain. The subject there was social mobility, and this time Mr Ayckbourn has nothing so topical to exercise his wit. If his characters were to interest the sociologists at all, it would be as case-studies for that burgeoning sub-branch of the industry known as victim-ology. As in *Absurd Person* and the earlier *Time and Time Again*, he tends to divide them into two categories, those who exploit and those who are exploited, with scarcely a murmur from the middle ground between. The most absolute victim in *The Norman Conquests* is probably Reg, who dances attendance in a natty blazer, genially admitting to thinking that 'if no-one told me what to do, I'd never do anything at all'; but the one who mainly demands our attention (and probably our concern) is Annie. Miss Kendal saunters through the part with casual but touching bravado: a girl whose recent history has consisted of taking medicine to the hag upstairs, being neglected by her boyfriend, patronised by her relatives and had on the sitting-room rug by her brother-in-law. Her future seems scarcely less bleak, judging by the first two plays. It could be, of course, that doggy Tom will propose at the end of *Round and Round the Garden*; but I hope not. Mr Ayckbourn might try to pass that off as a happy ending, and a happy ending would neutralise what is, at best, a pretty acid account of the loving British family.

(From: Benedict Nightingale, *New Statesman*, 31 May, 1974)

The Beast
Snoo Wilson
November 1974   The Place

Nothing in Wilson's hands is totally dull, though. He cares little for consistency; he will introduce a comic line in any genre, even one borrowed from another author, if it will attract our attention.
(From: B.A. Young, *The Financial Times*, 19 November, 1974)

The Beast . . . with such gifted players as Richard Pasco, Brenda Bruce, Tony Church and Rosemary McHale among the nonplussed personnel, strikes me as the sort of thing they should leave to the remoter outposts of the 'fringe', where tastes are notoriously as indulgent as they are bizarre . . . as aimless and trivial as it is dreary.
(From: Kenneth Hurren, *The Spectator*, 30 November, 1974)

The trouble is, of course, that a dreary subject makes for a dreary evening, in spite of Mr Wilson's undoubted flair with words. . . But what's the object of it all? To remind us, yet again, of the supposed banality of evil? Or suggest that 'evil' is really psychosis, and a bit pathetic? Or, perhaps, show the sterility of seeking revolutionary answers in either sex or astrology, as many now do? I left The Place feeling that someone had been endlessly sniffing around the bottom of my trousers; but why, I could not tell.
(From: Benedict Nightingale, *New Statesman*, 22 November, 1974)

Mountaineer, Swinburnian versifier, journalist, magician: these are some of the authenticated masks of Aleister Crowley before we even get to the legends (Dylan Thomas claimed to have seen him sitting on the surface of his own bath water). But whatever one's idea of 'The Great Beast' it is a shock to see him dancing on, wearing a kilt and tam o'shanter (with attached toupé) to an accompaniment of 'Swanee' from a posse of Belgian gendarmes.

Brutal vaudeville has cropped up in earlier plays by Snoo Wilson, but never more appropriately than here. It is easy to put Crowley down as a self-publicizing mountebank until you move in close; then those eyes start making their effect. And in any case, his life was too public, too single-minded, and too long to amount to no more than confidence trickery.

If you want some explanation for the sources of his obsession, Mr Wilson supplies it by citing his Plymouth Brethren childhood, where the creation of the world in 4004 BC corresponds to the dating of the new age from his magical transcription of the 'Thelematic' Law in 1904, and from Crowley's attachment to the Golden Dawn movement in the nineties. Lacking the literary talents of Yeats and company, he moved into the role of omniscient mage, and lingered on until the 1940s as the ultimate and most spectacularly dilapidated instance of *fin de siècle* decadence.

Mr Wilson, however, is not a reductive writer; he wants to recreate Crowley, not to explain him away. And to that task he brings a cinematic skill in story-telling, and a talent for grand-scale grotesque effect which never wholly parts company from common human feelings.

(From: Irving Wardle, *The Times*, 19 November, 1974)

1975

There is a sense, engendered by reading the notices of the most lauded theatrical event of the year – Pinter's No Man's Land – of relief. This is occasioned by the fact that the huge excellence of John Gielgud's and Ralph Richardson's acting and the absolute requirement that it should be suitably celebrated critically, seems to have convinced the majority of reviewers that they were absolved from attempting to explain the play, to justify it, even to understand it. The acting was enough and, after all, Pinter was an actor's playwright – a near aphorism that gradually almost became a convenient cliché.

In a sense the reviewers were right. These two performers outshone anything else in the theatre of that year. They remind us, in a very timely way, that the sixties and seventies, whatever the vicissitudes of playwrights, were marked by the glory of great and good acting by more individuals than in any other era in the British theatre, except perhaps the last decade of the sixteenth, and the first of the seventeenth centuries.

While noting this, it is justice to record the extent and quality of the critics' recognition of this histrionic greatness. They do not strut, they often, indeed, wax lyrical and perceptive about the acting that flourished in their midst. It was, indeed, a fine time to go to a first night.

One wonders, in fact, whether the second significant event in the theatrical year – Trevor Griffiths's Comedians – wasn't watered and sustained by the same source. The acting of Jonathan Price, Jimmy Jewel, Ralph Nossek seems now to have dominated the reviews – though Robert Cushman is typically and refreshingly sceptical. Yet it is not No Man's Land but Comedians which has entered into the pantheon of amateur repertory – the sure sign of acceptance which needs only 'O' or 'A' level recognition to give it a blue riband. It is very difficult, reading the reviews, to estimate what the critics really thought of the plays in a comparative assessment. Benedict Nightingale, as usual, dives deepest, but even he gives evidence of perilous swimming in waters where it is difficult to know whether he is waving with assurance or drowning in perturbation.

Comedians
Trevor Griffiths
February 1975   Nottingham Playhouse

Trevor Griffiths is not the most waggish and carefree of
contemporary dramatists; and, on the face of it, it's as odd that he
should set a play in a school for comedians as it would be if Brian
Rix set a farce in a school for urban guerrillas. But he is, of
course, after something more than our laughter. Among other
things, he wants us to think about the social function of humour
itself. . . .

At times he's surely too solemn and severe; but often he is, of
course, perfectly right. Who still thinks it funny to hear of
Irishmen recovering their good spirits on being told they're too
sick ever to work again, or someone publishing a book called *The
Wit and Wisdom of the Irish: 20 Years of Social Security*? These are
what the teacher of the class irrefutably calls 'stereotype' jokes:
glib lies designed to buy the audience's favour by pimping for its
prejudices. In his view, good comedians tell benign and healing
truths about things that worry or frighten their listeners. They
relieve tension, undermine bigotry. 'Comedy is medicine,' he
declares, 'not coloured sweeties to rot the teeth with.' I must admit
that, for all my happy memories of his radio shows with Ben
Warris, these opinions didn't instantly put me in mind of Jimmy
Jewel. But he it is who materialises in suit and tie at Nottingham
Playhouse, to prowl around the desks, cite Freud and gently
harangue his budding Dodds and Morecambes about the affection due to their audiences. He does it all pretty well, too, though
with a face so chalky and glum he could use it to scribble a suicide
note on the classroom blackboard.

What mainly upsets him is the arrival of an old professional
enemy, played with a sort of breezy slyness by Ralph Nossek. He's
there to evaluate six pupils on behalf of the London agents; and
it's soon clear that he regards comedians primarily as commercial
travellers, taking canned and cartoned jokes from club to club.
'Escape' is what people want and must be given. 'I'm not looking
for philosophers,' he tells the boys, 'I'm looking for comics.' So
two of them promptly salt their acts with cracks about indolent
blacks, nagging wives and insatiable mistresses, and are accepted
onto the agents' books. Three others stick more or less to their
principles, and are rejected. That leaves one, a very long, thin,
shiny-headed young man, a kind of human harpoon, played by
Jonathan Pryce. He disguises himself as a football hooligan, hoists
a couple of nattily-dressed dummies onstage, and proceeds to
insult and threaten them: a performance of such venom that both
Nossek and Jewel are appalled.

So there it is. We'd been beginning to suppose there was no third alternative to humour-as-therapy and humour-as-product; and now Mr Pryce gives us one, humour-as-scourge or humour-as-bomb. Audiences aren't to be soothed, sentimentalised, or contemptuously exploited: they're to be relentlessly radicalised with shouts of 'there's people would call this envy, it's not, it's *hate*'. Now, this may be fine in principle; but I have two objections to the way Mr Griffiths sees it in practice. First, the bitterness he thrusts into Mr Pryce's curled mouth isn't very funny. In fact, it isn't funny at all. Second, it seems inconsistent, to say the least, to condemn 'category-jokes' about Jews, Irishmen and women while positively welcoming them when they're about the middle class, upper class, or whatever the two dummies are supposed to represent. Not all well-dressed people are bland and snobbish, any more than all Scots are mean or all Italians lecherous. Prejudice seems to me no better for coming from the Left rather than the Right. In fact, it is worse, since we look to the Left to break barriers, build bridges, and do all those things which will eventually produce a man who is 'sceptreless, free, unencumbered, equal, classless, tribeless and nationless'.
(From: Benedict Nightingale, *New Statesman*, 28 February, 1975)

By a pleasing irony the only prominent character not required to perform as a stand-up comic is played by the only actor who actually was one; Jimmy Jewel brings off beautifully the business of presenting a tired man without seeming merely limp, showing us without actually doing anything, through his warm, cracked voice and seamed, kind face, a battered but indomitable strength within. Opposite him, too, Ralph Nossek draws a neat sharp portrait of the agent, himself a former comic, who has put himself entirely at the service of showbiz as a commercial machine ('We're not missionaries, we're suppliers of laughter') – no villain, quite a decent chap really, his beaky, flash-hatted ruthlessness reflecting efficiency rather than spite.

And snarling among the rest of the aspirant comics like a cheetah among tabby kittens Jonathan Pryce's Gethin makes Max von Sydow and Nicol Williamson look and sound like the Cheeryble Brothers. (Why are near-psychotic characters in today's British theatre practically always represented as, or by, Welshmen?) In a spectacular role Mr Pryce gives a spectacular performance, and much more.

Tall, beanpole thin, hollow-cheeked, black hair cropped to a Mephistophelian peak, ranging the stage like an athlete limbering up, freezing into an icicle with electric eyes, Mr Pryce's Gethin speaks, I suspect, in every angry gesture and inflection, in every raging quiver, for Mr Griffiths' *idée fixe*; but then Mr Griffiths' humanity has seen to it that this would-be laser-beam aimed at existing society doesn't win the day. Gethin's idea of a comic turn is desperately chilling, his barely controlled, racked personality virtually disintegrates, until a temporary reprieve, along with his flailing limbs before our very eyes. Here, stunningly projected, is yet another anti-hero, yes; but much the most interesting since Jimmy Porter hit us between the eyes.

(From: J.W. Lambert, *The Sunday Times*, 23 February, 1975)

Two decades ago, in *The Entertainer*, John Osborne was content to plant the dying music hall on the stage before us and trust to its power as an image. Mr Griffiths tries something more disturbing; the tradition he explores is, for better or worse, still alive. The implication of the play is that it is very much for worse; Mr Griffiths is far more concerned than was Mr Osborne with the quality of laughter. Nobody found Archie Rice funny; it was almost his dramatic point that he played to tiny audiences who were only there for the nudes. But whatever the individual quality of Mr Griffiths's jesters, the breed they aspire to join is flourishing.

Their medium is one-line quick-change patter; the man from London castigates one aspirant for maintaining continuity in his material. People get bored, and they do not want to be burdened with a comic's individuality. So, goes the advice, fire your shots from as many angles as possible, but always at the same targets. We are now a multi-racial society, and afraid of it, so racist jokes go down well; if an anti-Irish joke is told by an Irishman, the savour, so long as he does not so to speak harp on it, is all the sweeter. We can even congratulate him and ourselves on our sportsmanship. We profess to be liberated about sex and are even more afraid of that; so jokes that manage to be both risqué and evasive – elaborate euphemisms – are also in order.

Within his own terms, the visitor offers brilliant analyses of the turns presented to him, and the excellence of the writing and acting (by Ralph Nossek) of this role is matched by that of his subjects; one may not agree with his judgment of them, but one can see what has prompted it in each case. Richard Eyre's direction of the various comics can hardly be faulted, and several of the performances are memorable: Dave Hill an engaging loser, Stephen Rea a coruscating winner, and, in a category of his own, Jonathan Pryce.

Mr Pryce looks and snarls like an emanciated Nicol Williamson; he is lankier, nearly as powerful, and more controlled. His nose is long and sharp, his death's head shaven, his face, when he does his routine, white, and his body trim and grotesquely flexible. He plays the one clown who rebels, breaks taboos, and dredges up the undertow of all the other acts. He brings on two prosperously dressed cut-out figures and attacks them: 'It's not envy, it's hate.' His punchline is 'National Unity: Up yours, sunshine.' He naturally disgusts the agent (who has exhorted this crew of pawky or abrasive northerners to emulate Max Bygraves, the archetype of southern blandness) and shocks the old pro instructor who cautions that 'if you hate your audience, you'll end up hating yourself.'

Mr Pryce seems to me to prove him right (I didn't like his act much, either). But I hesitate to draw definite conclusions, since the scene in which they thunder out their differences, though powerful in a generalised way, is muddy. The acoustics of the Playhouse are unkind to unfocused rhetoric and Jimmy Jewel, though he looks suitably careworn, is over-ingenious casting for the teacher.

Trevor Griffiths has, on this showing, written another impenetrably private play on a public theme; but one worth following as far as possible. He is, when he chooses, a very funny writer; while his protagonists knock themselves out for laughs, his minor characters effortlessly achieve them. A school caretaker (Richard Simpson) looks disapprovingly on, a bingo caller (John Joyce) stolidly announces the acts that have so rudely interrupted the real business of his evening, and a passing Pakistani (Talat Hussain), telling an adapted Jewish joke, wraps up the racial theme on which Mr Griffiths has played inventive variations throughout.

(From: Robert Cushman, *The Observer*, 23 February, 1975)

No Man's Land
Harold Pinter
April 1975   Old Vic

Pinter-fanciers will have a great time with this. The piece will be debated again and again; its non-sequiturs, its catalogues, its false alarms, its fantasies, its conversation at cross-purposes, its elaborated jokes, its obliquities, its anecdotes, its deeply impaired style.

Yes, but does it really matter, and what will it be like when actors without the clear theatrical genius of Gielgud and Richardson take over the parts, and there is no Peter Hall to direct. . . . One has a suspicion, almost a certainty, that these plays, for all their top-dressing of style, are fast becoming clichés themselves.

(From: J.C. Trewin, *Birmingham Post*, 24 April, 1974)

[One actor is in a tree] a telescope to his eyes and a fiendish grin across his five o'clock shadow, watching the animals as they paw the ground, butt, tussle, and chase one another off limits. . . . [The other] is at the tiny rococo table, a glass of Pernod on his left, the works of Proust in a dainty pile on his right, his nose twitching at old evocative smells and a sad, woozy smile on his face as he dreams of times past, times remembered, times not quite remembered and times all but forgotten.

(From: Benedict Nightingale, *New Statesman*, 2 May, 1975)

The last time we saw John Gielgud and Ralph Richardson together they were keeping each other company in David Storey's *Home*. In Harold Pinter's *No Man's Land* (Old Vic) they appear to be in Sir Ralph's home; Sir John has been invited in for a drink.

Sir Ralph plays a wealthy and successful literary man named Hirst, Sir John an extremely seedy one called Spooner. The contrast is piquant; we are used to seeing Richardson on the skids (and as this evening wears on he does take some tremendous alcoholic falls), and Gielgud aloof and dominant. Sir John's new role inspires in him some brilliant variations on his familiar stage persona. His suit and his face are equally crumpled; what with the faded pin-stripes of the one and the furrows and wrinkles of the other, the actor wears as many lines as he speaks. But there remains a certain jauntiness, and the mellifluous voice has taken on a plaintiveness that makes it if anything more persuasive.

As a house-guest uncertain of how long his welcome will last, Spooner needs persuasiveness. His situation strongly recalls that of Davies, the intrusive cuckoo-tramp of *The Caretaker*. Like Davies, he finds his tenure of his new premises threatened by prior occupants. Hirst already retains a spiv and a thug (antique but useful terms) beneath his roof and their demeanour towards Spooner is not welcoming. . . .

Altogether Spooner must rank in Gielgud's performance among Mr Pinter's finest creations. Hirst, despite Sir Ralph's massive presence, may prove less memorable, but each has been neatly deposited at his own station (on the Northern Line). From Chalk Farm, where Spooner earns a crust by clearing pub tables, to Hampstead, where Hirst exists as a Beckettian recluse with added alcohol, is a short but steep ascent. . . .

But there is, unfortunately, more to it than that. Mr Pinter's titles are a good index to the progress of his art: once they referred to characters, objects or events, now to abstractions. *No Man's Land* may denote the area of ground – Hirst's house – in which the characters are struggling to gain or retain a footing. (Mr Pinter's plays are frequently described as territorial battles. The description holds good, as it does – drama being conflict and stages spaces – for most plays.) But when the phrase actually occurs in the dialogue it is used of a state of mind: a sense of time having ceased and all memories having jelled into a single immovable instant.

Pinter has treated of this instant before; the irony is that he defined it most clearly in *Silence*, a play which, however interesting philosophically, proved dramatically unsatisfactory and possibly unworkable. The references in *No Man's Land*, though climatically placed, are self-contained globules, failing to connect with the personal conflict that occupies us elsewhere. So what might have been a synthesis of the two main currents in his work looks more like a frayed re-hash. Certainly the two minor characters, despite Michael Feast's whinnying smoothness and Terence Rigby's threatening grunts, are like ghosts of more substantial figures in earlier plays. When Hirst remarks that he would like to change the subject 'for the last time,' they hold him to it. There will be no alteration in the *status quo*; and the play is resolved on a metaphysical quibble.

But the language yields much pleasure; among other things it amusingly characterises Spooner as a minor-league Eliot, parodying the *Four Quartets* ('now and in England and in Hampstead and for all eternity') and pronouncing sternly-rhymed judgment as Hirst makes a drunken exit on all fours ('I have known this before. The exit through the door, by way of belly and floor'). Peter Hall delivers his usual (in these circumstances) impeccable production and benefits, again as usual, from a stylish enclosure of a setting designed by John Bury. (Future title for a Pinter play: *Buried Alive*.).

(From: Robert Cushman, *The Observer*, 27 April, 1975)

The essence of Gielgud's performance is its contrast between high and low status behaviour. Dressed in crumpled pin-stripes, he speaks in stiltedly bookish English; and, when under attack, withdraws into hooded disdainful silence like a moulting eagle. Left alone, he instantly starts filching handfuls of cigarettes; but when one of the roughs serves him a champagne breakfast, he takes it in his stride with the supercilious inquiry, 'Is it cold?'

In this performance, the character has a consistent life. Whether this would appear from the text is another matter, as there are striking incongruities. In his dialogue, for instance, Spooner seems pure Georgian, but when he goes into verse soliloquy, it is pastiche Eliot.

Nor do the Eliot echoes end there. Like the mazes and rose gardens invoked by that poet and others of his generation, the play seeks to locate spiritual malaise in some concrete image, and fails to find one. Even Terence Rigby, as one of the servants, gets involved in this pursuit with a speech about finding an elusive street. At one time, that would have been a cue for one of Pinter's virtuoso idiomatic rifts; now the language is heavy, and straining towards wider significance. The feeling, in general, is that having located his territory and got to know its inhabitants, Pinter is now trying to extract meaning from them.

He also seems to know his own rules too well. Mr Rigby tells an improbable tale about his first meeting with the other servant; then remarks: 'His story would be different'. Formerly we would have had the alternative story from Michael Feast, without knowing comments. Nor is it any surprise when Richardson, having brought in Spooner as a down-and-out and then disowned him, strides on with outstretched hand, booming, 'Charles! How nice of you to drop in.'

Another literary presence is Beckett, never more insistent in Pinter than in this play. Richardson's Hirst, immobile in his chair and relentlessly gulping whiskies amid lines like, 'Somebody's doing me a death', and, 'I am sitting here for ever', is a direct echo of Hamm calling for his painkiller in *Endgame*.

No Man's Land remains palpably the work of our best living playwright in its command of language and its power to erect a coherent structure in a twilight zone of confusion and dismay. And it receives a production of burnished precision from Peter Hall, who, as in the past, excels in resolving this author's ambiguities in a flowing dramatic line; and exploiting John Bury's semi-circular windowed set, both as a sunlit refuge and an inescapable cell. The play makes its effects with total confidence: the objection is that effect has been raised into a first priority.

(From: Irving Wardle, *The Times*, 24 April, 1975)

1976

In 1976 two kinds of drama new to the British tradition established themselves. They were (not in order of importance); what has been called the 'second angry wave', and the drama of woman's liberation written by women.

By the 1980s the second angry wave had become absolutely established as a dominant feature of British drama But in 1976 its harbinger was David Edgar. He and his contemporaries (for example, Brenton, Snoo Wilson, Poliakoff, Halliwell) seemed determined to write plays which eschewed charm and humour, and completely rejected the notion of drama as an escapist excuse to anaesthetise the theatre-goer from the increasingly arduous features of everyday existence. Indeed, on the contrary, Edgar's Destiny and others were only too concerned to disturb the uneven tenor of many people's lives even more, in a society rapidly dividing itself into irreconcilable ideological, political and economic segments. This drama is often bad-tempered, irrational in its proselytising, careless of form and language and grimly sincere in the assertion of its commitment to ameliorating or revealing the ills of society. Theatregoing, after 1976, often became a kind of obstacle race, as the theatregoing was battered by the insistent puritanism (because this is, in a sense, what it amounted to) of the new wave. Some critics welcomed it, others were wary, some were hostile, but it could not be ignored because there was so much of it and because it was, so to say, very noisy. Its chief virtue was its sincerity, its chief vices its uncontrolled excess, its intellectual exaggeration, its emotional waywardness. Destiny is a good example of it, and Edgar one of the best exponents.

Women's Lib cracked out of its egg and made its first really audible cry in the accents of Pam Gems' Dusa, Fish, Stas and Vi. The reviews indicate that the critics didn't quite know what to make of it. Michael Coveney kept his balance best, but most of the others faltered and fumbled.

From 1976 the ferocious convictions of Women's Lib – which in some later plays, by Pam Gems and, notably, Olwen Wymark, were tempered by a thoughtful sensibility – existed side by side with the equally ferocious sincerity of the second angry wave, whose height and force was increased by the baleful weight of Edward Bond. In fact, from 1976 it has been a tough time for theatregoers – they have increasingly been asked, sometimes *explicitly, to participate in the author's wallowing preoccupation with what he or she deems to be an inimical society. Indeed, one never knew, especially with the growth of Studio theatre, when one's innocent visit to a new play was going to end in a seatless, demanding, uncomfortable, embarrassingly active participation in some piece whose author was not only determined to castigate society but also to break the mould of theatre presentation. From 1976 the whole notion of what we mean by a theatrical performance began to be questioned. It may turn out (for the process goes on) to be a new beginning — or it may be the chaos of an ending.*

Destiny
David Edgar
September 1976   The Other Place

David Edgar is a man who puts his boots on to go play writing and he requires his audience to do the same ... for all its documentary qualities it (*Destiny*) is a hate-filled piece.
(From: Irving Wardle, *The Times*, 29 September, 1976)

... the first play I have seen to deal in detail with the workings of the extreme Right wing in Britain today ... easily the most mature work yet to be given us.
(From: Michael Billington, *The Guardian*, 29 September, 1976)

The surprise here is that Mr Edgar presents blinkered and racist arguments with such conviction that his play would be, I am sure, cheered to the echo in all the industrial centres of Britain. Perhaps the expression of extreme points of view comes easily to him; and as one of his more or less left-wing characters exclaims of the other side, 'It's just like looking in a mirror'.
(From: J.C. Lambert, *The Sunday Times*, 3 October, 1976)

David Edgar's *Destiny* is a wide-ranging examination of the far Right in Britain now. It begins simply, with the independence of India, whose returning British troops furnish Mr Edgar with many of his main characters; and it ends simplistically. But what comes between is astonishingly complex; no play of this generation has had so powerful a sense of the criss-crossing of ideologies. 'Drop the wog-bashing and it could be *Tribune*,' complains a *National* Socialist of the manifesto drawn up by a National *Socialist*.

The man for whom they have least time is the local Conservative, whose Labour opponent is brought by his wife to realise that racism cannot be laughed away; it exists in unfanatical British minds. A Left activist looks at a Right, and reports that it was like looking in a mirror. The spirit, and the peculiar passion of the play are crystallised by an old officer who speaks of the terrible moment 'when you realise you have more regard for your enemies than those you view as friends'.

This speech, which is nearly crushed by tears, is the crown of a superb ramrod-spirited performance by Michael Pennington. Bob Peck as a Fascist visionary and Ian McDiarmid as a Fascist dupe add to their already remarkable records. Ron Daniels's production gives sharp and solid reality to a script short on human detail and even sometimes on narrative, but brilliantly adept in scenes of debate, manipulation and intellectual shock.

(From: Robert Cushman, *The Observer*, 3 October, 1976)

Dusa, Fish, Stas and Vi
Pam Gems
December 1976   Hampstead Theatre

. . . for all its fashionable trappings, we have seen a play which falls squarely within the category labelled by male chauvinist pigs as women's fiction.
(From: Frank Marcus, *The Sunday Telegraph*, 12 December, 1976)

What matters is that the play pulsates with humanity.
(From: John Peter, *The Sunday Times*, 12 December, 1976)

It's reasonable to expect (designed, acted, costumed, directed by women) that such a production will tell us something about what women are thinking today, and I have an awful fear that it does.
(From: Ted Whitehead, *The Spectator*, 18 December, 1976)

I believed in Miss Gems's characters, though I wasn't always sure of her purpose in introducing them to us.
(From: Benedict Nightingale, *New Statesman*, 17 December, 1976)

Pam Gems is an avowedly feminist playwright or, to put it more accurately, she writes passionately for actresses. Here we have four characters, glorying in the names of the above title, sorting their lives out in a communal flat. Dusa (Brigit Forsyth) is lately divorced and her ex-husband has made off with the children to foreign parts; Fish (Alison Fiske) has a heavy number for Rosa Luxembourg but is sexually dependent on men, for all her suede shoes and dufflecoats; Stas (Diane Fletcher) is an extremely sexy high-class whore with a straight line in brain-damaged children; and little Vi (Mary Maddox) is into quality dope, meditation and joss-sticks.

If the West End can have its plays about middle-class marital tribulations there is certainly room for so fresh and accurately written a piece as this. Not since David Hare's *Slag* have we seen a play that really digs into the lives of women living together and, although Pam Gems is enormously flattered by the brilliance of Nancy Meckler's direction, there is no denying the tough urgency of what she has to say about girls under one roof.

Men come into it, of course, but they do so even more effectively for remaining unseen. For, above all else, the play insists that to live alone as a woman is to live as a second-class citizen. Stas wants to specialise in marine biology in Hawaii and has to whore to get there; Fish was married briefly to 'some gink' but has left him and spies on her new man's girlfriends before taking reckless action; Dusa is a born mother but silly enough to suggest she may be wrong; Vi needs hospitalisation before she enters hilariously employed as a traffic warden ('I hate cars').

But there is a physical dimension to the show that is, in itself, remarkable. The designer, Tanya McCallin, is rapidly becoming the queen of antiseptic chic and her apartment is lavishly white, beautifully proportioned and somehow bigger than it should be. A clothes cupboard, essential to the play, becomes an excitingly lit Aladdin's cave. And Lindy Hemming's costumes are a continual delight both in themselves and in the way they are worn. There is some pleasant sound dressing courtesy of Capital Radio with Cyril Fletcher on gardening and Jackie Stewart on seat-belts. One day Pam Gems will write a really excellent play; but she may never get a better production.

(From: Michael Coveney, *The Financial Times*, 9 December, 1976)

1977

In some sense Abigail's Party *is the characteristic play of the seventies. It is an emblem of permissiveness – a way of life, behaviour and habit spawned in the sixties and nurtured during the following decade. Permissiveness lies at the play's heart and it survives on impulse circulated by improvisation.*

Few arts can be more permissive than the play which is sketchy in preparation and relies heavily on spontaneous contributions from individual actors. Form, design, theme, language, plot, character, are at the mercy of instant response. Mick Leigh, the 'chairman', as it were, of the improvised sessions out of which Abigail's Party *emerged, is a sensitive specialist in, and, one guesses, exercises careful artistic discipline on, a mode dedicated to 'spontaneity'. He was able to produce a sense of immediacy, of stark actuality, of tingling energy. In this work, improvisation strikes hard and keen, but the reviews clearly show that it leaves absolutely nothing behind, after all its unpredictabilities and its vivid incandescence – like Bengal matches flaring up, only to end as charred sticks.*

Alan Bennett (The Old Country) *entered the affections of theatre-goers at a very early point in his career, and has never been ousted. This does not help assessment, for between the critic and the object, lie the allurements of Bennett's zany, vulnerable television personality – a kind of winsome but cheeky mole – and the mixture of parody, sentimentality and a kind of muted patriotism which sounds quietly in his plays. To a few he was and is anathema – the play 'never really extricates itself from the conventional sludge that has been holding it up. . .' (B.A. Young), but the majority greeted what became a very popular play with enthusiasm, and reminded us that plays often survive not because they possess certain excellences, but because some appealing aura surrounding the author predisposes audiences to sympathy and acceptance.*

1977

Abigail's Party
Mike Leigh
April 1977   Hampstead Theatre

. . . he has given improvisation a good name and removed it from the realm of nebulous theory and special pleading.

(From: Nicholas de Jongh, *The Guardian*, 23 April, 1977)

. . . gets stuck on a grim plateau of social mannerism that completely neglects the heart of the matter . . . this is behaviourist drama without compassion or insight.

(From: Victoria Radin, *The Observer*, 1 May, 1977)

'The show is not the show, but those who go'; this week's theatre has provided a most interesting set of variations on that theme, and if you will bear with me, I propose to run through some of them today.

At *Abigail's Party* (Hampstead) an observant playgoer can derive a fascination even deeper than that of the play, which itself has the hypnotic quality said to be exerted by a rattlesnake (though I am happily unable to confirm that traditional ascription from my own experience), by studying the audience. The play (something of a collective effort, its largely improvised construction refined into its present form by Mike Leigh, who also drew up the original scheme) presents an appallingly plausible quartet of monsters, together with what poker-players call a kicker – the one human being, who is also, I think significantly, the one failure as a character. The four are two couples from a newly-affluent suburb ('And God!' as Belloc sang, 'the dreadful things that dwell therein!'); Abigail is entertaining her contemporaries down the road, which is why her mother, the human being, has joined the monsters for an evening of aimlessness: 'We are not *here* to have a conversation' snarls the hostess (a performance of lethal perfection by Alison Steadman) at her husband when he complains about the record-player's volume, 'we are here to *enjoy* ourselves'.

She can say that again; indeed, she does, several times. The whole of one act, and fully three-quarters of the other, consists *entirely* of the fly-blown small-talk of those who have gathered not for conversation but for enjoyment, and are getting none of that, either. Interested in nothing, relating to nothing, touched by nothing, they string together only clichés of response, scraped from the surface of their deadened lives. Very, very slowly, the tension rises, as they flail in unconscious self-hate and project their lack of feeling on each other, and even when death joins the party, the response does not change; the fear, remorse and tears that ensue are without substance or depth. Rightly; people who

224

do not even know they are alive can hardly be expected to notice when others are not.

Horror and pity contend for mastery in one's breast; and that is where the audience I sat among became the actors. For most of them greeted most of the play, line after line, with screams, with howls, with very paroxysms, of mirth and glee. Among exchanges (and I have not excised anything from any of them) that produced such reactions were:

'What kind of business are you in?' – 'Computers'.

'Where do you shop?' – 'Sainsbury's'.

'Would you like another drink?' – 'Yes, please' – 'What would you like?'

Now when uncontrollable laughter, on the edge of hysteria, greets such lines, an explanation is required. And very soon, I realised what it was. The stage had become a mirror, wherein the spectators saw themselves, and did not like what they saw, the recognition being so painful that it had to be walled in by the defence-release of laughter. And what made the experience so extraordinary was that the spark that leaped between actors and audience was a recognition not of the characters' unreal reality – their attachment to objects, their plastic imitation of friendship, their empty minds – but of the deep truth about them, of which all those things were but symptoms.

In organic terms, these people lack roots; in terms of energy, they are unearthed. Their problem is our world's; they are torn loose from history, faith, spirit and even language, because they are torn loose from themselves. Only when they (and they are we) can identify with themselves – not with the chromium-plated egos on show but with the true inner and incorporeal reality that is part of a universal human self – will they be able to abandon these lives of noisy desperation. *Abigail's Party* offers no cure for its characters' sickness, or for the contagion its audience feels; but its diagnosis is faultless.

(From: Bernard Levin, *The Times*, 1 May, 1977)

The Old Country
Alan Bennett
September 1977   Queen's

I felt I should have absorbed most of the play as well by radio.
(From: B.A. Young, *The Financial Times*, 8 September, 1977)

Alan Bennett has written nothing so subtle and powerfully

225

imagined . . . a wise literate play that does honour to our theatre.
(From: J.C. Trewin, *Birmingham Post*, 8 September, 1977)

Bennett's plays have always been marked by an irrepressible gift
for parody underscored by elegiac melancholy. I believe him to be
a theatrical poet whose flair for Betjemanesque decoration keeps
getting in the way. In this piece too, the pendulum swings
between moments of atmospheric incandescence and prolonged
evocations of Ruislip on a dull afternoon. But never has Bennett
found an apter form for the things he does best: Hilary
improvizing a *Times* obituary, or a mock-Buchan Buchan thriller,
or isolating the fatuities of English good manners in the
unlikeliest context.

Built around the theme of repatriation, the action involves two
other couples: a miserable working-class defector who detests his
Russian wife, and Hilary's smart metropolitan sister whose
baronet husband is pulling the strings for Hilary's return. The
plot is well prepared and equipped with a neat sting in the tail, but
at the time you hardly notice it: it supplies just enough
momentum to carry the satire and debate on English values that
are Bennett's main concern.

(From: Irving Wardle, *The Times*, 8 September, 1977)

1978

If ever proof were needed of the main route being followed by dramatists in the seventies, it would be amply provided by two plays of 1978. They were not the best plays, but they were the most characteristic.

The first, **Deeds**, in its multiple authorship – Brenton, Griffiths, Campbell and Hare – emphasises the mutuality of individual estimates of the function of drama. Irving Wardle clearly expresses it – 'the play amounts to an enraged scream of pain from someone at the bottom of the social heap against the forces that allegedly control our lives'. Levin expressed it less gently: there is, he wrote '. . . a depressing unanimity in their striking of the most timidly conformist left-wing attitude. . . .'

Not to put too fine a point on it, a good many of the plays of the younger generation amounted to political and/or ideological propaganda, expressed usually with hard mordant humour and a relentless puritanism.

Artistic delicacy, verbal sensitivity, were not marked characteristics of the 'new' drama. Whitehead (**Spectator**) complained that the second play, Hare's **Plenty** '. . . never quite becomes organic growth'. This is generally true, but because of a remarkable phenomenon, many such plays were presented in an environment which tended to disguise the absence of the customary virtues of dramatic writing. This phenomenon was the swift growth in the seventies of small, low-budget, studio theatres, with the minimum of facilities, and some seating barely a hundred spectators. The proximity of the audience and players, the frequently militant visual and verbal presentation, the absence of sophisticated sets, quickly set up an atmosphere of lean, assured, no-nonsense purposefulness. The effects of propaganda are the greater the nearer the recipients are to the source. The studio theatre ensured that, at last, those who wanted to use drama to incite social action would no longer dissipate their strength in the wide spaces of large comfortable auditoriums which, in any case, were deemed by some dramatists to be elitist mausoleums.

Deeds
Richard Eyre
March 1978   Nottingham Playhouse

. . . a depressing unanimity, in the striking of the most timidly conformist left-wing attitudes. . . Do you suppose they have ever spent half an hour in the company of anyone who disagreed with them?. . . There is only one part not beneath contempt.
(From: Bernard Levin, *The Sunday Times*, 12 March, 1978)

It's an exceptionally powerful, unsettling, funny short play.
(From: Jeremy Treglown, *New Statesman*, 17 March, 1978)

For all its variety of tone and divided authorship, the play amounts to an enraged scream of pain from someone at the bottom of the social heap against the forces that allegedly control our lives: hospitals, MPs, police, giant corporations. One can sympathize with that, but not with the authors' readiness to substitute hatred and contempt for enlightenment. I would like to know the scientific evidence against baby milk: I am not interested to see the fictitious head of a baby milk firm trapped in a bathroom with a couple of call-girls.

I regret this ungenerous response towards the [sic] production as scrupulously considered as Mr Eyre's. Its flow of inset scenes, reduced to solid essentials in John Gunter's sets, supplies the physical appearance of an inexorable cycle of events which the text fails to deliver. An energetically doubling company is led by Mick Ford whose Ken likewise proceeds from innocent shock to missionary obsession without the advantage of clearcut evidence.
(From: Irving Wardle, *The Times*, 10 March, 1978)

It would be idle to pretend the play offers detailed argument and characterisation. It is much more a product of the New Expressionism dealing with essences rather than psychological subtleties, panoramic views rather than private lives. Its weakness is that you feel that one phone call to a newspaper or TV company by its hero would have achieved everything he set out to do and that he himself would have had the shrewdness to realise this. But its great theatrical strength is that it combines a single-minded purpose with a wide angled lens.

And it vividly creates the impression of a society where compassion is always under pressure: a hospital doctor is constantly at the mercy of a bleeping phone, a nurse is too exhausted to help, an MP is more concerned with answering his 300 letters a week than actually achieving change. The scope of the play is quite extraordinary. And, despite the multiple authorship, you feel it drives logically and cohesively to its conclusion: that only direct action can lead to change.

Richard Eyre's production, beautifully designed by John Gunter, is also an astonishingly economic epic: an Eyre, you might say, on a shoe-string. But how remarkably it uses the wide, deep, Nottingham stage so that Hyde Park is evoked through a couple throwing a Frisbee or a prison yard by isolated figures picked out under spotlights. Mick Ford as the hero also has just the right tow haired unyielding obsessiveness and there is good support from Nick le Prevost, Roger Sloman and Ralph Nossek all proving that at Nottingham one man in his time plays many parts. *Deeds* may not be the best play Eyre has done at Nottingham; but the real test of its strength, as Shaw said of *A Dolls House*, will be the work it does in the world.

(From: Michael Billington, *The Guardian*, 10 March, 1978)

Plenty
David Hare
April 1978   National

. . . a good rule when unable to guess what a play is about is to assume that it was not about anything. The suspicion will often prove to be well-founded . . . what does the author want us to think, to feel? Language, story-line, characters, are admirably clear. Stephen Moore, when the curtain rises, is discovered lying stark naked, bum upwards. He then rolls over so that other parts, equally naked, are upwards. There is no explanation anywhere in the play for this striking deshabille, and in view of my oft repeated assertion that the only players ever asked to take their clothes off are the prettier actresses, I suspect that someone is trying to make a fool of me. I warn you, I won't stand for it.

(From: Bernard Levin, *The Sunday Times*, 16 April, 1978)

David Hare is the most brilliant of the young playwrights currently trying to express their disillusion, and consequent desperation, about post-war England . . . he has found a new way of saying this.

(From: John Barber, *The Daily Telegraph*, 15 April, 1978)

. . . beneath the glacially witty dialogue of this play is a dangerous nostalgia and a deep sense of exhaustion, with a patrician-romantic distaste that is thoroughly English in tone. The National production is extremely sumptuous. What better place to hurl

229

subsidised abuse at the ruling class?
(From: Ted Whitehead, *The Spectator*, 22 April, 1978)

Mr Hare has chosen for his subject the eternal favourite of the British theatre, the marital affairs of the middle classes.

He has, of course, treated it in a very individual way. The numerous changes of scene, where Haydn Griffin's designs test the resources of the Lyttleton stage to their limit, and the occasional use of flashback, hint at the film technique that Mr Hare used in his fine television piece, *Licking Hitler*, a rather similar story. And no attempt is made to clear up loose ends. What became of Alice, what became of Brock, what became indeed of Susan, are matters that are left to our imagination. A brief outline of the plot might suggest a play like *Flare Path*: but its only real point of resemblance is the choice of milieu – married life in a Service family.

Mr Hare is his own director, imaginative yet certain. But I found a curious veil lying over the acting for much of the first act. The players, even Kate Nelligan as Susan and Stephen Moore as Brock, speak as if there were no punctuation in their lines. When Susan says 'I want to move on' (she is working in an office and she adds that she wants *desperately* to move on) she uses the empty sound of Garbo's 'I want to be alone'. In the same scene, Brock tells her 'I triple my income. What can I do?' in a tone that puts hyphens between the last five words. As this characteristic is common to Susan and Brock and to Julie Covington's Alice, I take it to be Mr Hare's version of alienation.

Later on it disappears. Miss Nelligan's trips into hysteria are most beautifully graded, at the embarrassing dinner-party with the Ambassador (a beautiful performance by Basil Henson) and the Burmese, and later in the interview with the F.O. where she seeks to speed Brock's promotion and only hastens his resignation. Brock too emerges from his chrysalis, though his special talent, masterfully displayed by Stephen Moore, is diplomatic impassivity in the face of daunting troubles.

Julie Covington's character has the function of a confidante only, but without much to do she projects a vivid personality, proceeding along the drop-out route to social service with occasional aimless lesbian associations. It is characteristic of Mr Hare's writing that such matters drift in and out of the play without comment or consequence. There is little social criticism in the play – the usual mockery of the Diplomatic (usually in the mouths of diplomats), some acid hindsight about Eden's Suez venture. But mostly this is a play about people, not about affairs: and deeply interesting most of them are. I did not descry a false note all evening, apart from Susan's brief reunion with the agent

Lazar at the end. As an examination of the effects of Susan's wartime adventures, it seems to be fascinating.

(From: B.A. Young, *The Financial Times*, 13 April, 1978)

I try to resist the frivolous fancy that David Hare is McCartney to Howard Brenton's Lennon. It's something to do with Hare's apparently effortless passage from portable Theatre and the fringe through the Court to the West End, the BBC and the National. On the way he has developed the patina of the well-made playwright and gained the opportunity, both on stage and on telecine, to direct his own work.

Has this passage been at some cost? Brenton has not been so readily embraced by the establishment. Is he then a lesser writer? Or do his plays bristle more and concede less? At any rate, I sat through *Plenty* with a growing sense of unease. Whilst admiring again the austerity of Hare's technique (which, as in the BBC film *Licking Hitler*, chimes extraordinarily with the austerity of Kate Nelligan's technique), I found the politics of the play, both on its own terms and in the context of the National, incomprehensible. . . .

Plenty is a considerable piece of writing – I wouldn't quote so much from it or worry at its threads if I didn't think so – but the sum is frustrating and perplexing. In a sense it makes me want to seek the happy and stupid and to respond to critical invocations of Rattigan and Osborne with 'well, serve him right'. For if it's a play about England and money and being divorced from political reality then it's not clearly so, it lacks a polemical edge it really needs to cut through. And if it's a portrait of a woman in crisis, then the weight of sympathy is diffuse and so who cares? Whereas *Licking Hitler* was suffused with the virtue of control, *Plenty* seems to suffer the concomitant vice of calculation – there are portentous moments in writing and staging – without the complementary clarity.

Meanwhile, Hare is off in the States on what I suspect will be the crucial year of his career. I have this notion that we'll next hear of him as the author (and perhaps the director) of a Hollywood movie for Faye Dunaway. That would be a rather McCartney thing to do.

(From: Stephen Gilbert, *Plays and Players*, June, 1978)

1979

Two sharply contrasted plays catch the eye in a generally undistinguished year. Cloud Nine by Caryl Churchill was judged by Peter Jenkins to be a 'mere sequence of acting exercises', 'loosely plotted' and its language unable to rise above a 'portentous banality of social, political and philosophical comment'. He concludes with the comforting remark that the evening 'when awful was very very awful but when good was marvellous'. In short we are deep in the territory of the new drama where permissiveness allows dramatic faults and excellences to fall over one another so regularly, as if to make a point that tripping up is a virtue in itself.

On the other hand, Ayckbourn's Joking Apart is the work of a master-craftsman. Of that the critics have no doubt. What seems to worry them all, to a degree, is the puzzle of how seriously to take him. They are agreed that his farcical mode has a harder, even grimmer reality – but few seem to be confident that they have found its nature.

Ayckbourn has remained for some considerable time the darling of the critics. At the beginning of the eighties there was no indication of his losing their approbation and warm respect. One wonders indeed whether this status has been preserved because Ayckbourn as a technician and word-monger has never dropped below a high standard, while all around him his younger contemporaries have fervently clung to the belief that the nearer art is to the inchoate structure and communication of 'real' life the better art it is likely to be. Perhaps the critics have subconsciously recognised the contrast.

Joking Apart
Alan Ayckbourn
March 1979   Globe

As the title may suggest, this is Ayckbourn in his sociological mood again . . . the familiar comic skills flicker across the stage.
(From: B.A. Young, *The Financial Times*, 8 March, 1979)

232

He tells us in his plays more about 'the human condition' than any of the dramatists who have used that irritating cliché pretentiously.

(From: J.C. Trewin, *Birmingham Post*, 8 March, 1979)

Why then the grudging reviews that their [the actors] collective efforts received to date?

In two words, preconception and prejudice. For some, Ayckbourn is a bravura funny-man wilfully denying paid-up audiences their quota of escape. For others, he is simply a commercial farceur with ideas above his station, which is (so to speak) East Cheam and not Waterloo. Well *Joking Apart* seems to me to answer both factions more than adequately. . . In fact, I have a strong suspicion that the play as a whole is his best so far, and that means it is very interesting indeed.

(From: Benedict Nightingale, *New Statesman*, 16 March, 1979)

Here as before we watch 'characteristic' behaviour dissolve, scene by scene. But the being behind behaviour is exposed and real emotion felt after the curtain falls. His sour endings are as satisfying and as necessary to his West End audiences as the happy endings of sentimental comedy once were. His laughing patrons are given intimations of truth without being forced to witness it. That is flair indeed.

(From: Authur Schmidt, *Plays and Players*, April, 1979)

The implications of Alan Ayckbourn's title *Joking Apart* (Globe) is that there comes a point at which the laughing has to stop.

I like it best myself when that moment is deferred for as long as possible: say until the last seconds of the play, as in *Bedroom Farce* when we survey the exhausted, sleepless company and ponder on how rocky their relationships really are. In *Joking Apart* Mr Ayckbourn comes perilously close to telling us instead of letting us find out for ourselves. Perilously close be damned: he *does* tell us.

There are seven principal characters in the play and at its end one of them is laughing uncontrollably. This is not because she has a sunny outlook on life; it is because she is on the wrong kind of pills. Her plight is not unlike that of the wife in *Just Between Ourselves* who declined in catatonia. The implication is that these are doubly shocking events because we have hitherto thought of them as comic characters.

The reason we have thought of them as comic characters is that they are in an Ayckbourn play. If we neglected to read the author's name on the programme, a whole dramatic dimension would be lost. No other playwrights claim special marks for mentioning or dramatising depressive states (which is just as well, as many of them do it all the time). Actually it's unfair to say that he claims them: rather say that the critics insist on awarding them to him.

(From: Robert Cushman, The Observer, 11 March, 1979)

There comes a point in most comic writers' careers when they seem to feel almost guilty at their capacity to make people laugh. Playing for higher stakes, they ease up on the jokes. It happened, I recall, with Neil Simon in an indifferent play about a modern job. And, less alarmingly, Alan Ayckbourn's *Joking Apart* is, as the title indicates, a bid for seriousness. It's an interesting, always enjoyable play. But my own feeling is that Ayckbourn says most about human behaviour, the nearest he comes to downright farce.

In *Joking Apart* the technical high-jinks are kept to a minimum. Admittedly, the play covers a time-span of twelve years in which the characters age from their late twenties to early forties. But Ayckbourn's chief concern is with the unjust distribution of human luck. Richard and Anthea, in whose spacious garden the play is set, are a couple who sail through life surrounded by a halo of good fortune. Their friends and neighbours, whose lives they increasingly dominate with a tyrannical bonhomie, are however all losers gradually reconciling themselves to their own mediocrity and mishap.

Let me say at once that Ayckbourn hits several nails squarely on the head. In *Bedroom Farce* he dealt with the tyranny of the weak. Here he shows the monopolistic destructiveness of the nice and the good.

(From: Michael Billington, The Guardian, 8 March, 1979)

Some people have all the luck and the charm and the talent, and it all sits on them lightly. Others, who fall admiringly under their spell, cannot help a feeling of resentment.

That is all *Joking Apart*, Alan Ayckbourn's new play at the Globe, seems to be about. But it is enough to make this comedy of uncomfortable home truths grate even while we laugh at it.

Although it is amusingly and sharply observed as a study of middle-class suburban jealousy there is something so strangely bland and baleful about the characterisation that it freezes our smiles.

There is no one to whom our hearts can go out more than briefly, and although almost everyone seems to be drawn from life they are drawn perhaps too closely for real fun.

In other words, Mr Ayckbourn here returns to something that came out in *Just Between Ourselves* – the inadvertent tendency of contented and successful people to overlook the pain they may be

causing in others.
(From: Eric Shorter, *The Daily Telegraph*, 8 March, 1979)

Cloud Nine
Caryl Churchill
March 1979   Royal Court

. . . this second half is almost the best thing to arrive in the London theatre this young and dismal year.
(From: Robert Cushman, *The Observer*, 1 April, 1979)

I learnt nothing, I'm afraid. . . If the aim is to show, as the theme song suggests, that any kind of sexual union may be blissful, this is old news by now.
(From: B.A. Young, *The Financial Times*, 30 March, 1979)

What does one call this? A treatise on bisexuality? A view of parents and children? Anyway, it strikes me as superfluous. I am sure members of the versatile Joint Stock Company would be better employed in reading Shaw's preface to *Misalliance* among themselves.

Parents and children certainly, with a variety of sexual sidelines. The first hour, Victorian, is spent in some African area of the far-flung Empire. By this time I would have thought the comic-Empire joke was well over – recent history has hardly suggested any marked improvement since the atlases were revised.

Still, it is unfashionable to think in these terms. One must be fashionable at all costs, especially at the Royal Court. So the dramatist, Caryl Churchill, begins with a full-hearted parody, complete with frustration, hysterics, and perversions. To make it brighter, an effeminate boy is played by an actress and a Victorian wife is played by a man.

In the second half we are as contemporary as we can be, with the comic official who bore the white man's burden (Anthony Sher) now appearing as a peculiarly horrible girl-child.

During this section, where the language is resolutely and tediously uninhibited, the first act mother is now the son and the son the mother. It turns into a wholly muddled fantasy that remains superfluous, though such people – directed by Max Stafford-Clark – as Julie Covington, Carole Hayman and Tony Rohr try their hardest to clear a path through changing and merging identities.
(From: J.C. Trewin, *Birmingham Post*, 30 March, 1979)

235

Joint Stock starts with the acting. The style has become established, almost stylised, but is still quite different to what most
theatre goers are used to seeing. The actors have helped to shape
the characters they are acting, from outside as well as from the
inside; in effect they have helped to write the play. In part the
inspiration was Brechtian, the actor stepping back from the part
and helping the audience to break the spell of theatrical illusion;
partly it derived from an American fashion for acting out
everyday experiences and partly also from a British desire to be
topical and political.

Cloud Nine by Caryl Churchill brings out the virtues and
exposes the vices of the Joint Stock technique. Its most constant
danger is degeneration into a mere sequence of acting exercises,
or cabaret turns, loosely plotted together. The element of
improvisation is liable to take on an air of school-play larkishness
unless the proceedings are structured with a good deal more art
than meets the eye. Another trouble is that however perceptive
and sensitive the performers may be for the purpose of capturing
daily experience or speech they can not be guaranteed to rise
above a portentous banality of social, political and philosophic
comment – but then some of our theatre writers have no need of
the assistance of actors to that end.

Caryl Churchill's play is her second for Joint Stock and is
heavily contrived as a vehicle for the company's and Max
Stafford-Clark's talents. The theme is sex – sex of all manner and
variety – and the perennial hypocrisy towards it.

(From: Peter Jenkins, *The Spectator*, 7 April, 1979)

1980

It is, although accidentally achieved, fitting that the period in review should end with two plays which emblematise so much of what eventually developed – partly from and partly despite – the shifts of mode and changes of motivation of modern dramatic history. Commitments, by Dusty Hughes, who was to emerge later as one of the best-regarded of the younger dramatists, is, as James Fenton remarks, 'a sharp and highly accurate political play'. Its one obvious and saving difference from so many of a similar genre was its sense of humour, and, blessedly, its sense of words. In a minor way it firmly made a point – that the overwhelming pressures of ideological and political theory and sociological rhetoric which characterised so much of the drama of the seventies were capable of being refined by an alert and informed artistic imagination; and that, in the final analysis, there is no incompatibility between artistic finesse and ideological fervour.

Most of the reviews of The Romans are a tacit confirmation of two realities – first, that the stress of permissiveness and the refusal to accept a self-imposed censorship of morality and emotional and verbal taste, by some writers and directors, had become a lamentable feature of the drama of the late twentieth century. If we are remembered for our 'political' plays we may also be remembered for our scatological ones.

Secondly, however, the reviews are a tribute to most of our critics, because they so decidedly condemn what was not only bad morally but also bad art. Throughout the period under review, time and again some critic or other, or a group, have extricated themselves from too slavish an adherence to the wilder lurchings of theatrical modes and gimmicks and have taken a straight unblinking look, writing down what they saw with precise, rational and imaginative integrity.

What The Romans in Britain actually offered, through its dismal, ill-presented, banal and obscene existence, was an opportunity for the critics to reach into their proper selves, to exercise their elusive art and craft, and thus to honour their profession.

Commitments
Dusty Hughes
June 1980   Bush

. . . a sharp and highly accurate political play.
>   (From: James Fenton, *The Sunday Times*, 29 June, 1980)

The play is a still life, but I say this in no adverse way. I found it magnetic to watch the development of these different people through crises.
>   (From: B.A. Young, *The Financial Times*, 24 June, 1980)

Extreme left wing politics are usually a humourless business but Hughes gets some laughs out of his subject.
>   (From: Peter Jenkins, *The Spectator*, 5 July, 1980)

Mr Hughes, who was once *Time Out*'s principal theatre critic and then worked as one of the Bush Theatre's artistic directors, has written a first play which is far more impressive in its establishment of the situation and character than in its development and resolution. The ironic title is the clue to the play's aim and aspiration, for it questions the methods and hardships of any form of commitment and the competition between incompatible demands.

The play's command both of character and dialogue, with its self satire, wit and pressing sexual and political anxiety, all in competitive arrangements, making Mr Hughes sound like one of David Mercer's heirs, is not aided by a real thematic development.

Despite the need for pruning it is served in Richard Williams's fluent production by performances of outstanding ease and conviction in which Alan Rackman's disenchanted weariness as Hugh is a foil to Paola Dionisotti's impassioned daughter of a revolution which fails to arrive.
>   (From: Nicholas de Jongh, *The Guardian*, 24 June, 1980)

The Romans in Britain
Howard Brenton
October 1980   National

. . . homosexual rape, bloody violence, frequent obscenity, and political signifying do not necessarily make for a mature play and so many of his parallels are driven home with a bludgeon that his regard for an adult audience must be questioned.
>   (From: Ned Chaillet, *The Times*, 17 October, 1980)

As in the outfitting of *The Titanic*, no expense has been spared on this prodution. Sadly, it meets with a fate not dissimilar.

(From: Francis King, *The Sunday Telegraph*, 19 October, 1980)

I accept totally that Mr Brenton finds the hunger for empire anathema; but in order to savage such a crucial historical phenomenon I suggest you first have to understand it.

(From: Michael Billington, *The Guardian*, 17 October, 1980)

. . . it is hard to understand why Howard Brenton occupies the quasi-official position that he does at the National; he has shown no sign of being able to write a play so far and the reiterated limitations of class confusion and socio-sexual immorality are stridently boring. . . It is wrong of the G.L.C. leader to wave the grant at the National as a warning, but equally irritating of the National to put critics in the position of having to defend in principle the poor practice of their pet young poet.

(From: Bryan Robertson, *The Spectator*, 25 October, 1980)

Each time I see a new play by Howard Brenton I feel a slight sense of reassurance. Could *The Churchill Play* have been quite as appalling as I thought? Why, yes – here is *Sore Throats* to confirm my judgment. But suppose *Sore Throats* was really a little better than it seemed to me? Well, there is nothing in *The Romans in Britain* which opened on Thursday at the Olivier to suggest any such thing. Its three hours are devoid of wit, beauty or drama, and the message it appears to offer us only surfaces in the closing scenes. Whatever weaknesses there may be in Mr Brenton's writing, inconsistency isn't one of them.

(From: B.A. Young, *The Financial Times*, 18 October, 1980)

. . . has nothing at all to do with naked Romans and Celts going up each other like knives, nor yet to do with theatrical censorship. The scandal here concerns an artistic director engaged abroad when he could or at least should have been expecting trouble at home, and more importantly the artistic administration of a state-subsidised company which could allow this play to get beyond the Xerox machine, let alone into first rehearsal. Not because it is scandalous, or tasteless, or shocking, but because it is an underwritten and overproduced pageant which would look inadequate if performed as a school play.

(From: Sheridan Morley, *Punch*, 29 October, 1980)

What I call the Amadeus Defence works in the following way: you are concerned to forestall criticism of the strikingly bad play you are about to write; so you make the work as obscene as you can,

239

with the result that any critic who objects to it lays himself open to charges of puritanism and narrow-mindedness. The aim is to make the general public say to itself: 'If we are having a perfectly horrible time, this must be in the cause of Great Art.'

What I call the Brenton Variation throws in left-wingery and the Irish dimension, so that the audience should feel: 'If, when we are not bored rigid by this play, we find it utterly repugnant, that is because we are imperialist pigs who do not care two hoots about the crimes the British Army is committing in our name.'

Neither the Defence nor the Variation should be effective against a little calm self-questioning. Ask yourself, in Howard Brenton's *The Romans in Britain*, the new play at the National Theatre which has so upset Mary Whitehouse and Sir Horace Cutler, leader of the Greater London Council, what is the purpose of this obscenity, and what is the value of this violence.

Do we for instance care anything about the Celtic criminal who is strung up by the feet while his throat is cut? If the odd Roman soldier sodomised the odd Druid, what is that to us? Answer: nothing. . .

The directing is quite deficient in its grasp of reality. We are shown a man standing over a diseased corpse, which stinks so foully that it makes him retch. But at the end of his retching the man continues to stand right over the corpse chatting away about this and that. This indicates to me that the director has had the luck never to smell a corpse.

This play is a nauseating load of rubbish from beginning to end. It is written in a ludicrous pseudo-poetic yob-talk; such themes as it possesses are banal beyond belief; and the intended bravery of the acting company amounts to no more than an embarrassing exhibitionism.

It is advertised as unsuitable for children. It is unsuitable for anyone. If I were Sir Peter Hall and had instigated such a production, I would take myself out to dinner and very tactfully but firmly sack myself over the desert.

That said, I should make it clear that I in no way support either those who wish to use this production as an excuse to cut funds to the National, or those who on hearing the word 'nudity' will at once dial 999. Not that I think that the police should not go to the National. I think that the police should throng to the National, every night of the week.

And I strongly recommend that they should see Michael Gambon's performance in *Galileo*, which is quite the best thing in town. Mrs Whitehouse should stop persecuting the police. She should not force them to sit through *The Romans in Britain*.

(From: James Fenton, *The Sunday Times*, 19 October, 1980)

APPENDIXES

The Plays

Forty Years On (p. 158)	Alan Bennett	October 1968
Home (p. 170)	David Storey	June 1970
Homecoming, The (p. 131) ·	Harold Pinter	June 1965
Hostage, The (p. 77)	Brendan Behan	October 1958
I'm Talking About Jerusalem (p. 94)	Arnold Wesker	April 1960
Joking Apart (p. 232)	Alan Ayckbourn	March 1979
Jumpers (p. 185)	Tom Stoppard	February 1972
Knuckle (p. 197)	David Hare	March 1974
Krapp's Last Tape (p. 80)	Samuel Beckett	October 1958
Life Class (p. 199)	David Storey	April 1974
Little Malcolm and his Struggle Against the Eunuchs (p. 141)	David Halliwell	February 1966
Look Back in Anger (p. 50) ·	John Osborne	May 1956
Man for All Seasons, A (p. 100)	Robert Bolt	July 1960
Narrow Road to the Deep North (p. 157)	Edward Bond	July 1968
National Health, The (p. 164)	Peter Nichols	October 1969
Next Time I'll Sing to You (p. 116)	James Saunders	January 1963
No Man's Land (p. 215)	Harold Pinter	April 1975
Norman Conquests, The (p. 202)	Alan Ayckbourn	May 1974
Old Country, The (p. 225)	Alan Bennett	September 1977
Old Times (p. 177)	Harold Pinter	June 1971
One Way Pendulum (p. 90)	N.F. Simpson	December 1959
Plenty (p. 229)	David Hare	April 1978
Resounding Tinkle, A (p. 59)	N.F. Simpson	December 1957
Romans in Britain, The (p. 238)	Howard Brenton	October 1980
Roots (p. 85)	Arnold Wesker	May 1959
Rosencrantz and Guildenstern Are Dead (p. 149)	Tom Stoppard	April 1967
Royal Hunt of the Sun, The (p. 126)	Peter Shaffer	July 1964
Ruling Class, The (p. 161)	Peter Barnes	October 1968
Saved (p. 135)	Edward Bond	November 1965
Semi-Detached (p. 113)	David Turner	June 1962
Serjeant Musgrave's Dance (p. 88)	John Arden	October 1959
Staircase (p. 145)	Charles Dyer	November 1966
Taste of Honey, A (p. 66)	Shelagh Delaney	May 1958
West of Suez (p. 181)	John Osborne	April 1971
Workhouse Donkey, The (p. 119)	John Arden	July 1963
Yard of Sun, A (p. 172)	Christopher Fry	July 1970
Zigger Zagger (p. 152)	Peter Terson	August 1967

The Playwrights

ARDEN, John   b. 1930
Serjeant Musgrave's Dance, October 1959, Royal Court
The Workhouse Donkey, July 1963, Festival Theatre, Chichester

AYCKBOURN, Alan   b. 1939
The Norman Conquests, May 1974, Greenwich Theatre
Joking Apart, March 1979, Globe

BARNES, Peter   b. 1931
The Ruling Class, November 1968, Nottingham Playhouse

BECKETT, Samuel   b. 1906
Krapp's Last Tape, October 1958, Royal Court

BEHAN, Brendan   1923–1964
The Hostage, October 1958, Theatre Royal, Stratford East

BENNETT, Alan   b. 1934
Forty Years On, October 1968, Apollo
The Old Country, September 1977, Queens

BOLT, Robert   b. 1924
A Man for All Seasons, July 1960, Globe

BOND, Edward   b. 1934
Saved, November 1965, Royal Court
The Narrow Road to the Deep North, June 1968, Belgrade, Coventry
Bingo, November 1973, Northcott, Exeter

BRENTON, Howard   b. 1942
The Churchill Play, May 1974, Nottingham Playhouse
Deeds (with Griffiths, Campbell and Hare), March 1978, Nottingham Playhouse
The Romans in Britain, October 1980, National Theatre

CAMPBELL, Ken   b. 1941
Deeds, (*see* Brenton)

CHURCHILL, Caryl   b. 1938
Cloud Nine, March 1979, Royal Court

DELANEY, Shelagh   b. 1939
A Taste of Honey, May 1958, Theatre Royal, Stratford East

DYER, Charles   b. 1928
Staircase, November 1966, Aldwych

EDGAR, David   b. 1948
Destiny, September 1976, The Other Place

ELIOT, T.S.   1888–1965
The Elder Statesman, August 1958, Lyceum, Edinburgh; September 1958, Cambridge, London

FRY, Christopher   b. 1907
A Yard of Sun, July 1970, Nottingham Playhouse

GEMS, Pam   b. 1925
Dusa, Fish, Stas and Vi, December 1976, Hampstead Theatre

GRIFFITHS, Trevor   b. 1935
Comedians, February 1975, Nottingham Playhouse
Deeds (*see* Brenton)

HALLIWELL, David   b. 1936
Little Malcolm and his Struggle Against the Eunuchs, Dublin, 1965; February 1966, Garrick

HARE, David   b. 1947
Knuckle, March 1974, Comedy
Deeds (*see* Brenton)
Plenty, April 1978, National Theatre

HUGHES, Dusty   b. 1947
Commitments, June 1980, Bush

LEIGH, Mike   b. 1943
Abigail's Party, April 1977, Hampstead

LIVINGS, Henry   b. 1929
Big Soft Nellie, September 1961, Arts, Cambridge; November 1961, Theatre Royal, Stratford East)
Eh?, October 1964, Aldwych

MCGRATH, John   b. 1935
Events While Guarding the Bofors Gun, April 1966, Hampstead Theatre Club

MERCER, David   b. 1928
Belcher's Luck, November 1966, Aldwych

NICHOLS, Peter   b. 1927
The National Health, October 1969, Old Vic

ORTON, Joe   1933–1967
Entertaining Mr Sloane, May 1964, New Arts

OSBORNE, John   b. 1929
Look Back in Anger, May 1956, Royal Court
The Entertainer, April 1957, Royal Court
West of Suez, August 1971, Royal Court

PINTER, Harold   b. 1930;
  The Birthday Party, April 1958, Lyric, Hammersmith
  The Caretaker, April 1960, Arts
  The Homecoming, June 1965, Aldwych
  Old Times, June 1971, Aldwych
  No Man's Land, April 1975, National Theatre

RUDKIN, David   b. 1936
  Afore Night Come, June 1962, Arts

SAUNDERS, James   b. 1925
  Next Time I'll Sing to You, January 1963, Arts

SHAFFER, Peter   b. 1926
  Five Finger Exercise, July 1958, Comedy
  The Royal Hunt of the Sun, July 1964, Festival Theatre, Chichester
  Equus, July 1973, National Theatre

SIMPSON, N.F.   b. 1919
  A Resounding Tinkle, December 1957, Royal Court
  One Way Pendulum, December 1959, Royal Court

STOPPARD, Tom   b. 1937
  Rosencrantz and Guildenstern Are Dead, April 1967, Old Vic
  Jumpers, February 1972, Old Vic

STOREY, David   b. 1933
  Home, June 1970, Royal Court
  Life Class, April 1974, Royal Court

TERSON, Peter   b. 1932
  Zigger Zagger, August 1967, Jeannetta Cochrane

TURNER, David   b. 1927
  Semi-Detached, June 1962, Belgrade, Coventry; December 1962, Saville

WESKER, Arnold   b. 1932
  Chicken Soup with Barley, July 1958, Belgrade, Coventry; Royal Court
  Roots, May 1959, Belgrade, Coventry; June 1959, Royal Court
  I'm Talking About Jerusalem, April 1960, Belgrade, Coventry; June 1960, Royal Court (the *Trilogy*)
  Chips With Everything, April 1962, Royal Court; Playhouse, Sheffield; Glasgow Citizens'

WHITING, John   1917–1963
  The Devils, February 1961, Aldwych

WILSON, Snoo   b. 1948
  The Beast, November 1974, The Other Place

WOOD, Charles   b. 1933
  Dingo, April 1967, Bristol Arts Centre

The Theatres

ALDWYCH
The Devils, John Whiting, February 1961
Eh? Henry Livings, October 1964
The Homecoming, Harold Pinter, June 1965
Staircase, Charles Dyer, November 1966
Belcher's Luck, David Mercer, November 1966
Old Times, Harold Pinter, June 1971

APOLLO
Forty Years On, Alan Bennett, October 1968

ARTS
The Caretaker, Harold Pinter, April 1960 (Theatre Club)
Afore Night Come, David Rudkin, June 1962
Next Time I'll Sing to You, James Saunders, January 1963
Entertaining Mr Sloane, Joe Orton, June 1964

BELGRADE, (Coventry)
Chicken Soup With Barley, Arnold Wesker, July (Royal Court, July), 1958
Roots, Arnold Wesker, May (Royal Court, June) 1959
I'm Talking About Jerusalem, Arnold Wesker, April (Royal Court, *Trilogy*,
June) 1960
Semi-Detached, David Turner, June (Saville, December) 1962
The Narrow Road to the Deep North, Edward Bond, June 1968

BRISTOL ARTS CENTRE
Dingo, Charles Wood, April 1967

BUSH
Commitments, Dusty Hughes, June 1980

CAMBRIDGE (London)
The Elder Statesman, T.S. Eliot, September 1958 (from Lyceum,
Edinburgh)

COMEDY
Five Finger Exercise, Peter Shaffer, July 1958
Knuckle, David Hare, March 1974

FESTIVAL (Chichester)
The Workhouse Donkey, John Arden, July 1963
The Royal Hunt of the Sun, Peter Shaffer, July 1964

THE THEATRES

GARRICK
Little Malcolm and his Struggle Against the Eunuchs, David Halliwell, February 1966

GLASGOW CITIZENS'
Chips With Everything, Arnold Wesker, April 1962 (also Royal Court and Playhouse, Sheffield)

GLOBE
A Man for All Seasons, Robert Bolt, July 1960
Joking Apart, Alan Ayckbourn, March 1979

GREENWICH
The Norman Conquests, Alan Ayckbourn, May 1974

HAMPSTEAD
Events While Guarding the Bofors Gun, John McGrath, April 1966
Dusa, Fish, Stas and Vi, Pam Gems, December 1976
Abigail's Party, Mike Leigh, April 1977

JEANNETTA COCHRANE
Zigger Zagger, Peter Terson, August 1967

LYRIC (Hammersmith)
The Birthday Party, Harold Pinter, May 1958

LYCEUM (Edinburgh)
The Elder Statesman, T.S. Eliot, August (September, Cambridge Theatre, London) 1958

NATIONAL
Equus, Peter Shaffer, July 1973
No Man's Land, Harold Pinter, April 1975
Plenty, David Hare, April 1978
The Romans in Britain, Howard Brenton, October 1980

NORTHCOTT (Exeter)
Bingo, Edward Bond, November 1973

THE OLD VIC
Rosencrantz and Guildenstern Are Dead, Tom Stoppard, April 1967
The National Health, Peter Nichols, October 1969
Jumpers, Tom Stoppard, February 1972

THE OTHER PLACE (Stratford-upon-Avon)
The Beast, Snoo Wilson, November 1974
Destiny, David Edgar, September 1976

PLAYHOUSE (Nottingham)
The Ruling Class, Peter Barnes, October 1968
A Yard of Sun, Christopher Fry, July 1970
The Churchill Play, Howard Brenton, May 1974
Comedians, Trevor Griffiths, February 1975
Deeds, Howard Brenton, Ken Campbell, Trevor Griffiths and David Hare, March 1978

PLAYHOUSE (Sheffield)
Chips With Everything, Arnold Wesker, April 1962 (also at Royal Court and Glasgow Citizens')

QUEENS
The Old Country, Alan Bennett, September 1977

ROYAL COURT
Look Back in Anger, John Osborne, May 1956
The Entertainer, John Osborne, April 1957
A Resounding Tinkle, N.F. Simpson, December 1957
Chicken Soup With Barley, Arnold Wesker, July (from the Belgrade, Coventry) 1958
Krapp's Last Tape, Samuel Beckett, October 1958
Roots, Arnold Wesker, July (from the Belgrade, Coventry) 1959
Serjeant Musgrave's Dance, John Arden, October 1959
One Way Pendulum, N.F. Simpson, December 1959
I'm Talking About Jerusalem, Arnold Wesker, June (the *Trilogy*, from the Belgrade, Coventry), 1960
Chips With Everything, Arnold Wesker, April (also at the Playhouse, Sheffield and Glasgow Citizens') 1962
Saved, Edward Bond, November 1965
Home, David Storey, June 1970
West of Suez, John Osborne, August 1971
Life Class, David Storey, April 1974
Cloud Nine, Caryl Churchill, March 1979

SAVILLE
Semi-Detached, David Turner, December (from the Belgrade, Coventry) 1962

THEATRE ROYAL (Stratford East)
A Taste of Honey, Shelagh Delaney, May 1958
The Hostage, Brendan Behan, October 1958
Big Soft Nellie, Henry Livings, November 1961

The Critics

Allan, Walter
   Roots   New Statesman   11 July 1959

Alvarez, Alfred
   Serjeant Musgrave's Dance   New Statesman   31 Oct 1959
   The Caretaker   7 May 1960
   A Man For All Seasons   9 July 1960

Barber, John
   Home   Daily Telegraph   18 June 1970
   Old Times   2 June 1971
   Jumpers   3 Feb 1972
   Bingo   16 Nov 1973
   Plenty   15 Apr 1978

Billington, Michael
   Equus   Guardian   27 July 1973
   Bingo   16 Nov 1973
   Knuckle   5 Mar 1974
   Life Class   10 Apr 1974
   The Norman Conquests:
     Living Together   22 May 1974
     Round and Round the
     Garden   7 June 1974
   The Churchill Play   10 May 1974
   Destiny   29 Sept 1976
   Deeds   10 Mar 1978
   Joking Apart   8 Mar 1979
   The Romans in Britain   17 Oct 1980

Brahms, Caryl
   The Elder Statesman   Plays and Players   Nov 1958

Brien, Alan
   The Birthday Party   Spectator   30 May 1958
   A Taste of Honey   6 June 1958
   Five Finger Exercise   25 July 1958
   The Elder Statesman   5 Sept 1958
   The Hostage   17 Oct 1958
   Krapp's Last Tape   7 Nov 1958

Roots		10 July 1959
One Way Pendulum		1 Jan 1960
A Man for All Seasons		8 July 1960
Chips With Everything	Sunday Telegraph	6 May 1962
Afore Night Come		10 June 1962
The Workhouse Donkey		14 July 1963
Entertaining Mr Sloane		10 May 1964
The Royal Hunt of the Sun		12 July 1964
Saved		7 Nov 1965
Dingo		30 Apr 1967

Bryden, Ronald

The Royal Hunt of the Sun	New Statesman	17 July 1964
Homecoming		11 June 1965
Saved		12 Nov 1965
Little Malcolm and his		
Struggle Against the Eunuchs		11 Feb 1966
Staircase	Observer	6 Nov 1966
Zigger Zagger		3 Sept 1967
The Ruling Class		17 Nov 1968
A Yard of Sun		19 July 1970
Old Times		6 June 1971

Buckle, Richard

The Entertainer	Plays and Players	May 1957

Chaillet, Edward

The Romans in Britain	Times	17 Oct 1980

Chapman, Eric

Chips With Everything	Plays and Players	July 1962

Coveney, Michael

Dusa, Fish, Stas and Vi	Financial Times	9 Dec 1976

Craig, H.A.L.

The Devils	New Statesman	24 Feb 1961

Curtis, Anthony

The Homecoming	Sunday Telegraph	6 June 1965

Cushman, Robert

The National Health	Spectator	25 Oct 1969
Knuckle	Observer	10 Mar 1974
The Churchill Play		2 June 1974
Comedians		23 Feb 1975
No Man's Land		27 Apr 1975
Destiny		3 Oct 1976
Joking Apart		11 Mar 1979
Cloud Nine		1 Apr 1979

Darlington, W.A.

The Birthday Party	Daily Telegraph	20 May 1958
Entertaining Mr Sloane		7 May 1964

251

Saved		4 Nov 1965
Rosencrantz and Guildenstern Are Dead		12 Apr 1967

Dawson, Helen

The National Health	Plays and Players	Dec 1969
West of Suez	Observer	22 Aug 1969

D. – L., S

Big Soft Nellie	Daily Telegraph	29 Nov 1961

Dent, Alan

The Caretaker	Plays and Players	Jan 1961

Esslin, Martin

The Ruling Class	Plays and Players	Jan 1969

Evans, Gareth Lloyd

Roots	Guardian	26 May 1959
The Narrow Road to the Deep North		25 June 1968
A Yard of Sun		13 July 1970

Fenton, James

Commitments	Sunday Times	29 June 1980
The Romans in Britain		29 Oct 1980

Gascoigne, Bamber

Big Soft Nellie	Spectator	8 Dec 1961
Chips With Everything		11 May 1962
Afore Night Come		15 June 1962
Semi-Detached		14 Dec 1962

Gellert, Roger

Afore Night Come	New Statesman	15 June 1962
Semi-Detached		14 Dec 1962
Next Time I'll Sing To You		1 Feb 1963

Gibbs, Patrick

A Resounding Tinkle	Daily Telegraph	3 Dec 1957
Chicken Soup With Barley		15 July 1958
The Caretaker		28 Apr 1960

Gilbert, Stephen

Plenty	Plays and Players	June 1978

Granger, Peter

Look Back in Anger	Financial Times	10 May 1956
The Birthday Party		20 May 1958

Hobson, Sir Harold

The Entertainer	Sunday Times	14 Apr 1957
The Birthday Party		25 May 1958
Five Finger Exercise		25 July 1958

The Elder Statesman		31 Aug 1958
Serjeant Musgrave's Dance		25 Oct 1959
One Way Pendulum		27 Dec 1959
A Man for All Seasons		3 July 1960
Big Soft Nellie		3 Dec 1961
Chips With Everything		29 Aug 1962
Semi-Detached		9 Dec 1962
Next Time I'll Sing to You		27 Jan 1963
The Workhouse Donkey		11 July 1963
Entertaining Mr Sloane		10 May 1964
Eh?		1 Nov 1964
Little Malcolm and his Struggle Against the Eunuchs		6 Feb 1966
Events While Guarding the Bofors Gun		17 Apr 1966
Staircase		6 Nov 1966
Belcher's Luck		20 Nov 1966
Rosencrantz and Guildenstern Are Dead		16 Apr 1967
The Ruling Class		10 Nov 1968
The National Health		19 Oct 1969
A Yard of Sun		19 July 1970
Old Times		6 June 1971
Equus		29 July 1973
Bingo		18 Nov 1973
Knuckle		10 Mar 1974
The Churchill Play		2 June 1974

Holmstrom, John

Eh?	Plays and Players	Dec 1964

Hope-Wallace, Philip

Look Back in Anger	Manchester Guardian	10 May 1956
The Entertainer		11 Apr 1957
Five Finger Exercise	Guardian	17 July 1958
Serjeant Musgrave's Dance		23 Oct 1959
A Man for All Seasons		2 July 1960
Big Soft Nellie		29 Nov 1961
Semi-Detached		6 Dec 1962
The Homecoming		4 June 1965
Rosencrantz and Guildenstern Are Dead		12 Apr 1967
Forty Years On		1 Nov 1968
The National Health		17 Oct 1969

Hurren, Kenneth

Equus	Spectator	4 Aug 1973
Life Class		20 Apr 1974
The Norman Conquests		15 June 1974
The Beast		30 Nov 1974

253

Jackson, Peter
   Chicken Soup with Barley   Plays and Players   Sept 1958

Jenkins, Peter
   Cloud Nine   Spectator   7 Apr 1979
   Commitments   5 July 1980

Jones, D.A.N.
   Bingo   New Statesman   5 May 1967

de Jongh, Nicholas
   Abigail's Party   Guardian   23 Apr 1977
   Commitments   24 June 1980

King, Francis
   The Romans in Britain   Sunday Telegraph   19 Oct 1980

Lambert, J.W.
   I'm Talking About Jerusalem   Sunday Times   10 Apr 1960
   The Caretaker   1 May 1960
   Saved   7 Nov 1965
   West of Suez   22 Aug 1971
   Life Class   14 Apr 1974
   Living Together
     (The Norman Conquests)   26 May 1974
   Comedians   23 Feb 1975
   Destiny   3 Oct 1976

Levin, Bernard
   Abigail's Party   1 May 1977
   Deeds   12 Mar 1978
   Plenty   16 Apr 1978

Lewson, Charles
   Table Manners
     (The Norman Conquests)   Times   11 May 1974

Marcus, Frank
   The National Health   Sunday Telegraph   19 Oct 1969
   Home   21 June 1970
   Jumpers   6 Feb 1972
   Dusa, Fish, Stas and Vi   12 Dec 1976

Marowitz, Charles
   Afore Night Come   Plays and Players   Aug 1962
   Next Time I'll Sing to You   Mar 1963

Morley, Sheridan
   The Romans in Britain   Punch   29 Oct 1980

Muller, Robert
   The Devils   Daily Mail   21 Feb 1961

Nightingale, Benedict
   The Royal Hunt of the Sun   Guardian   18 July 1964

Forty Years On	New Statesman	8 Nov 1968
Old Times		11 June 1971
Bingo		23 Nov 1973
The Norman Conquests		31 May 1974
The Beast		22 Nov 1974
Comedians		28 Feb 1975
No Man's Land		2 May 1975
Dusa, Fish, Stas and Vi		17 Dec 1976
Joking Apart		16 Mar 1979

Olivier, Sir Laurence
Saved	Plays and Players (reprinted from Observer)	Jan 1966

Peter, John
Dusa, Fish, Stas and Vi	Sunday Times	12 Dec 1976

Radin, Victoria
Abigail's Party	Observer	1 May 1977

Roberts, Peter
Five Finger Exercise	Plays and Players	Sept 1958
Chips With Everything		July 1962
Jumpers		Apr 1972

Robertson, Bryan
The Romans in Britain	Spectator	25 Oct 1980

Rosselli, John
The Caretaker	Guardian	29 Apr 1960

Rundall, Jeremy
Events While Guarding the Bofors Gun	Plays and Players	June 1966

Schmidt, Arthur
Joking Apart	Plays and Players	Apr 1979

Shorter, Eric
The Homecoming	Daily Telegraph	4 June 1965
Dingo		30 Apr 1967
Zigger Zagger		22 Aug 1967
The Narrow Road to the Deep North		25 June 1968
The Ruling Class		9 Nov 1968
Joking Apart		8 Mar 1979

Smith, Lisa Gordon
The Hostage	Plays and Players	Dec 1958

Spurling, Hilary
Staircase	Spectator	11 Nov 1966
Belcher's Luck		25 Nov 1966

Rosencrantz and Guildenstern		
Are Dead		21 Apr 1967
Forty Years On		8 Nov 1968
Home		27 June 1970
Life Class		20 Apr 1970

Taylor, John Russell
Staircase	Plays and Players	Jan 1967

Treglown, Jeremy
Deeds	New Statesman	17 Mar 1978

Trewin, John
The Elder Statesman	Plays and Players	Oct 1958
Home	Birmingham Post	18 June 1970
A Yard of Sun		13 July 1970
Old Times		2 June 1971
West of Suez		18 Aug 1971
Jumpers		3 Feb 1972
Equus		27 July 1973
Life Class		10 Apr 1974
Table Manners		
(The Norman Conquests)		10 May 1974
No Man's Land		24 Apr 1975
The Old Country		8 Sept 1977
Joking Apart		8 Mar 1979
Cloud Nine		30 Mar 1979

Tynan, Kenneth
Look Back in Anger	Observer	13 May 1956
The Entertainer		14 Apr 1957
A Resounding Tinkle		8 Dec 1957
A Taste of Honey		1 June 1958
The Elder Statesman		31 Aug 1958
The Hostage		19 Oct 1958
Krapp's Last Tape		2 Nov 1958
The Caretaker		5 June 1960
Chicken Soup with Barley		12 June 1960
I'm Talking About Jerusalem		31 July 1960
Semi-Detached		9 Dec 1962

W., M.W.
The Birthday Party	Guardian	21 May 1958

Wardle, Irving
Rosencrantz and Guildenstern		
Are Dead	Times	12 Apr 1967
The Narrow Road to the Deep		
North		25 June 1968
The Ruling Class		9 Nov 1968
The National Health		17 Oct 1969
Home		18 June 1970

A Yard of Sun		13 July 1970
West of Suez		18 Aug 1971
Equus		27 July 1973
Bingo		15 Nov 1973
The Beast		19 Nov 1974
No Man's Land		24 Apr 1975
Destiny		29 Sept 1976
The Old Country		8 Sept 1977
Deeds		10 Mar 1978

Whitehead, Ted

Dusa, Fish, Stas and Vi	Spectator	18 Dec 1976
Plenty		22 Apr 1978

Worsley, T.C.

Look Back in Anger	New Statesman	19 May 1956
The Entertainer		20 Apr 1957
Five Finger Exercise		26 July 1958
The Devils	Financial Times	22 Feb 1961
The Workhouse Donkey		10 July 1963

Wraight, Robert

Roots	Star	1 July 1959

Young, B.A.

Eh?	Financial Times	31 Oct 1964
The Homecoming		5 June 1965
Little Malcolm and his Struggle Against the Eunuchs		5 Feb 1966
Dingo		29 Apr 1967
The Narrow Road to the Deep North		25 June 1968
The National Health		17 Oct 1969
Home		18 June 1970
Jumpers		3 Feb 1972
Knuckle		5 Mar 1974
The Norman Conquests:		
Table Manners		10 May 1974
Living Together		22 May 1974
Round and Round the Garden		7 June 1974
The Churchill Play		11 May 1974
The Beast		19 Nov 1974
The Old Country		8 Sept 1977
Plenty		13 Apr 1978
Joking Apart		8 Mar 1979
Cloud Nine		30 Mar 1979
Commitments		24 June 1980
The Romans in Britain		18 Oct 1980